A TREASURY OF Victorian MURDER
COMPENDIUM II

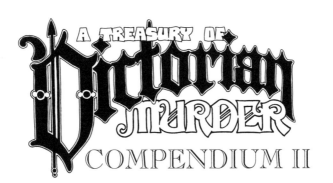

A TREASURY OF Victorian MURDER

COMPENDIUM II

Compiled and Illustrated by
RICK GEARY

ISBN 9781561639076
© Rick Geary 1997-2007
1st printing January 2015
Printed in China

Comicslit is an imprint
and trademark of

NANTIER · BEALL · MINOUSTCHINE
Publishing inc.
new york

Table of Contents

THE BORDEN TRAGEDY

ANDREW AND ABBY BORDEN

A MEMOIR of the INFAMOUS DOUBLE MURDER at FALL RIVER, MASS. 1892

EMMA

LIZZIE

ADAPTED AND ILLUSTRATED BY RICK GEARY

INTRODUCTION

The account presented in these pages of 19th Century America's most famous murder case is excerpted and adapted from the unpublished memoirs of a (thus far) unknown lady of Fall River, Massachusetts. Since the typewritten, unedited manuscript came to light at a 1990 estate sale, its provenance has been established to a satisfying degree. As part of the contents of an unopened trunk, it resided since the turn of the century in the basement of a private archive in Boston.

In the years since the public release of the memoirs, speculation has been lively among Bordenologists as to the identity of their mysterious authoress, who drops tantalizing hints throughout the text. Her apparent intimacy with the Borden family and her knowledge of Fall River's history and social structure have prompted theorists to champion several candidates, even the ambiguous and elusive "family friend," Miss Alice Russell. No hard evidence as yet points to any individual.

BIBLIOGRAPHY

The facts contained in the memoirs have been found to conform to the following sources:

Brown, Arnold R. *Lizzie Borden: The Legend, the Truth, the Final Chapter*. Nashville: Rutledge Hill Press, 1991.

Flynn, Robert A., *Lizzie Borden and the Mysterious Axe*. Portland, Maine: King Phillip Publishing Co., 1992.

Infamous Murders. London: Verdict Press, 1975.

Kent, David, *Forty Whacks: New Evidence in the Life and Legend of Lizzie Borden*. Emmaus, Pennsylvania: Yankee Books, 1992.

Kent, David, and Robert A. Flynn, *The Lizzie Borden Sourcebook*. Boston: Branden Publishing Co., 1992.

Lincoln, Victoria, *A Private Disgrace: Lizzie Borden by Daylight*. New York: G.P. Putnam's Sons, 1967.

Pearson, Edmund, "The Borden Case." Reprinted in *Unsolved!*, Richard Glyn Jones, ed. New York: Peter Bedrick Books, 1987.

Samuels, Charles and Louise, *The Girl in the House of Hate*. Mattituck, New York: Aeonian Press, Inc., 1953.

Spiering, Frank. *Lizzie*. New York: Random House, 1984.

Williams, Joyce G., J. Eric Smithburn and M. Jeanne Peterson, eds., Lizzie Borden: *A Casebook of Family and Crime in the 1890's*. Bloomington, Indiana, T.I.S. Publications, 1980.

Wilson Colin. *True Crime 2*. New York: Carroll and Graf, 1990.

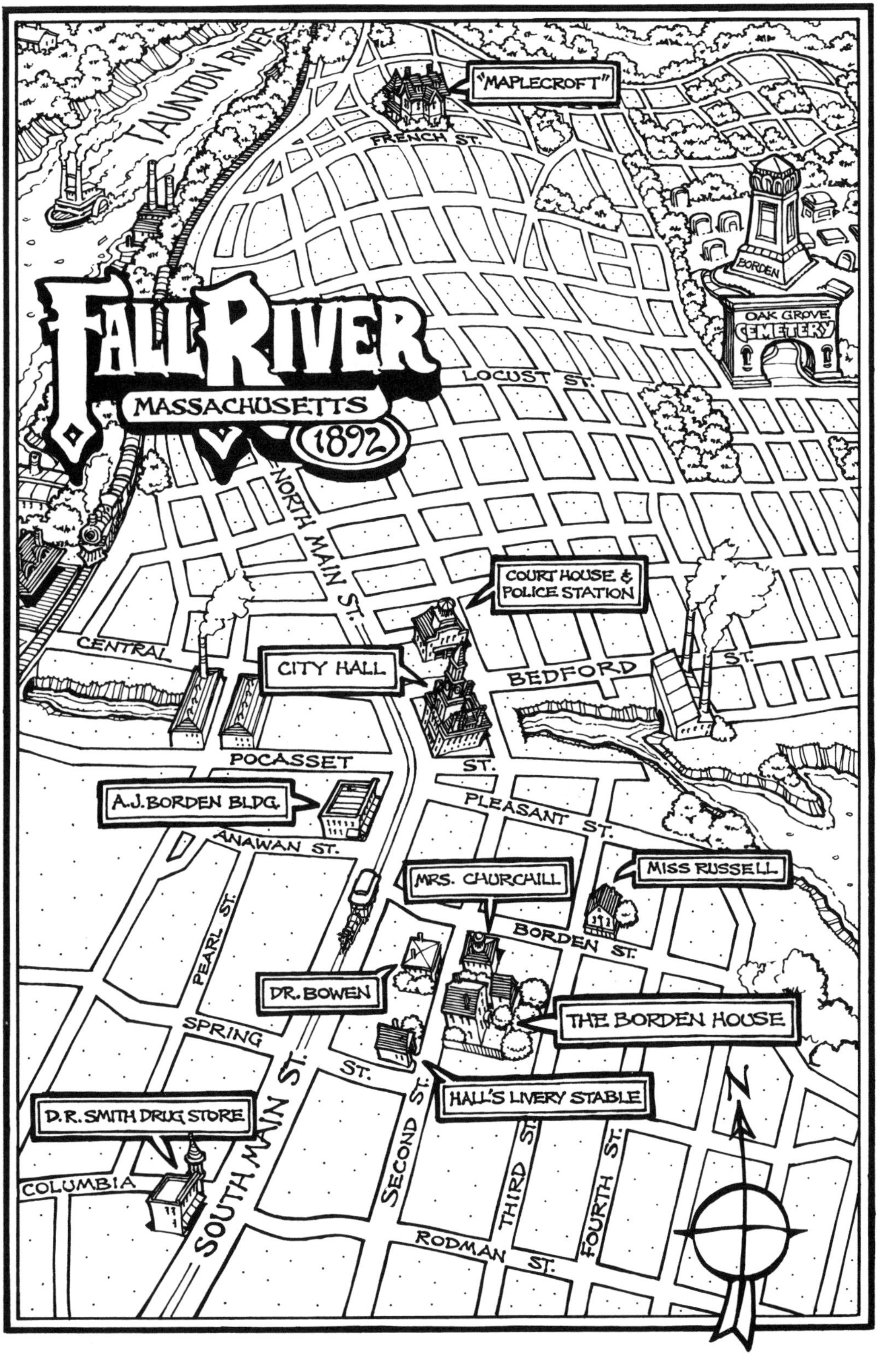

FALL RIVER
MASSACHUSETTS
1892
TAUNTON RIVER
"MAPLECROFT"
FRENCH ST.
BORDEN
OAK GROVE CEMETERY
LOCUST ST.
NORTH MAIN ST.
COURT HOUSE & POLICE STATION
CENTRAL
CITY HALL
BEDFORD
ST.
POCASSET
ST.
A.J. BORDEN BLDG.
PLEASANT ST.
ANAWAN ST.
MRS. CHURCHILL
MISS RUSSELL
PEARL ST.
BORDEN ST.
DR. BOWEN
THE BORDEN HOUSE
SPRING
ST.
SOUTH MAIN ST.
HALL'S LIVERY STABLE
SECOND ST.
THIRD ST.
FOURTH ST.
D.R. SMITH DRUG STORE
COLUMBIA
RODMAN ST.
N

THE GRIM AND SEETHING SUMMER OF 1892 WILL NEVER DEPART MY MEMORY...

NOR, I DARESAY, WILL IT BE EVER FORGOT BY THE GOOD CITIZENS OF FALL RIVER.

WITH TEMPERATURES ABOVE 100 DEGREES DAILY, THE PACE OF COMMERCIAL LIFE SLOWED TO A CRAWL.

HORSES COLLAPSED WHILE ATTEMPTING TO SCALE THE STEEPEST STREETS.

ON THAT STIFLING MORNING OF AUGUST 4, OUR 75,000 RESIDENTS WERE GOING ABOUT THEIR BUSINESS WITH NO INKLING THAT THEIR LIVES WERE ABOUT TO CHANGE UTTERLY AND FOREVER.

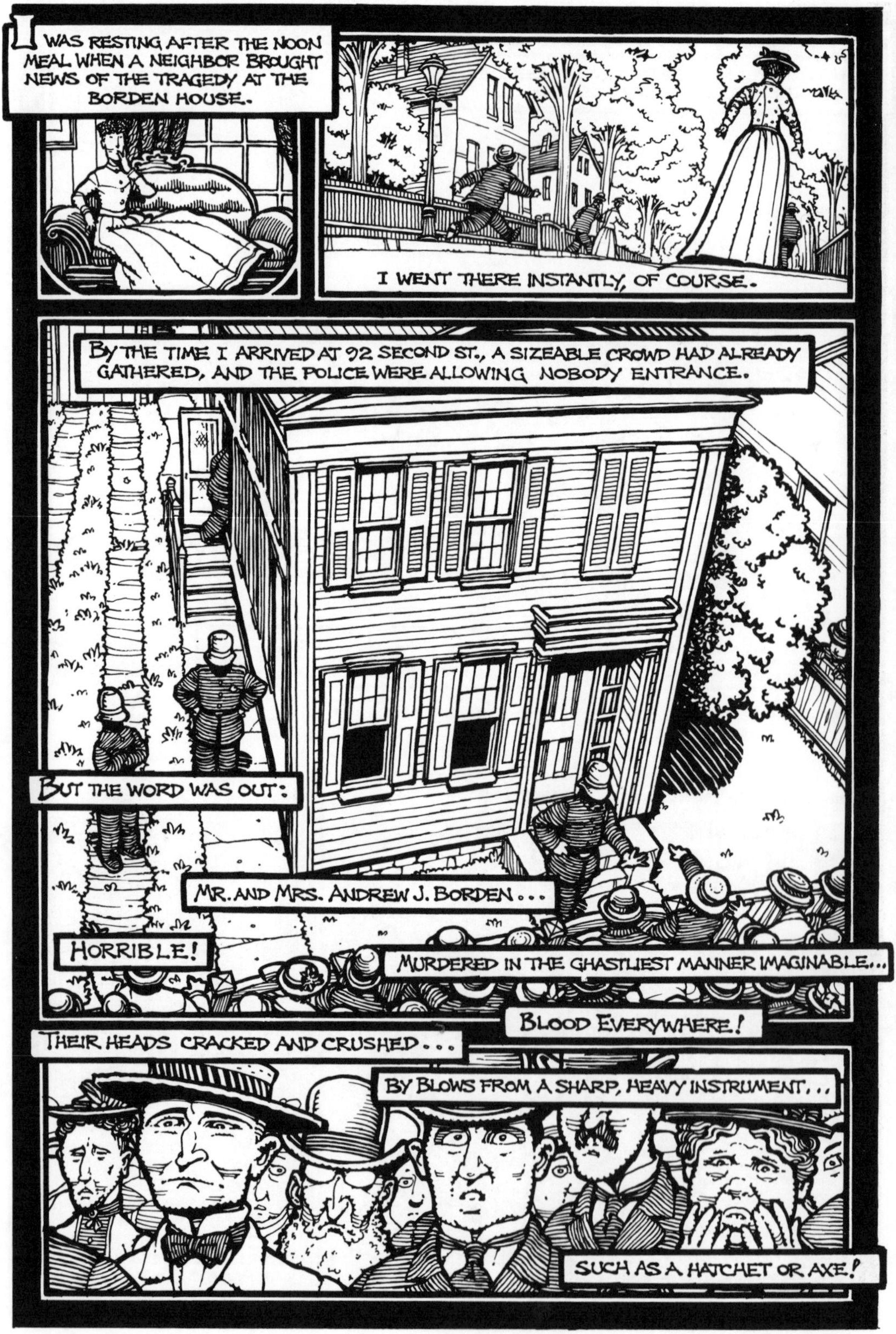
I WAS RESTING AFTER THE NOON MEAL WHEN A NEIGHBOR BROUGHT NEWS OF THE TRAGEDY AT THE BORDEN HOUSE.
I WENT THERE INSTANTLY, OF COURSE.
BY THE TIME I ARRIVED AT 92 SECOND ST., A SIZEABLE CROWD HAD ALREADY GATHERED, AND THE POLICE WERE ALLOWING NOBODY ENTRANCE.
BUT THE WORD WAS OUT:
MR. AND MRS. ANDREW J. BORDEN...
HORRIBLE!
MURDERED IN THE GHASTLIEST MANNER IMAGINABLE...
BLOOD EVERYWHERE!
THEIR HEADS CRACKED AND CRUSHED...
BY BLOWS FROM A SHARP, HEAVY INSTRUMENT...
SUCH AS A HATCHET OR AXE!

AT THAT TIME, APART FROM THE TWO VICTIMS, I KNEW THERE TO BE FOUR PERSONS RESIDENT IN THE BORDEN HOUSE —

ANDREW BORDEN

ABBY, HIS 2ND WIFE

THE IRISH HOUSEMAID BRIDGET

TWO DAUGHTERS BY HIS LATE 1ST WIFE: EMMA, THE ELDER...

AND THE YOUNGER, LIZZIE.

JOHN V. MORSE, A RELATION VISITING FROM NEW BEDFORD

I HAD THEN KNOWN THE BORDEN FAMILY FOR PERHAPS A SCORE OF YEARS, THE DAUGHTER LIZZIE BEING OF MY OWN AGE.

AS YOUNG LADIES, WE OFTEN ATTENDED THE SAME SOCIAL FUNCTIONS, AND HAD OCCASION, NOW AND THEN, TO SHARE OUR MOST INTIMATE THOUGHTS.

NONE OF THIS, HOWEVER, COULD GAIN ME ENTRANCE TO THE BORDEN HOUSE ON THAT DAY.

FOR THE REST OF THE AFTERNOON, POLICEMEN BY THE DOZENS TROOPED IN AND OUT.

LIGHTS IN THE HOUSE BURNED INTO THE SWELTERING NIGHT. "WHAT CAN BE HAPPENING IN THERE?" WE ALL WONDERED.

13

OVER THE NEXT SEVERAL DAYS, THE NORMAL ACTIVITY OF FALL RIVER GROUND TO A HALT, AS THE NEWS SPREAD FAR AND WIDE.

ANDREW BORDEN WAS OF COURSE WELL KNOWN FOR HIS STERN AND PENURIOUS WAYS. HE WAS MOURNED AS ONE OF THE TOWN'S LEADING CITIZENS.

JOURNALISTS FROM AS FAR AS BOSTON AND NEW YORK PROVED ASSIDUOUS IN FERRETING OUT RUMORS AND ACCUSATIONS.

AS WE AWAITED AN ARREST, DEBATE ON THE STREETS WAS LIVELY.

NINETEEN BLOWS!

NO..., TWENTY-ONE!

CONSENSUS OF OPINION AT FIRST HELD THE KILLER TO BE ONE OF THE FAST-BREEDING PORTUGESE FROM THE SOUTH END OF TOWN ...

OR, FAILING THAT, ONE OF THE VIOLENT-TEMPERED IRISH — PERHAPS THE FAMILY'S OWN HOUSEMAID!

LIZZIE BORDEN HERSELF WAS ALSO UNDER A CLOUD:

WORD SPREAD THAT SHE HAD ATTEMPTED TO PURCHASE POISON FROM A LOCAL DRUGGIST ON THE DAY BEFORE THE CRIMES.

AND WHAT OF THE SHADOWY CHARACTER OF JOHN V. MORSE (BROTHER OF ANDREW'S LATE FIRST WIFE AND UNCLE TO EMMA AND LIZZIE)?

SUPPOSEDLY, HE WAS PAYING A CALL ACROSS TOWN DURING THE TIME OF THE MURDERS.

ABOVE ALL, THE VISION OF A RAVING MAD-MAN AT LARGE IN THE COUNTRYSIDE AND SWINGING A BLOOD-SMEARED AXE, HAUNTED OUR DREAMS AND PRE-OCCUPIED OUR WAKING HOURS.

ON AUGUST 9-11, AN INQUEST, CLOSED TO THE PUBLIC, WAS CONDUCTED, DURING WHICH THE STATEMENTS OF ALL THOSE INVOLVED WERE PUT INTO LEGAL RECORD.

UPON ITS ADJOURNMENT, LIZZIE BORDEN WAS PLACED UNDER ARREST FOR THE MURDERS OF HER FATHER AND STEPMOTHER.

THIS ACTION, WE WERE TOLD, WAS BASED UPON SEVERAL INCONSISTENCIES IN HER TESTIMONY... IN ADDITION TO THE FACT THAT NOBODY ELSE SEEMED TO HAVE HAD THE OPPORTUNITY.

I WAS THUNDER-STRUCK! HOW COULD THIS WELL-BRED, CHURCHGOING LADY, TO WHOSE NAME NO BREATH OF SCANDAL WAS EVER ATTACHED—AND WHOM I HAD ONCE CONSIDERED CONFIDANTE—HAVE COMMITTED AN ACT OF SUCH STUNNING BRUTALITY?

MISS BORDEN ARRESTED.

IF TRUE, THERE WAS MORE RAGE AND HATRED WITHIN THAT HOUSE THAN I COULD EVER HAVE IMAGINED!

ON THAT DAY, I DETERMINED TO MYSELF THAT I HAD TO KNOW THE TRUTH OF WHAT HAPPENED ON THE MORNING OF AUGUST 4... AND THAT I WOULD FIND IT OUT, EVEN IF I HAD TO PLAY "DETECTIVE."

15

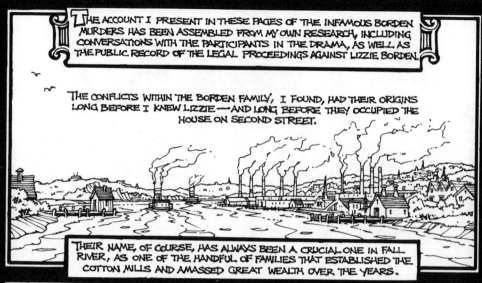

THE ACCOUNT I PRESENT IN THESE PAGES OF THE INFAMOUS BORDEN MURDERS HAS BEEN ASSEMBLED FROM MY OWN RESEARCH, INCLUDING CONVERSATIONS WITH THE PARTICIPANTS IN THE DRAMA, AS WELL AS THE PUBLIC RECORD OF THE LEGAL PROCEEDINGS AGAINST LIZZIE BORDEN.

THE CONFLICTS WITHIN THE BORDEN FAMILY, I FOUND, HAD THEIR ORIGINS LONG BEFORE I KNEW LIZZIE — AND LONG BEFORE THEY OCCUPIED THE HOUSE ON SECOND STREET.

THEIR NAME, OF COURSE, HAS ALWAYS BEEN A CRUCIAL ONE IN FALL RIVER, AS ONE OF THE HANDFUL OF FAMILIES THAT ESTABLISHED THE COTTON MILLS AND AMASSED GREAT WEALTH OVER THE YEARS.

HOWEVER, BY THE TIME OF ANDREW BORDEN'S BIRTH, HIS BRANCH OF THE FAMILY HAD FALLEN INTO POVERTY AND DISREPUTE...

FROM WHICH HE WAS FORCED TO CLIMB BY DINT OF THRIFT, SHREWDNESS AND HARD LABOR.

IN 1845, HE MARRIED A LOCAL WOMAN, SARAH MORSE.

THEIR UNION PRODUCED TWO DAUGHTERS: EMMA, BORN IN 1851...

AND LIZZIE, BORN IN 1860.

SARAH PASSED ON IN 1863...

AND TWO YEARS LATER, ANDREW MARRIED ABBY DURFEE GRAY, THE SPINSTER DAUGHTER OF ANOTHER PROMINENT FALL RIVER FAMILY.

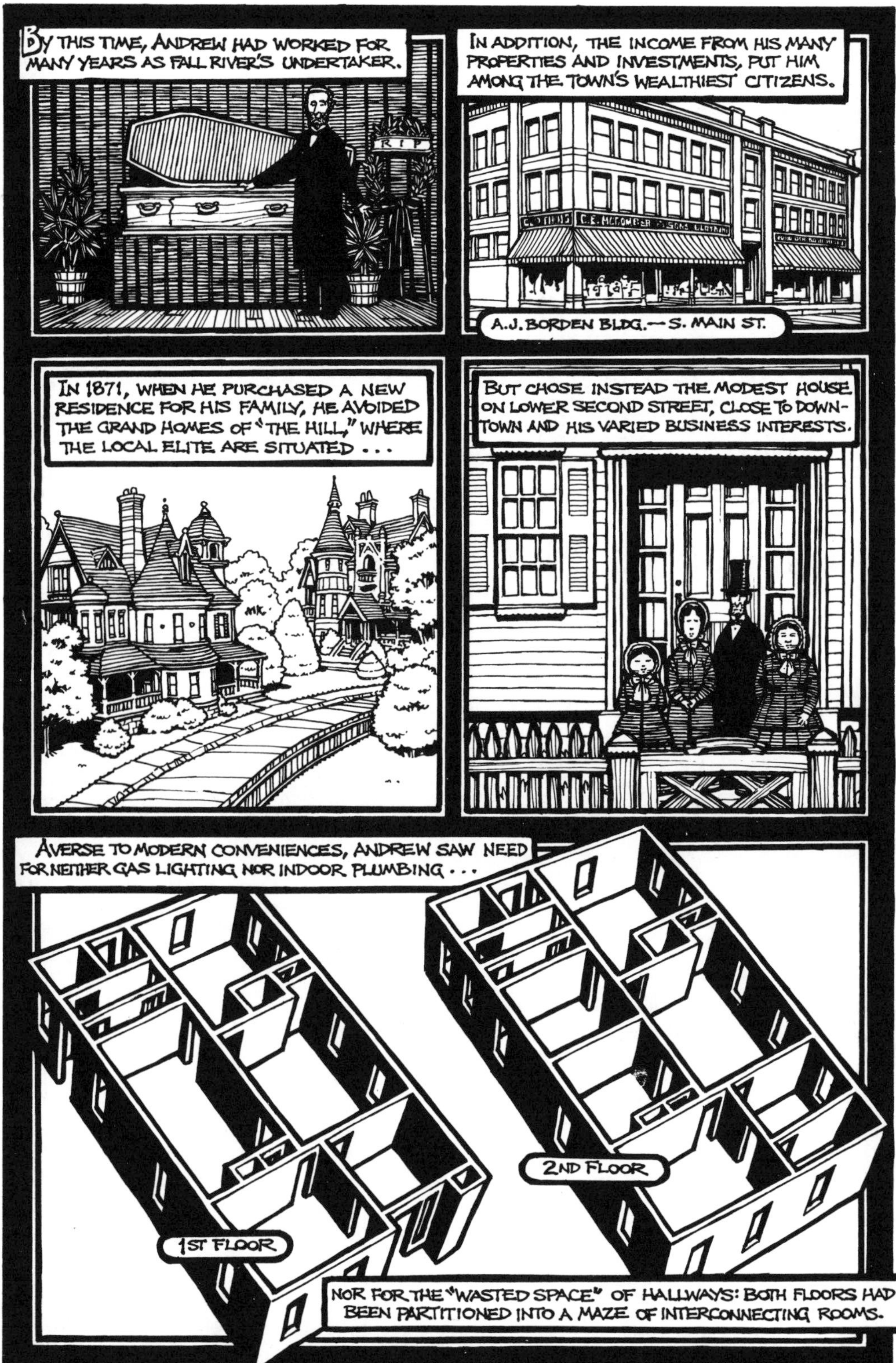
BY THIS TIME, ANDREW HAD WORKED FOR MANY YEARS AS FALL RIVER'S UNDERTAKER.
R.I.P.
IN ADDITION, THE INCOME FROM HIS MANY PROPERTIES AND INVESTMENTS, PUT HIM AMONG THE TOWN'S WEALTHIEST CITIZENS.
A.J. BORDEN BLDG.—S. MAIN ST.
IN 1871, WHEN HE PURCHASED A NEW RESIDENCE FOR HIS FAMILY, HE AVOIDED THE GRAND HOMES OF "THE HILL," WHERE THE LOCAL ELITE ARE SITUATED . . .
BUT CHOSE INSTEAD THE MODEST HOUSE ON LOWER SECOND STREET, CLOSE TO DOWNTOWN AND HIS VARIED BUSINESS INTERESTS.
AVERSE TO MODERN CONVENIENCES, ANDREW SAW NEED FOR NEITHER GAS LIGHTING NOR INDOOR PLUMBING . . .
2ND FLOOR
1ST FLOOR
NOR FOR THE "WASTED SPACE" OF HALLWAYS: BOTH FLOORS HAD BEEN PARTITIONED INTO A MAZE OF INTERCONNECTING ROOMS.

WHEN I FIRST KNEW LIZZIE, SHE WAS ROBUST AND VIVACIOUS, POSSESSED OF A PLAYFUL AND GENEROUS NATURE.

SHE COULD CERTAINLY BE WILLFUL AND STUBBORN, BUT HER MORAL CHARACTER WAS ALWAYS OF THE HIGHEST ORDER. SHE MAINTAINED MEMBERSHIP IN THE CENTRAL CONGREGATIONAL CHURCH, WHERE SHE SOMETIMES TAUGHT IN THE SUNDAY-SCHOOL.

AS SHE MATURED, LIZZIE HAD HER SHARE OF ESCORTS AND SUITORS -- BUT NONE, TO MY KNOWLEDGE, EVER PRODUCED A SERIOUS OFFER.

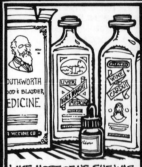

LIKE MOST OF US, SHE WAS SUBJECT TO THE OCCASIONAL "SPELL" OR BLACK MOOD. FOR THESE, YOUNG LADIES HAD NO END OF REMEDIES FROM WHICH TO CHOOSE.

WHEN SHE TURNED THIRTY YEARS, LIZZIE WAS SENT ON A GRAND TOUR OF EUROPE WITH SEVERAL OTHER FALL RIVER LADIES. THEREAFTER, SHE SEEMED RESIGNED TO A LIFE OF SPINSTERHOOD.

SUCH SEEMED ALSO THE CASE WITH HER OLDER SISTER EMMA, WHOM I RECALL AS GENTLE-NATURED AND SHY TO THE POINT OF RECLUSIVENESS.

SHE HAD FEW FRIENDS AND WAS APPARENTLY CONTENT TO SPEND HER DAYS AT HOME.

IN LOOKS, LIZZIE FAVORED HER LATE MOTHER — BUT SHE ALWAYS ENJOYED AN ESPECIAL BOND WITH HER FATHER.

TOGETHER THEY TOOK THE FISHING EXCURSIONS THAT WERE ANDREW'S ONLY PASTIME.

TO THE END OF HIS LIFE, HE WORE THE GOLDEN RING SHE HAD GIVEN HIM AS A GIRL.

BUT I OFTEN WONDERED: HOW CLOSE A BOND COULD ONE ESTABLISH WITH SUCH A DISTANT AND FORBIDDING MAN?

THE FEELINGS OF BOTH DAUGHTERS TOWARD THEIR STEP-MOTHER HAVE LIKEWISE BEEN MUCH SPECULATED UPON.

ABBY'S ARRIVAL, SO SOON AFTER THE DEATH OF THEIR DEAR MOTHER, COULD NOT HAVE BEEN ENTIRELY PLEASANT.

TO MY RECOLLECTION, ABBY BORDEN WAS A PLAIN AND UNREMARKABLE SOUL — BETTER SUITED TO HER ROLE AS HOUSE-WIFE AND HELP-MEET THAN AS THE DEVIOUS MANIPULATOR THAT SOME HAVE PORTRAYED HER.

I KNOW THAT SOME RESENTMENT SURFACED IN 1887, WHEN ANDREW TRANSFERRED OWNERSHIP OF A HOUSE ON FOURTH STREET TO ABBY'S SISTER, MRS. SARAH WHITEHEAD.

COULD THE TWO DAUGHTERS, GETTING OLDER AND WITH NO PROSPECTS OF MARRIAGE, HAVE ENVISIONED THEIR INHERITANCE VANISHING PIECE-BY-PIECE INTO THE HANDS OF THEIR STEP-MOTHER'S FAMILY?

AN APPARENT BURGLARY IN 1891 MUST HAVE ADDED TO AN ATMOSPHERE OF MISTRUST.

CASH MONEY AND SEVERAL ITEMS OF JEWELRY WERE TAKEN FROM A BUREAU IN THE MASTER BEDROOM— EVIDENTLY BY A THIEF WHO KNEW JUST WHERE TO LOOK.

IT SEEMS TO HAVE BEEN AN OPEN SECRET WITHIN THE FAMILY THAT LIZZIE WAS THE CULPRIT.

(SHE HAD, AFTER ALL, BEEN ACCUSED YEARS EARLIER OF SHOP-LIFTING BY A NUMBER OF LOCAL MERCHANTS)

AFTER THIS INCIDENT, ANDREW BORDEN INITIATED THE PRACTICE OF LOCKING THE DOOR TO THE MASTER BEDROOM...

AND LEAVING THE KEY IN PLAIN VIEW ON THE MANTLE-PIECE IN THE SITTING ROOM.

THE CONNECTING DOOR BETWEEN THE MASTER BEDROOM AND THE REST OF THE SECOND FLOOR WAS SEALED OFF AS WELL.

RELATIONS BETWEEN ABBY AND BOTH HER STEP-DAUGHTERS APPEAR TO HAVE BECOME MINIMAL AND PERFUNCTORY. WHENEVER POSSIBLE, THEY TOOK THEIR MEALS SEPARATELY.

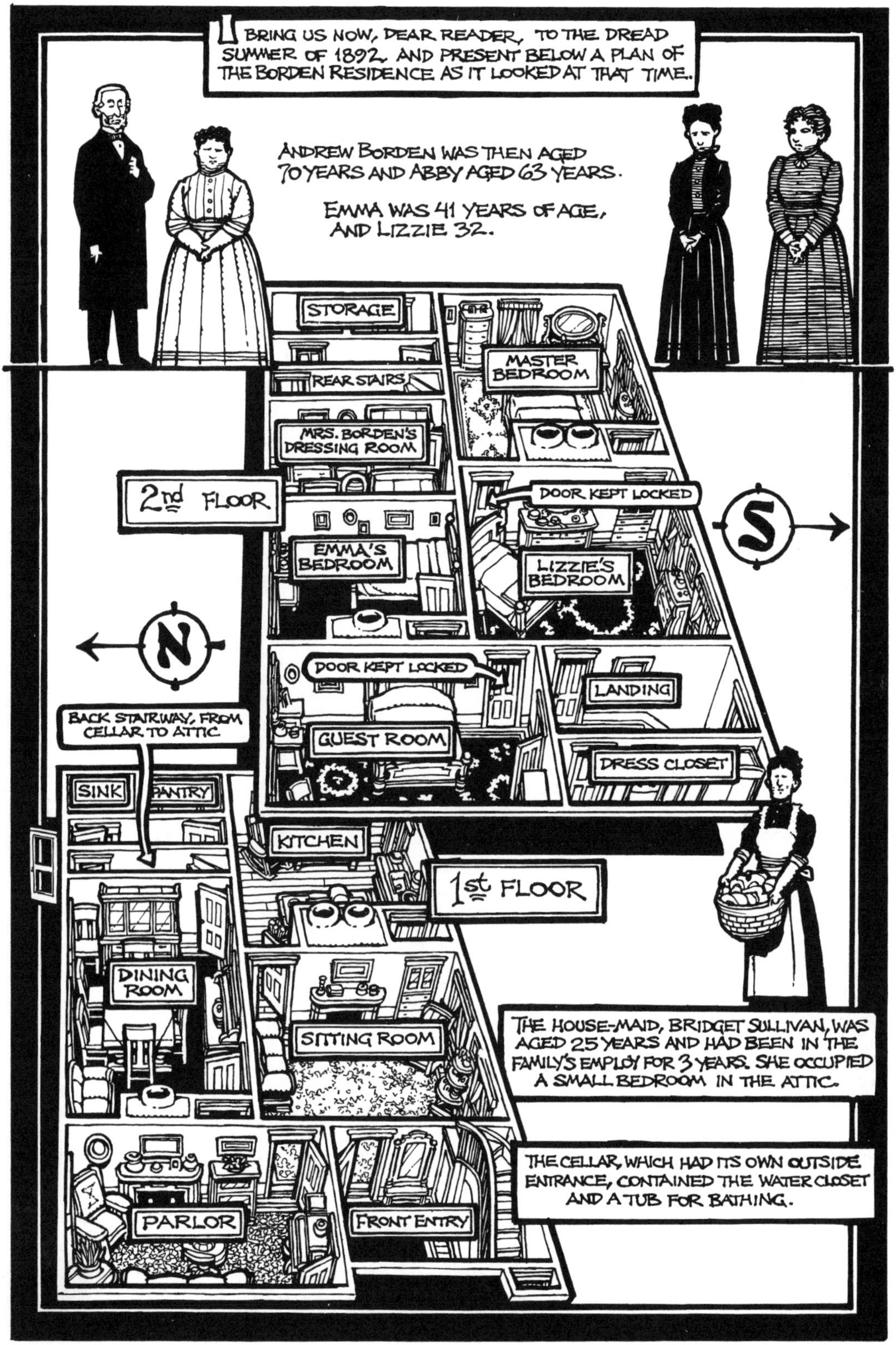
I BRING US NOW, DEAR READER, TO THE DREAD SUMMER OF 1892 AND PRESENT BELOW A PLAN OF THE BORDEN RESIDENCE AS IT LOOKED AT THAT TIME.
ANDREW BORDEN WAS THEN AGED 70 YEARS AND ABBY AGED 63 YEARS.
EMMA WAS 41 YEARS OF AGE, AND LIZZIE 32.
STORAGE
MASTER BEDROOM
REAR STAIRS
MRS. BORDEN'S DRESSING ROOM
2nd FLOOR
DOOR KEPT LOCKED
S
EMMA'S BEDROOM
LIZZIE'S BEDROOM
N
DOOR KEPT LOCKED
LANDING
BACK STAIRWAY, FROM CELLAR TO ATTIC
GUEST ROOM
DRESS CLOSET
SINK
PANTRY
KITCHEN
1st FLOOR
DINING ROOM
SITTING ROOM
THE HOUSE-MAID, BRIDGET SULLIVAN, WAS AGED 25 YEARS AND HAD BEEN IN THE FAMILY'S EMPLOY FOR 3 YEARS. SHE OCCUPIED A SMALL BEDROOM IN THE ATTIC.
THE CELLAR, WHICH HAD ITS OWN OUTSIDE ENTRANCE, CONTAINED THE WATER CLOSET AND A TUB FOR BATHING.
PARLOR
FRONT ENTRY

SOMETIME IN MAY, THERE OCCURRED AN EVENT THAT MANY PEOPLE BELIEVE SEVERED UTTERLY THE AFFECTIONS THAT LIZZIE HELD FOR HER FATHER.

LIZZIE, IT MUST BE REMEMBERED, WAS A FERVENT LOVER OF ALL ANIMALS. SHE KEPT A ROOST IN THE LOFT OF THE BARN FOR THE WILD PIGEONS OF THE NEIGHBORHOOD.

IT SEEMED THAT, ON TWO RECENT OCCASIONS, THE BARN HAD BEEN BROKEN INTO — NO DOUBT BY NEIGHBORHOOD BOYS HUNTING THE BIRDS.

AND SO, IN AN APPARENT EFFORT TO PREVENT FURTHER SUCH INTRUSIONS, ANDREW USED A HATCHET TO BEHEAD EVERY PIGEON!

ONE IS FREE TO SPECULATE UPON HOW LIZZIE, LONG ACCUSTOMED BY NOW TO HER FATHER'S VARIOUS MEANNESSES, WAS AFFECTED BY THIS ACTION.

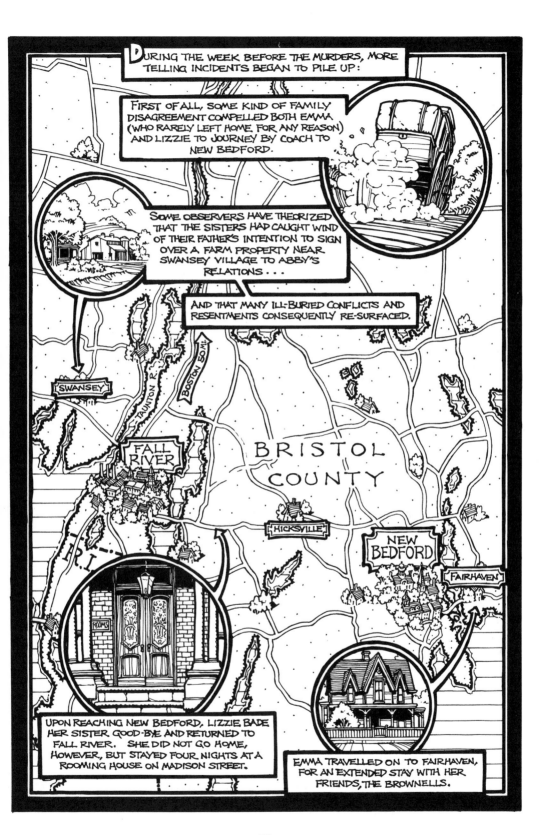

DURING THE WEEK BEFORE THE MURDERS, MORE TELLING INCIDENTS BEGAN TO PILE UP:

FIRST OF ALL, SOME KIND OF FAMILY DISAGREEMENT COMPELLED BOTH EMMA (WHO RARELY LEFT HOME FOR ANY REASON) AND LIZZIE TO JOURNEY BY COACH TO NEW BEDFORD.

SOME OBSERVERS HAVE THEORIZED THAT THE SISTERS HAD CAUGHT WIND OF THEIR FATHER'S INTENTION TO SIGN OVER A FARM PROPERTY NEAR SWANSEY VILLAGE TO ABBY'S RELATIONS . . .

AND THAT MANY ILL-BURIED CONFLICTS AND RESENTMENTS CONSEQUENTLY RE-SURFACED.

SWANSEY

TAUNTON R.

BOSTON 50 M.

FALL RIVER

BRISTOL COUNTY

HICKSVILLE

R.I.

NEW BEDFORD

FAIRHAVEN

UPON REACHING NEW BEDFORD, LIZZIE BADE HER SISTER GOOD-BYE AND RETURNED TO FALL RIVER. SHE DID NOT GO HOME, HOWEVER, BUT STAYED FOUR NIGHTS AT A ROOMING HOUSE ON MADISON STREET.

ROOMS

EMMA TRAVELLED ON TO FAIRHAVEN, FOR AN EXTENDED STAY WITH HER FRIENDS, THE BROWNELLS.

TUESDAY, AUGUST 2 — TWO DAYS BEFORE THE TRAGEDY.

ON THE MORNING AFTER LIZZIE'S RETURN HOME FROM HER STAY AT THE BOARDING HOUSE, BOTH ANDREW AND ABBY BORDEN AWOKE COMPLAINING OF STOMACH PAINS AND VOMITING IN THE NIGHT.

ABBY, IT SEEMED, HAD BEEN TAKEN WITH ESPECIAL VIOLENCE.

SHE WENT SO FAR AS TO WALK ACROSS THE STREET AND CALL UPON DR. SEABURY BOWEN, THE FAMILY'S FRIEND AND PHYSICIAN.

TO HIM, SHE CONFIDED HER SUSPICION THAT SHE AND HER HUSBAND HAD BEEN POISONED!

THE GOOD DOCTOR LISTENED SYMPATHETICALLY, BUT HE KNEW THAT SUCH STOMACH AILMENTS WERE NOT UNUSUAL DURING THE SUMMER MONTHS.

IN THOSE DAYS, AFTER ALL, FOOD PRESERVATION REMAINED IN A RATHER PRIMITIVE STATE. (A ROAST OF MUTTON, WHICH SUSTAINED THE FAMILY THROUGH SEVERAL MEALS THAT WEEK, WAS LATER ASSIGNED THE BLAME.)

ON THAT MORNING, A LADY (LATER IDENTIFIED BY SEVERAL WITNESSES AS LIZZIE BORDEN) ENTERED SMITH'S DRUG STORE ON SOUTH MAIN AT COLUMBIA STREET.

THIS ESTABLISHMENT, IT MUST BE NOTED, WAS FAR ENOUGH SOUTH ON MAIN ST. AS TO BE RARELY, IF EVER, PATRONIZED BY THE BORDENS OR ANYONE THEY KNEW.

THIS LADY ASKED TO PURCHASE PRUSSIC ACID — BUT THE PROPRIETOR, MR. ELI BENCE, REFUSED TO SELL HER THE DEADLY POISON WITHOUT A NOTE FROM A PHYSICIAN.

THE LADY PROTESTED INDIGNANTLY THAT SHE ONLY NEEDED "10 CENTS WORTH" TO CLEAN A SEALSKIN CAPE, THAT SHE NEVER HAD ANY TROUBLE OBTAINING IT BEFORE.... AT LAST, SHE TURNED AND WALKED OUT. (LIZZIE LATER DENIED HAVING MADE THIS VISIT.)

THAT AFTERNOON, BY ANOTHER TRICK OF PROVIDENCE, JOHN V. MORSE, UNCLE TO THE BORDEN SISTERS, ARRIVED BY RAIL-CAR FROM HIS HOME IN NEW BEDFORD.

LITTLE IS KNOWN TODAY ABOUT THIS MAN — THEN AGED ABOUT 69 YEARS.

HE DRESSED SHABBILY, NEVER TOOK A WIFE. REPORTEDLY, HE HAD SPENT SEVERAL YEARS IN IOWA AS A HORSE TRADER.

UPON HIS RETURN TO THE EAST, HE AND ANDREW BECAME INVOLVED IN VARIOUS INVESTMENT SCHEMES — THUS NECESSITATING HIS INFREQUENT VISITS TO FALL RIVER.

AT ABOUT 7:00 PM THAT EVENING, LIZZIE PAID A CALL UPON MISS ALICE RUSSELL, A MAIDEN LADY WHO LIVED IN A SMALL HOUSE OFF OF THIRD STREET.

ALTHOUGH I KNEW HER ONLY SLIGHTLY, MISS RUSSELL HAD BEEN FOR YEARS THE CLOSEST OF FRIENDS TO BOTH EMMA AND LIZZIE.

AS MISS RUSSELL REMEMBERED IT, LIZZIE SEEMED NERVOUS THAT EVENING, AND OVERTAKEN BY A STRONG SENSE OF FOREBODING.

OH ALICE, I FEEL DEPRESSED — AS IF SOMETHING IS HANGING OVER ME — AND I CAN'T THROW IT OFF.

SHE RELATED THE FACTS OF HER FAMILY'S RECENT ILLNESS—

LAST NIGHT, FATHER AND ABBY WERE SO SICK... SOMETIMES I THINK OUR MILK MIGHT BE POISONED.

AND SHE TOLD OF HOW THE BORDEN HOUSE AND BARN HAD BEEN BROKEN INTO IN RECENT MONTHS.

I FEEL AFRAID THAT FATHER HAS AN ENEMY... HE HAS SO MUCH TROUBLE WITH THE MEN WHO COME TO SEE HIM.

THERE WAS ONE MAN WHO CAME BY. I DIDN'T SEE HIS FACE, BUT HE AND FATHER HAD A TERRIBLE ARGUMENT OVER SOME PROPERTY.

As she parted from Miss Russell, Lizzie made a final grim prediction:

OH ALICE, I'M AFRAID SOMEBODY WILL DO SOMETHING! I DON'T KNOW BUT WHAT SOMEBODY WILL DO SOMETHING!

She arrived home about 9:00 PM, triple-locking the front door, as was the family's custom.

Andrew and Abby and John Morse talked in the sitting room as Lizzie, paying them no greeting, climbed the stairs to her bedroom.

She recalled later that, as she prepared for bed, she could hear her father, uncle and step-mother in loud, heated discussion below...

But she could not make out precisely what they were saying.

One final incident should be mentioned at this point: at about 11:00 PM, Mrs. Chagnon and her daughter, who occupied the property adjacent to the Borden back yard, heard a distinct and sustained pounding — lasting some five minutes...

And coming from the direction of the tall wooden fence that separated their property from the Bordens'.

27

THE FOLLOWING ACCOUNT OF THE EVENTS OF
THURSDAY, AUGUST 4
IS THE MOST ACCURATE AND COMPLETE THAT CAN BE
ASSEMBLED THUS FAR.

AS THE SUN ROSE THAT MORNING, THE AIR WAS ALREADY STIFLING, AND THE TEMPERATURE CLIMBING TOWARD 90 DEGREES.

THERE WAS NO RELIEF IN SIGHT.

OTHERWISE, THE DAY BEGAN AS A PERFECTLY ORDINARY ONE FOR FALL RIVER.

AT THE BORDEN HOUSE ON SECOND STREET, FIVE PEOPLE AWOKE.

SHORTLY AFTER 6:00AM, JOHN V. MORSE, WHO SLEPT IN THE GUEST ROOM ON THE SECOND FLOOR, WAS DRESSED AND DOWNSTAIRS. HE OCCUPIED HIMSELF IN THE SITTING ROOM.

AT ABOUT THE SAME TIME, BRIDGET SULLIVAN AWOKE IN HER ATTIC ROOM. FEELING ILL AND DIZZY, SHE KNEW THAT THE FAMILY'S SICKNESS HAD CAUGHT UP TO HER.

WITH GREAT EFFORT, SHE TRUDGED DOWNSTAIRS, FIRST BRINGING COAL AND WOOD UP FROM THE CELLAR TO START THE KITCHEN FIRE.

AT ABOUT 6:30 AM, ABBY BORDEN CAME DOWN TO THE KITCHEN. THERE SHE GAVE BRIDGET HER INSTRUCTIONS FOR THE MORNING:

AFTER BREAKFAST, I WANT YOU TO WASH ALL THE DOWNSTAIRS WINDOWS, INSIDE AND OUT.

SHORTLY THEREAFTER, ANDREW BORDEN DESCENDED, LOOKING THE WORSE FOR HIS LINGERING ILLNESS.

HE EMPTIED HIS NIGHT-MUG IN THE BACK YARD BEFORE JOINING HIS WIFE AND JOHN MORSE IN THE SITTING ROOM.

AT ABOUT 7:00 AM, THE THREE SAT DOWN TO BREAKFAST. THE BILL OF FARE (WHICH HAS SINCE BECOME NOTORIOUS) CONSISTED OF: THE MUTTON ROAST (BY NOW SOME FIVE DAYS OLD) AND MUTTON BROTH, BREAD AND JOHNNY-CAKES, BANANAS, ORANGES, COOKIES AND COFFEE.

AFTER BREAKFAST, ANDREW AND JOHN RETIRED AGAIN TO THE SITTING ROOM...

WHILE ABBY BEGAN HER HOUSE-CLEANING CHORES DOWNSTAIRS.

WHILE CLEARING THE TABLE, BRIDGET SULLIVAN WAS SUDDENLY COMPELLED TO RUN INTO THE BACK YARD...

AND SPEND SEVERAL MINUTES AGAINST THE REAR FENCE RETCHING VIOLENTLY.

BY 8:45 AM, BRIDGET WAS BACK IN THE KITCHEN...

AS JOHN MORSE LEFT THE HOUSE BY WAY OF THE REAR SCREEN DOOR. ANDREW SOON FOLLOWED.

THEY THEN STOOD OUTSIDE TALKING: JOHN WAS ON HIS WAY TO VISIT RELATIONS ACROSS TOWN AND INVITED ANDREW TO JOIN HIM.

ANDREW DECLINED, BUT INVITED JOHN BACK FOR THE NOON MEAL.

ANDREW THEN CAME BACK INSIDE, HOOKED THE SCREEN DOOR...

AND CLIMBED THE REAR STAIRS TO HIS BEDROOM.

AT THIS TIME —ABOUT 9:00 AM— LIZZIE BORDEN CAME DOWN THE FRONT STAIRS. (EMMA BORDEN, THE READER WILL RECALL, WAS STILL WITH THE BROWNELLS AT FAIRHAVEN.)

WHAT WAS LIZZIE WEARING THAT MORNING? THE QUESTION HAS BECOME ONE OF INCREASING DISPUTE — BUT, FOR PRESENT PURPOSES, I WILL PLACE HER IN A LIGHT BLUE COTTON HOUSEDRESS.

AVOIDING THE MUTTON, SHE CONSUMED A LIGHT BREAKFAST OF COOKIES AND COFFEE.

After several minutes, Andrew returned downstairs, dressed immaculately as always — even to his Prince Albert coat, despite the vicious heat!

He conferred with Abby about the noon meal; Lizzie gave him some letters to post for her.

He then left, via the rear door.

At about 9:30 AM, Abby continued her housecleaning by climbing the front stairs to the guest room...

While Bridget Sullivan grudgingly went outdoors to begin washing the windows.

And Lizzie, having finished breakfast, remained in the dining room to iron some handkerchiefs.

Thus was the stage set for the first murder.

FOR NEARLY ONE HOUR, BRIDGET WORKED ON THE WINDOWS, BEGINNING ON THE SOUTH SIDE AND MOVING, IN TURN, TO THE WEST AND NORTH...

IT WAS AN ARDUOUS CHORE, WHICH NECESSITATED SEVERAL TRIPS TO THE PUMP IN THE BARN...

AT WHICH TASK SHE WAS SEEN BY SEVERAL PASSERS-BY ON SECOND STREET.

FROM WHICH VANTAGE POINT SHE WOULD PRESUMABLY HAVE NOTICED ANYBODY ENTERING OR LEAVING THE HOUSE.

BETWEEN TRIPS, SHE CHATTED OVER THE FENCE WITH THE MAID FROM THE KELLY HOUSE TO THE SOUTH.

AS SHE WORKED, BRIDGET COULD PEER INTO THE ROOMS OF THE FIRST FLOOR, WHERE SHE NOTED NO ACTIVITY AT ALL.

INSIDE THE HOUSE, LIZZIE'S MOVEMENTS ARE, OF COURSE, UNACCOUNTED FOR BY ANYBODY BUT HERSELF.

AS SHE LATER TOLD IT, ABBY WAS CALLED TO THE FRONT DOOR BY A MESSENGER WITH A NOTE.

THE NOTE, ABBY SAID, SUMMONED HER OUT TO VISIT A SICK FRIEND.

BUT WHETHER ABBY ACTUALLY LEFT, LIZZIE COULD NOT SAY, FOR SHE THEN WENT TO HER ROOM TO SORT SOME LAUNDRY.

SOMETIME DURING THE HOUR OF 9:30-10:30 AM, AS ABBY BORDEN CLEANED THE GUEST ROOM, SOMEBODY ATTACKED THE BACK OF HER HEAD WITH A HATCHET...

NINETEEN BLOWS IN ALL!

ABBY MUST HAVE BEEN TAKEN COMPLETELY UNAWARES. BUT WAS IT A SURPRISE ATTACK BY A STRANGER — OR WAS SHE VISITED BY A PERSON SHE KNEW, WHO SIMPLY WAITED FOR THE RIGHT MOMENT?

AND WHERE WAS LIZZIE? IF SHE WAS IN HER ROOM, OR ANYPLACE IN THE HOUSE, HOW COULD SHE HELP BUT HAVE HEARD SUCH A FURIOUS ASSAULT? (ABBY'S BULK, HITTING THE FLOOR MUST HAVE SHAKEN THE RAFTERS!)

33

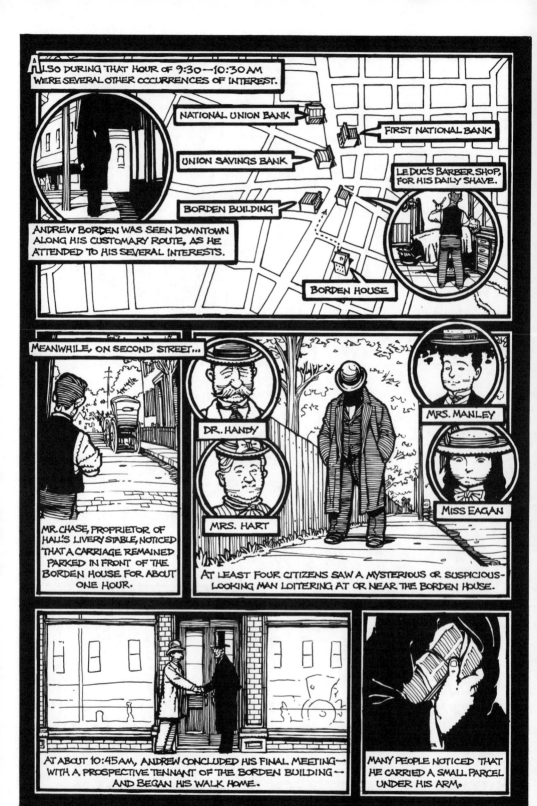

ALSO DURING THAT HOUR OF 9:30—10:30 AM WERE SEVERAL OTHER OCCURRENCES OF INTEREST.

NATIONAL UNION BANK

FIRST NATIONAL BANK

UNION SAVINGS BANK

LE DUC'S BARBER SHOP, FOR HIS DAILY SHAVE.

BORDEN BUILDING

ANDREW BORDEN WAS SEEN DOWNTOWN ALONG HIS CUSTOMARY ROUTE, AS HE ATTENDED TO HIS SEVERAL INTERESTS.

BORDEN HOUSE

MEANWHILE, ON SECOND STREET...

DR. HANDY

MRS. HART

MRS. MANLEY

MISS EAGAN

MR. CHASE, PROPRIETOR OF HALL'S LIVERY STABLE, NOTICED THAT A CARRIAGE REMAINED PARKED IN FRONT OF THE BORDEN HOUSE FOR ABOUT ONE HOUR.

AT LEAST FOUR CITIZENS SAW A MYSTERIOUS OR SUSPICIOUS-LOOKING MAN LOITERING AT OR NEAR THE BORDEN HOUSE.

AT ABOUT 10:45AM, ANDREW CONCLUDED HIS FINAL MEETING— WITH A PROSPECTIVE TENANT OF THE BORDEN BUILDING— AND BEGAN HIS WALK HOME.

MANY PEOPLE NOTICED THAT HE CARRIED A SMALL PARCEL UNDER HIS ARM.

At about this same time, Bridget Sullivan came indoors to wash the interior side of the windows ...

Locking the screen door behind her.

Shortly thereafter, Andrew Borden arrived home. He first tried the rear screen door ...

And then walked around to the front door, which was still triple-locked from the night before.

Finding he could not open the front door, he knocked heavily upon it ...

Bringing Bridget from her work.

As the maid struggled with the locks, she uttered a mild curse of frustration ...

PSHAW!

Upon which she heard a curious, muted laugh from the direction of the upstairs landing.

KEE, KEE!

She could not see from whom it emanated, but assumed it to have been Lizzie.

At last, Andrew entered the house ...

Carrying, Bridget noticed, a small wrapped parcel.

WHERE WAS LIZZIE WHEN HER FATHER ARRIVED HOME?

SHE LATER CLAIMED TO HAVE BEEN IN THE KITCHEN READING.

IN ANY CASE, SHE APPEARED IN THE DINING ROOM TO SPEAK BRIEFLY WITH HIM...

MENTIONING CASUALLY THAT ABBY HAD RECEIVED A MESSAGE AND GONE OUT.

AFTER SPENDING SOME MINUTES UPSTAIRS. ANDREW CAME DOWN TO THE SITTING ROOM.

AS HE RECLINED ON THE SOFA, LIZZIE CAME IN TO HELP HIM.

DO YOU WANT THE WINDOW LEFT LIKE THIS?

SHE REMOVED HIS SHOES...

FOLDED HIS COAT UNDER HIS HEAD...

AND THE STAGE WAS SET FOR THE SECOND MURDER.

BY NOW IT WAS ALMOST 11:00 AM. LIZZIE RETURNED TO THE DINING ROOM AND ENGAGED BRIDGET IN CONVERSATION.

MAGGIE,* ARE YOU GOING OUT THIS AFTERNOON?

I DON'T KNOW... I MIGHT AND I MIGHT NOT. I DON'T FEEL WELL.

* ADAPTOR'S NOTE: BOTH BORDEN SISTERS CALLED BRIDGET "MAGGIE," WHICH WAS THE NAME OF THE FAMILY'S LONGTIME FORMER HOUSE-MAID.

WELL, IF YOU DO BE SURE AND LOCK THE DOOR. MRS. BORDEN HAS GONE OUT ON A SICK CALL, AND I MIGHT GO OUT TOO.

THERE'S A CHEAP SALE OF DRESS GOODS AT SARGENT'S TODAY — ONLY EIGHT CENTS A YARD.

THEN I'M GOING TO HAVE ONE!

EAGER FOR A CHANCE TO REST BEFORE THE NOON MEAL, BRIDGET CLIMBED THE BACK STAIRS TO HER ATTIC ROOM, WHICH MUST HAVE BEEN LIKE A BLAZING OVEN.

BEFORE DOZING OFF, SHE REMEMBERED HEARING THE CITY HALL CLOCK STRIKE ELEVEN.

37

AT ABOUT THAT VERY MOMENT, SOMEBODY ENTERED THE SITTING ROOM — OR MERELY LEANED AROUND THE DOORWAY FROM THE DINING ROOM...

AND DISPATCHED ANDREW BORDEN WITH A HATCHET.

TEN FIERCE AND HEAVY BLOWS TO THE HEAD AND FACE!

SUCH A MASSIVE FRONTAL BARRAGE COULD ONLY HAVE TAKEN ANDREW AS HE SLUMBERED PEACEFULLY ON THE SOFA.

WHERE WAS LIZZIE AT THE TIME HER FATHER WAS MURDERED? SHE CLAIMED, THEN AND EVER AFTER, THAT SHE WAS OUTSIDE THE HOUSE.

A PASSING ICE CREAM VENDOR, MR. LUBINSKY, SAW A WOMAN IN THE BORDEN YARD AT ABOUT THAT VERY TIME.

WHEN SHE CAME BACK INSIDE — VIA THE REAR SCREEN DOOR — SHE PASSED THROUGH THE SITTING ROOM ON THE WAY TO THE FRONT STAIRS.

GLANCING TO HER LEFT, SHE DISCOVERED THE GRISLY REMAINS OF HER FATHER.

BRIDGET WAS JOLTED AWAKE BY LIZZIE'S CRIES.

MAGGIE, COME DOWN!

COME QUICK! FATHER'S DEAD! SOMEBODY KILLED HIM!

BRIDGET CAME DOWNSTAIRS TO CONFRONT LIZZIE IN THE REAR HALLWAY.

HE'S IN THE SITTING ROOM, BUT DON'T LOOK. GO FIND DR. BOWEN.

AS SHE DASHED FROM THE HOUSE, BRIDGET NOTED THAT THE SCREEN DOOR HAD BEEN UNHOOKED.

FINDING THE DOCTOR OUT (AND LEAVING AN URGENT MESSAGE WITH MRS. BOWEN) BRIDGET RETURNED TO THE REAR DOOR.

WHAT HAPPENED, MISS? DID YOU SEE?

NO—I WAS OUT IN THE YARD. I HEARD A GROAN AND CAME IN. NOW GO FETCH MISS RUSSELL.

MRS. ADELAIDE CHURCHILL, A WIDOW WHO OCCUPIED THE HOUSE NORTH OF THE BORDENS, HAD BEEN WATCHING THE ACTIVITY NEXT DOOR. SHE WALKED OVER AS BRIDGET DEPARTED AGAIN.

LIZZIE, WHAT'S THE MATTER?

TO HER, LIZZIE APPEARED DAZED AND STUNNED.

OH, MRS. CHURCHILL... SOMEONE HAS KILLED FATHER.

MRS. CHURCHILL BROUGHT LIZZIE INTO THE KITCHEN AND SAT HER IN THE ROCKER THERE.

AND THEN PEERED INTO THE SITTING ROOM TO CONFIRM THE HORRIBLE TALE.

TO MRS. CHURCHILL'S INQUIRIES, LIZZIE REPLIED: THAT SHE HAD BEEN OUT IN THE BARN, LOOKING FOR "IRONS," AND HAD HEARD NOISES COMING FROM THE HOUSE...

AND NO, ABBY WAS NOT AT HOME, HAVING RECEIVED A MESSAGE AND GONE OUT.

AT THIS POINT, IT MUST BE MENTIONED THAT MRS. CHURCHILL — WHO ARRIVED NO MORE THAN TEN MINUTES AFTER ANDREW'S MURDER — SAW NO BLOOD ON LIZZIE'S DRESS, SKIN OR HAIR, AND HER HAIR NEATLY PINNED UP, WITH NO SIGN OF HAVING BEEN RECENTLY WASHED.

MRS. CHURCHILL THEN LEFT LIZZIE ALONE AND WALKED DOWN SECOND STREET TO HALL'S LIVERY STABLE.

THERE, SHE FOUND HER HIRED MAN AND ORDERED HIM TO GO FIND A DOCTOR, THERE HAD BEEN "TROUBLE" AT THE BORDEN HOUSE.

SHE ALSO SUGGESTED THAT SOMEBODY TELEPHONE THE POLICE.

THIS WAS AT 11:15 AM.

DR. BOWEN ARRIVED, WITH MRS. BOWEN...

BRIDGET SULLIVAN RETURNED FROM MISS RUSSELL'S HOUSE...

AND, SHORTLY THEREAFTER, MISS RUSSELL HERSELF ARRIVED.

THE DOCTOR, AFTER SATISFYING HIMSELF AS TO ANDREW BORDEN'S DECEASE, CALLED FOR A SHEET TO PLACE OVER THE BODY...

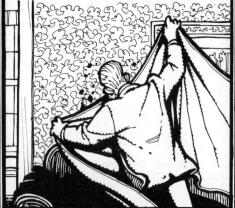

WHILE, IN THE KITCHEN, THE WOMEN ATTEMPTED TO COMFORT LIZZIE. WHEN MISS RUSSELL REACHED TO LOOSEN HER COLLAR, LIZZIE STOPPED HER.

I'M NOT FAINT.

AT THAT POINT, DR. BOWEN REMOVED LIZZIE TO A SMALL DIVAN IN THE DINING ROOM.

SHE TOLD HIM THAT SHE HAD BEEN OUT IN THE BARN, "LOOKING FOR IRONS" WHEN HER FATHER WAS KILLED.

SHE THEN SENT THE DOCTOR OUT TO TELEGRAPH THE TERRIBLE NEWS TO EMMA IN FAIRHAVEN...

PERHAPS ALSO TO NOTIFY JOHN MORSE AT THE HOME OF HIS RELATIONS ON WEYBOSSET STREET.

42

AS DR. BOWEN LEFT ON HIS MISSION, THE FIRST POLICE OFFICER ARRIVED.

THIS WAS OFFICER GEORGE ALLEN, WHO WAS THE ONLY MAN ON DUTY AT THE STATION...

(BECAUSE, ON THAT VERY DAY, MOST OF THE FALL RIVER POLICE FORCE WERE ON THEIR ANNUAL OUTING TO ROCKY POINT!)

HE TOOK A LOOK AT THE CORPSE...

SEARCHED THE FIRST FLOOR FOR ANY LURKING INTRUDER (ALTHOUGH NOT THE SECOND FLOOR OR THE CELLAR)...

AND DEPARTED TO LOCATE MORE OFFICERS, LEAVING A BURLY CITIZEN, MR. CHARLES SAWYER, TO GUARD THE DOOR.

IN THE DINING ROOM, MEANWHILE, MRS. CHURCHILL WONDERED AGAIN ABOUT ABBY BORDEN'S WHEREABOUTS. LIZZIE REPLIED OFFHANDEDLY:

I THOUGHT I HEARD HER COME IN THE FRONT DOOR.

AND SO, WITH DREAD IN THEIR HEARTS, MRS. CHURCHILL AND BRIDGET SULLIVAN ASCENDED THE FRONT STAIRS.

LOOKING INTO THE GUEST ROOM AT FLOOR LEVEL, MRS. CHURCHILL KNEW AT ONCE WHAT SHE SAW...

THE BUTCHERED REMAINS OF ABBY BORDEN!

AT 11:35 — 11:45 AM, AS A SIZEABLE CROWD GATHERED OUTSIDE THE BORDEN HOUSE, POLICE OFFICERS BEGAN TO ARRIVE IN NUMBERS.

OFFICER WIXON

OFFICER DOHERTY

OFFICER MULLALY

DEPUTY MARSHAL FLEET

OFFICER MEDLEY

OFFICER DEVINE

OFFICER WILSON

SGT. HARRINGTON

By AN ASTONISHING CO-INCIDENCE, THE MEDICAL EXAMINER OF BRISTOL COUNTY, DR. WILLIAM DOLAN, HAPPENED TO BE PASSING DOWN SECOND STREET. HE KNEW AT ONCE SOMETHING WAS AMISS.

THE POLICE INITIATED A THOROUGH SEARCH OF THE HOUSE...

WHILE LIZZIE, IN HER FIRST OFFICIAL INTERVIEW, (FROM OFFICER MEDLEY), TOLD OF HER TRIP TO THE BARN DURING THE TIME HER FATHER WAS KILLED. SHE CLIMBED TO THE LOFT, SHE SAID, IN SEARCH OF IRON PIECES TO USE AS SINKERS FOR AN UPCOMING FISHING EXCURSION.

SHE FIGURED SHE WAS THERE FOR FIFTEEN OR TWENTY MINUTES.

IN THE MEAN-TIME, JOHN V. MORSE, HAVING RETURNED BY STREET-CAR, APPROACHED THE HOUSE CAUTIOUSLY.

SEVERAL PEOPLE SAW HIM LOITERING AT THE SIDE OF THE HOUSE, AND IN THE BACK YARD BEFORE HE FINALLY ENTERED.

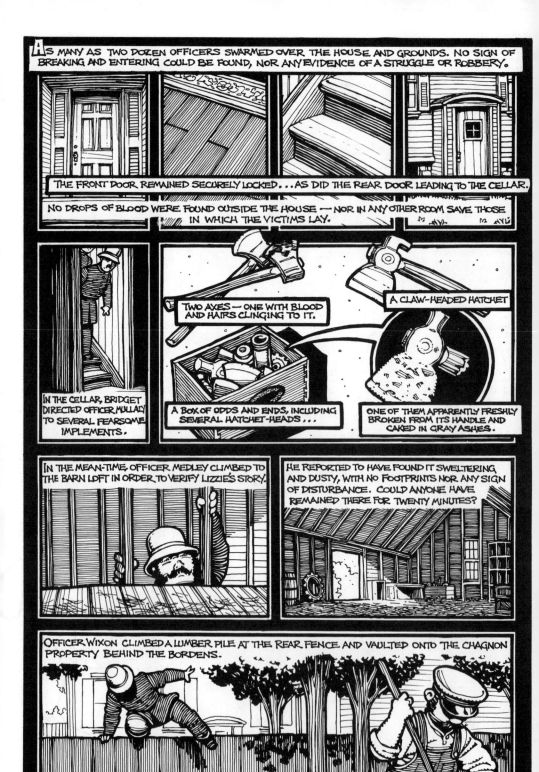

As many as two dozen officers swarmed over the house and grounds. No sign of breaking and entering could be found, nor any evidence of a struggle or robbery.

The front door remained securely locked... as did the rear door leading to the cellar.

No drops of blood were found outside the house — nor in any other room save those in which the victims lay.

In the cellar, Bridget directed Officer Mullaly to several fearsome implements.

Two axes — one with blood and hairs clinging to it.

A box of odds and ends, including several hatchet-heads...

A claw-headed hatchet

One of them apparently freshly broken from its handle and caked in gray ashes.

In the mean-time, Officer Medley climbed to the barn loft in order to verify Lizzie's story.

He reported to have found it sweltering and dusty, with no footprints nor any sign of disturbance. Could anyone have remained there for twenty minutes?

Officer Wixon climbed a lumber pile at the rear fence and vaulted onto the Chagnon property behind the Bordens.

Workers there reported having seen or heard nothing unusual all morning.

46

THE MEDICAL EXAMINER, AFTER A PRELIMINARY SCRUTINY OF THE BODIES, ANNOUNCED TWO IMMEDIATE CONCLUSIONS:

MRS. BORDEN WAS KILLED SOME TIME BEFORE HER HUSBAND — PERHAPS TWO HOURS!

(IF SO, COULD A MURDERER HAVE HIDDEN WITHIN THE HOUSE FOR THAT LENGTH OF TIME — OR DEPARTED AND RETURNED WITHOUT BEING SEEN?)

EACH ATTACK WAS OF SUCH FEROCITY THAT THE FIRST BLOW WAS SUFFICIENT TO CAUSE DEATH.

(IN OTHER WORDS, THIS WAS THE PRODUCT OF NO COMMONPLACE FELONY — BUT THE KIND OF OVER-KILL THAT MARKS THE WORK OF A HOPELESS MANIAC.)

THE POLICE PHOTOGRAPHER ARRIVED TO CAPTURE IMAGES OF THE TWO VICTIMS, AS THEY LAY WHERE THEY WERE FOUND.

THE PHOTOGRAPHS BECAME THE TALK OF FALL RIVER.

It was brutal mid-afternoon when the bodies were at last brought into the dining room, laid out upon the table, stripped and washed. Dr. Dolan, assisted by Dr. Bowen and five other physicians performed the post-mortem.

Townspeople jockeyed for a view through the wide-open windows...

While countless flies, attracted by the blood, filled the stifling air within the house.

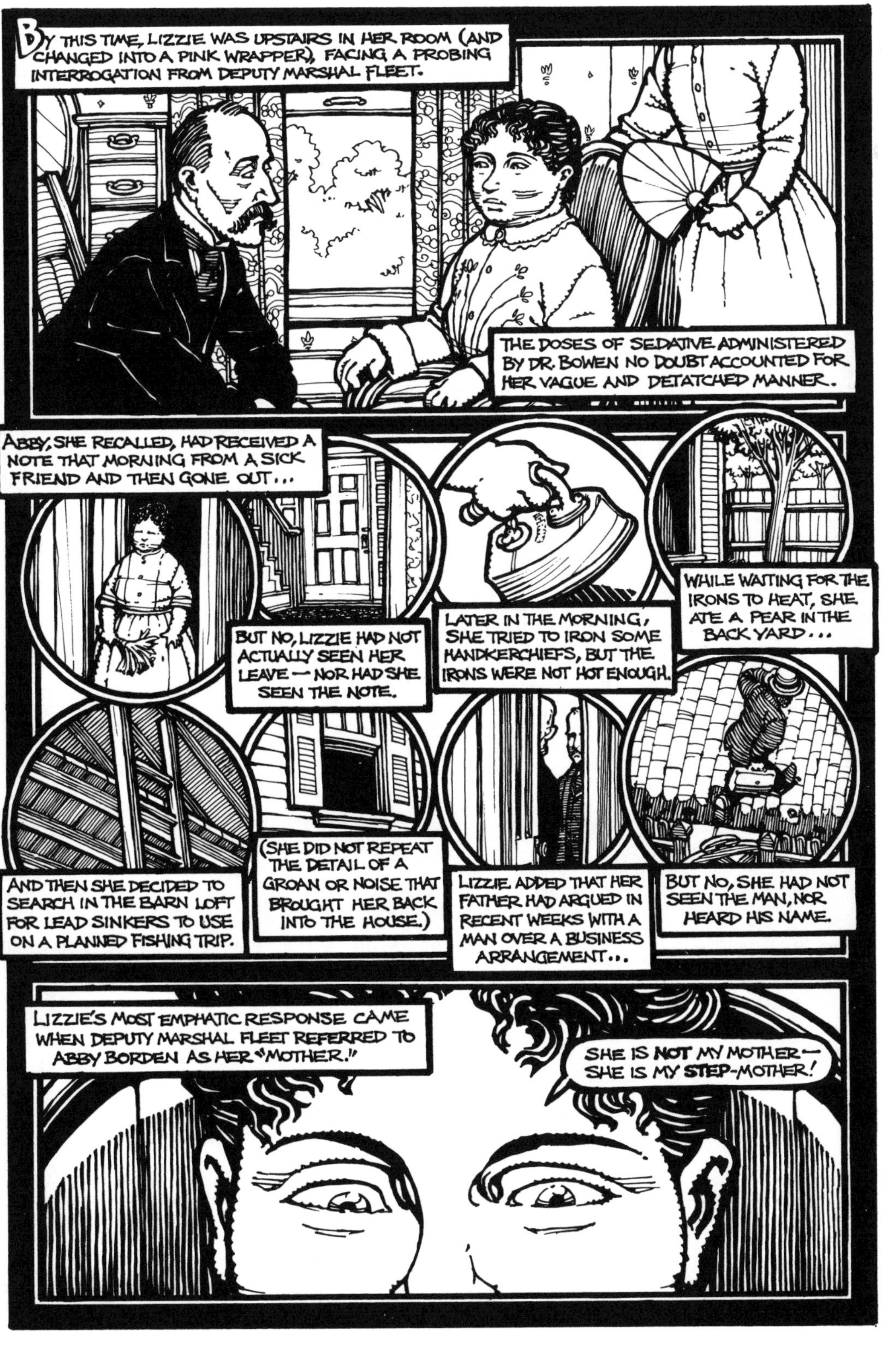
BY THIS TIME, LIZZIE WAS UPSTAIRS IN HER ROOM (AND CHANGED INTO A PINK WRAPPER), FACING A PROBING INTERROGATION FROM DEPUTY MARSHAL FLEET.
THE DOSES OF SEDATIVE ADMINISTERED BY DR. BOWEN NO DOUBT ACCOUNTED FOR HER VAGUE AND DETATCHED MANNER.
ABBY, SHE RECALLED, HAD RECEIVED A NOTE THAT MORNING FROM A SICK FRIEND AND THEN GONE OUT...
BUT NO, LIZZIE HAD NOT ACTUALLY SEEN HER LEAVE — NOR HAD SHE SEEN THE NOTE.
LATER IN THE MORNING, SHE TRIED TO IRON SOME HANDKERCHIEFS, BUT THE IRONS WERE NOT HOT ENOUGH.
WHILE WAITING FOR THE IRONS TO HEAT, SHE ATE A PEAR IN THE BACK YARD...
AND THEN SHE DECIDED TO SEARCH IN THE BARN LOFT FOR LEAD SINKERS TO USE ON A PLANNED FISHING TRIP.
(SHE DID NOT REPEAT THE DETAIL OF A GROAN OR NOISE THAT BROUGHT HER BACK INTO THE HOUSE.)
LIZZIE ADDED THAT HER FATHER HAD ARGUED IN RECENT WEEKS WITH A MAN OVER A BUSINESS ARRANGEMENT...
BUT NO, SHE HAD NOT SEEN THE MAN, NOR HEARD HIS NAME.
LIZZIE'S MOST EMPHATIC RESPONSE CAME WHEN DEPUTY MARSHAL FLEET REFERRED TO ABBY BORDEN AS HER "MOTHER."
SHE IS NOT MY MOTHER — SHE IS MY STEP-MOTHER!

AT 7:00 PM, EMMA BORDEN ARRIVED FROM FAIRHAVEN

THE SISTERS' REUNION TOOK PLACE IN THE PARLOR...

AS THE HOUSE UNDERWENT ANOTHER TOP-TO-BOTTOM SEARCH:

ESPECIAL ATTENTION WAS PAID TO BUREAUS AND CLOSETS, IN SEARCH OF BLOOD-SPATTERED CLOTHING.

A GREAT EFFORT WAS MADE TO FIND THE NOTE THAT LIZZIE SAID HER STEP-MOTHER HAD RECEIVED.

IT MUST BE MENTIONED, HOWEVER, THAT NO SUCH NOTE WAS EVER FOUND, NOR ANY MESSENGER OR SICK FRIEND OF ABBY'S.

THE FIREPLACES AND ASH-BINS WERE SIFTED FOR TRACES OF THE MURDER WEAPON.

THAT EVENING, IN THE KITCHEN, SGT. HARRINGTON WATCHED DR. BOWEN RIP SEVERAL PAGES FROM HIS NOTE-BOOK AND DROP THEM INTO THE FIRE.

THE CROWD OUTSIDE THE BORDEN HOUSE DIMINISHED ONLY SLIGHTLY WHEN DARKNESS FELL.

AS POLICE OFFICERS STOOD WATCH DOWNSTAIRS, EMMA AND LIZZIE RETIRED TO THEIR BEDROOMS.

JOHN V. MORSE AGAIN OCCUPIED THE GUEST ROOM . . .

AND MISS ALICE RUSSELL BEGAN AN EXTENDED STAY IN THE MASTER BEDROOM.

ONLY BRIDGET SULLIVAN REFUSED TO SPEND ANOTHER NIGHT IN THE HOUSE. SHE FOUND QUARTERS IN THE HOME OF A NEIGHBOR.

COULD ANY OF THEM HAVE SLUMBERED PEACEFULLY THAT NIGHT?

ANDREW AND ABBY BORDEN REMAINED UPON THE TABLE FROM WHICH THEY HAD CONSUMED BREAKFAST THAT VERY MORNING!

FOR THE ENTIRETY OF FRIDAY, AUGUST 5, THE BORDEN SISTERS STAYED INDOORS, AS REPORTS OF THE GRUESOME DOUBLE MURDER SPREAD ACROSS THE NATION AND THE WORLD.

THE CURIOUS KEPT THEIR VIGIL OUTSIDE, WHILE POLICE SUBJECTED THE HOUSE TO YET ANOTHER THOROUGH SEARCH.

THE IGNORANCE OF THOSE WITHIN THE HOUSE AS TO THE EXTENT OF PUBLIC ATTENTION CAN BE SEEN IN THE FACT THAT JOHN V. MORSE THOUGHT NOTHING OF GOING OUT IN THE EVENING TO POST A LETTER.

HE WAS PURSUED BY A MOB OF ANGRY CITIZENS FOR SEVERAL BLOCKS BEFORE HIS RESCUE BY POLICE.

THE MORNING OF SATURDAY, AUGUST 6 SAW AN EDITORIAL IN THE FALL RIVER GLOBE, CHIDING THE POLICE FORCE FOR ITS INACTION THUS FAR.

EVERYBODY WONDERED WHEN AN ARREST WOULD BE MADE.

AT 10:00 AM, A SMALL, PRIVATE FUNERAL SERVICE WAS HELD AT THE BORDEN HOUSE.

THE CASKETS WERE DISPLAYED IN THE SITTING ROOM.

AFTERWARD, A PARADE OF CARRIAGES FOLLOWED THE TWIN HEARSES TO OAK GROVE CEMETERY.

THRONGS OF CITIZENS LINED THE ROUTE.

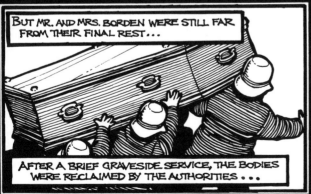

BUT MR. AND MRS. BORDEN WERE STILL FAR FROM THEIR FINAL REST...

AFTER A BRIEF GRAVESIDE SERVICE, THE BODIES WERE RECLAIMED BY THE AUTHORITIES...

AND REMOVED TO AN EMPTY TOMB FOR FURTHER EXAMINATION!

AT ABOUT THAT SAME MOMENT, CITY MARSHAL RUFUS HILLIARD, IN FRUSTRATION, CONDUCTED ANOTHER SEARCH OF THE BORDEN HOUSE . . .

DOWN TO THE SLIGHTEST BUMP IN THE WALLPAPER!

HE TOOK WITH HIM THE BLUE COTTON-AND-SILK DRESS THAT LIZZIE CLAIMED TO HAVE WORN ON THE MORNING OF THE MURDER.

THAT EVENING, MARSHAL HILLIARD RETURNED WITH MR. JOHN COUGHLIN, THE MAYOR OF FALL RIVER. EVERYBODY GATHERED IN THE PARLOR.

WHEN THE MAYOR SUGGESTED THAT THE FAMILY REMAIN INDOORS FOR THE NEXT SEVERAL DAYS, LIZZIE CHALLENGED HIM:

WHY? IS ANYBODY IN THIS HOUSE SUSPECTED?

IN VIEW OF WHAT HAPPENED TO MR. MORSE LAST NIGHT, THE INFERENCE MIGHT BE JUSTIFIED.

LIZZIE WOULD NOT BACK DOWN.

I WANT TO KNOW THE TRUTH! IS ANYBODY SUSPECTED?

WELL, MISS BORDEN, I REGRET TO ANSWER . . . BUT YES, YOU ARE SUSPECTED.

LIZZIE CALMLY ROSE AND EXTENDED HER WRISTS.

I AM READY TO GO NOW.

THE MAYOR AND MARSHAL HILLIARD HASTENED TO ASSURE HER THAT SHE WAS NOT UNDER ARREST, AND THAT THEIR CONCERN WAS ONLY FOR THE FAMILY'S SAFETY.

AND THEN THEY POLITELY TOOK THEIR LEAVE.

ON SUNDAY, AUGUST 7, THERE OCCURRED AN INCIDENT THAT WAS TO REFLECT BADLY UPON LIZZIE IN THE MONTHS TO COME. ON THAT MORNING, SHE AND EMMA WORKED IN THE KITCHEN.

WHAT ARE YOU GOING TO DO WITH THAT?

I'M GOING TO BURN THIS OLD THING UP. IT'S COVERED WITH PAINT.

AND SO, SHE BEGAN TO DROP PIECES OF A BLUE CORDUROY DRESS INTO THE FLAMES.

AT THIS POINT, MISS ALICE RUSSELL, STILL STAYING WITH THE SISTERS, ENTERED THE ROOM.

LIZZIE, WHAT ARE YOU DOING?

JUST BURNING UP THIS OLD DRESS.

I WOULDN'T LET ANYBODY SEE ME DOING THAT IF I WERE YOU.

AT THIS, LIZZIE APPEARED TRULY SURPRISED.

OH NO! WHY DIDN'T YOU TELL ME BEFORE? WHAT HAVE I DONE?

MISS RUSSELL WOULD NOT FORGET WHAT SHE HAD SEEN.

THAT EVENING, EMMA BORDEN, WITH PAIL AND BRUSH, WASHED THE BLOOD-STAINS FROM THE WALLS AND FLOORS OF BOTH MURDER CHAMBERS.

ON MONDAY, AUGUST 8, THE BORDEN HOUSE WAS PUT TO A FINAL SEARCH. (BUT IT MUST BE MENTIONED THAT, AFTER THE FIRST DAY, NO FURTHER PERTINENT EVIDENCE WAS EVER FOUND.)

THE VARIOUS AXES AND HATCHETS FROM THE CELLAR WERE SENT TO THE HARVARD MEDICAL SCHOOL FOR SCIENTIFIC TESTS.

TUESDAY, AUGUST 9, SAW THE OPENING OF THE INQUEST AT THE FALL RIVER COURT BUILDING.

UNDER THE QUESTIONING OF DISTRICT ATTORNEY HOSEA KNOWLTON, LIZZIE GAVE HER ONLY OFFICIALLY-DOCUMENTED ACCOUNT OF THE MURDER MORNING.

THE BORDEN SISTERS ARRIVED IN THE COMPANY OF THE FAMILY'S LAWYER, MR. ANDREW JENNINGS (WHO WAS PROHIBITED FROM ATTENDING THE PROCEEDINGS).

HER SOMETIMES CONFUSED AND CONTRADICTORY RESPONSES WERE MOST LIKELY THE RESULT OF THE STEADY DOSES OF MORPHINE ADMINISTERED OVER THE PRECEEDING WEEK.

FURTHER WITNESSES HEARD FROM DURING THE COURSE OF THE INQUEST:

BRIDGET SULLIVAN

DR. SEABURY BOWEN

MRS. CHURCHILL

JOHN V. MORSE

MR. HIRAM HARRINGTON, A BROTHER-IN-LAW OF ANDREW BORDEN, DESCRIBED WHAT HE SAW AS YEARS OF ILL-FEELING BETWEEN LIZZIE AND HER STEP-MOTHER.

ON THURSDAY, AUGUST 11, (ONE WEEK AFTER THE MURDERS), THE INQUEST STOOD ADJOURNED.

WITH THE TOWN NEAR HYSTERIA, LIZZIE BORDEN WAS PLACED UNDER ARREST BY MARSHAL HILLIARD.

SHE WAS ALLOWED TO SPEND ONE FINAL NIGHT IN HER HOME...

AND, ON FRIDAY, AUGUST 12, SHE RETURNED WITH MR. JENNINGS TO ENTER A FORMAL PLEA OF "NOT GUILTY."

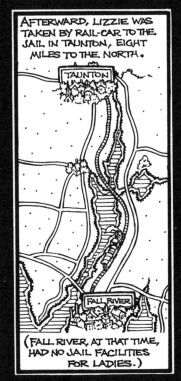

AFTERWARD, LIZZIE WAS TAKEN BY RAIL-CAR TO THE JAIL IN TAUNTON, EIGHT MILES TO THE NORTH.

(FALL RIVER, AT THAT TIME, HAD NO JAIL FACILITIES FOR LADIES.)

THERE SHE REMAINED, IN A SMALL CELL, FOR THE NEXT NINE DAYS

UNTIL RETURNED FOR THE PRELIMINARY HEARING...

WHICH CONVENED ON MONDAY, AUGUST 22, JUDGE JOSIAH BLAISDELL PRESIDING (AS HE HAD OVER THE INQUEST).

THE HEARING, ALTHOUGH A RATHER PERFUNCTORY AFFAIR, WAS OPENED TO THE PUBLIC. I SAT IN THE PACKED, STEAMING COURT-ROOM FOR THE ENTIRE DAY.

MR. KNOWLTON CAREFULLY LAID OUT THE COMMON-WEALTH'S WEB OF CIRCUMSTANTIAL EVIDENCE.

BUT DR. EDWARD WOOD, OF THE HARVARD MEDICAL SCHOOL, INTRODUCED INFORMATION BENEFICIAL TO THE DEFENSE.

A MICROSCOPIC EXAMINATION OF THE AXES AND HATCHETS FROM THE BORDEN CELLAR REVEALED NO BLOOD OR TISSUE RESIDUE AT ALL.

THE AUTOPSIES PERFORMED ON BOTH VICTIMS SHOWED NO TRACES OF POISON OF ANY KIND.

BLOOD AND HAIRS ON ONE AXE WERE FOUND TO BE THOSE OF A COW.

DR. WOOD

THE DAY CONCLUDED WITH MR. JENNINGS' RINGING SPEECH FOR THE DEFENSE.

THE HEARING RE-CONVENED THE NEXT MORNING LONG ENOUGH FOR THE JUDGE TO PRONOUNCE LIZZIE "PROBABLY GUILTY."

SHE WAS RETURNED TO POLICE CUSTODY, PENDING A MEETING OF THE GRAND JURY IN NOVEMBER.

THAT EVENING, SHE WAS REMOVED TO HER CELL IN TAUNTON.

OVER THE ENSUING WEEKS, I WAS ONE OF SEVERAL OLD FALL RIVER FRIENDS WHO VISITED LIZZIE IN THAT BARE LITTLE ROOM.

HER IMPRISONMENT WAS BEGINNING TO TELL ON HER: I SAW FEW TRACES OF THE OLD ROBUSTNESS AND GOOD HUMOR.

IN THE MEAN-TIME, LIFE IN FALL RIVER HAD BEEN TRANSFORMED.

NO TWO PEOPLE COULD MEET WITHOUT A THOROUGH AIRING OF THE BORDEN CASE.

BOARDING HOUSE DINNER TABLES WERE THE SCENES OF IMPASSIONED DEBATE.

WHO ELSE COULD HAVE DONE IT? IT **HAD** TO HAVE BEEN SHE!

BUT NO LADY COULD WIELD A HATCHET IN SO BRUTAL A MANNER!

THE BLOOD-PATTERNS INDICATE A LEFT-HANDED ASSAILANT.

ON EVERY STREET CORNER COULD BE HEARD THE POPULAR CHILDRENS' SONG, WHICH APPEARED OUT OF NOWHERE.*

LIZZIE BORDEN TOOK AN AXE AND GAVE HER MOTHER FORTY WHACKS; WHEN SHE SAW WHAT SHE HAD DONE, SHE GAVE HER FATHER FORTY-ONE!

* TO THE TUNE OF: "TA-RA-RA-BOOM-DE-AY!"

THE POPULAR FEELING AGAINST LIZZIE WAS NOT ALLEVIATED IN OCTOBER, WHEN THE BOSTON GLOBE (THERETOFORE HIGHLY RESPECTED) PRINTED A SERIES OF SCANDALOUS ARTICLES. SEVERAL NEWLY-UNCOVERED WITNESSES CLAIMED, AMONG OTHER THINGS:

LIZZIE HAD A SECRET.
Mr. Borden Discovered It. Then a Quarrel.
Startling Testimony of 25 New Witnesses.

ON THE NIGHT BEFORE THE MURDERS, LIZZIE HAD INFORMED HER FATHER THAT SHE WAS WITH CHILD, AND THEY QUARRELED VIOLENTLY.

THE BORDEN SISTERS PAID A FANTASTIC SUM TO BRIDGET SULLIVAN FOR HER SILENCE.

LIZZIE WAS SEEN THE NEXT MORNING, PEERING FROM AN UPSTAIRS WINDOW, A HOOD OVER HER HEAD.

THE STORIES WERE SOON RETRACTED AS COMPLETE FABRICATIONS — AND THEIR AUTHOR SHORTLY DIED, UNDER QUESTIONABLE CIRCUMSTANCES.

LIZZIE CERTAINLY HAD HER DEFENDERS — AND THEY POINTED TO CERTAIN UNASSAILABLE FACTS:

NO MURDER WEAPON NOR BLOOD-STAINED CLOTHING WERE EVER FOUND IN THE BORDEN HOUSE OR YARD.

NO BLOOD WAS SEEN ON LIZZIE'S SKIN, HAIR OR CLOTHING BY THOSE SHE ENCOUNTERED ONLY MINUTES AFTER THE MURDERS.

SHE WAS SEEN IN THE YARD BY A PASSING VENDOR AT THE VERY TIME SHE CLAIMED TO HAVE BEEN THERE.

MANY PEOPLE REPORTED HAVING SEEN A SUSPICIOUS-LOOKING MAN LOITERING NEAR THE BORDEN HOUSE.

LIZZIE SHARED A CLOSE BOND WITH HER FATHER — AND HAD NO DISPUTE WITH HER STEP-MOTHER THAT SHOULD HAVE LED TO MURDER.

HAD SHE COLDLY PLANNED THE CRIMES, LIZZIE WOULD HAVE PLACED EVIDENCE ABOUT THAT WOULD POINT TO AN INTRUDER.

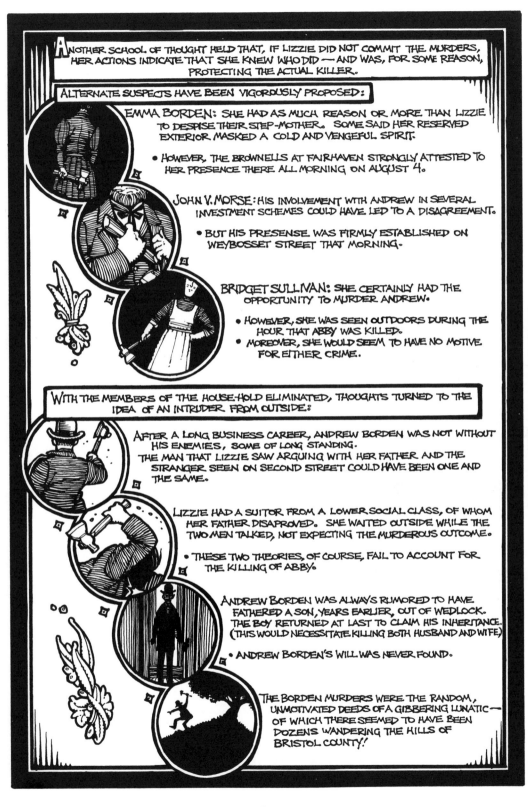

ANOTHER SCHOOL OF THOUGHT HELD THAT, IF LIZZIE DID NOT COMMIT THE MURDERS, HER ACTIONS INDICATE THAT SHE KNEW WHO DID — AND WAS, FOR SOME REASON, PROTECTING THE ACTUAL KILLER.

ALTERNATE SUSPECTS HAVE BEEN VIGOROUSLY PROPOSED:

EMMA BORDEN: SHE HAD AS MUCH REASON OR MORE THAN LIZZIE TO DESPISE THEIR STEP-MOTHER. SOME SAID HER RESERVED EXTERIOR MASKED A COLD AND VENGEFUL SPIRIT.

- HOWEVER, THE BROWNELLS AT FAIRHAVEN STRONGLY ATTESTED TO HER PRESENCE THERE ALL MORNING ON AUGUST 4.

JOHN V. MORSE: HIS INVOLVEMENT WITH ANDREW IN SEVERAL INVESTMENT SCHEMES COULD HAVE LED TO A DISAGREEMENT.

- BUT HIS PRESENSE WAS FIRMLY ESTABLISHED ON WEYBOSSET STREET THAT MORNING.

BRIDGET SULLIVAN: SHE CERTAINLY HAD THE OPPORTUNITY TO MURDER ANDREW.

- HOWEVER, SHE WAS SEEN OUTDOORS DURING THE HOUR THAT ABBY WAS KILLED.
- MOREOVER, SHE WOULD SEEM TO HAVE NO MOTIVE FOR EITHER CRIME.

WITH THE MEMBERS OF THE HOUSE-HOLD ELIMINATED, THOUGHTS TURNED TO THE IDEA OF AN INTRUDER FROM OUTSIDE:

AFTER A LONG BUSINESS CAREER, ANDREW BORDEN WAS NOT WITHOUT HIS ENEMIES, SOME OF LONG STANDING. THE MAN THAT LIZZIE SAW ARGUING WITH HER FATHER AND THE STRANGER SEEN ON SECOND STREET COULD HAVE BEEN ONE AND THE SAME.

LIZZIE HAD A SUITOR FROM A LOWER SOCIAL CLASS, OF WHOM HER FATHER DISAPROVED. SHE WAITED OUTSIDE WHILE THE TWO MEN TALKED, NOT EXPECTING THE MURDEROUS OUTCOME.

- THESE TWO THEORIES, OF COURSE, FAIL TO ACCOUNT FOR THE KILLING OF ABBY.

ANDREW BORDEN WAS ALWAYS RUMORED TO HAVE FATHERED A SON, YEARS EARLIER, OUT OF WEDLOCK. THE BOY RETURNED AT LAST TO CLAIM HIS INHERITANCE. (THIS WOULD NECESSITATE KILLING BOTH HUSBAND AND WIFE)

- ANDREW BORDEN'S WILL WAS NEVER FOUND.

THE BORDEN MURDERS WERE THE RANDOM, UNMOTIVATED DEEDS OF A GIBBERING LUNATIC — OF WHICH THERE SEEMED TO HAVE BEEN DOZENS WANDERING THE HILLS OF BRISTOL COUNTY!

THE GRAND JURY CONVENED AT NEW BEDFORD DURING THE WEEKS OF NOVEMBER 7-21...

AND ADJOURNED, AS MOST EVERYONE EXPECTED, HAVING ISSUED NO INDICTMENT AGAINST LIZZIE BORDEN.

BUT TEN DAYS LATER, THE GRAND JURY RECONVENED...

AND MISS ALICE RUSSELL TOOK THE WITNESS STAND.

APPARENTLY ABLE TO KEEP HER SILENCE NO LONGER, SHE TOLD OF WHAT SHE HAD SEEN ON THAT SUNDAY MORNING AFTER THE MURDERS.

ZIE, WHAT ARE
U DOING?

JUST BURNING THIS OLD DRES

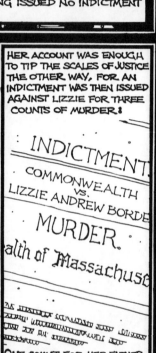

HER ACCOUNT WAS ENOUGH TO TIP THE SCALES OF JUSTICE THE OTHER WAY, FOR AN INDICTMENT WAS THEN ISSUED AGAINST LIZZIE FOR THREE COUNTS OF MURDER:

INDICTMENT

COMMONWEALTH
VS.
LIZZIE ANDREW BORDE

MURDER.

alth of Massachuse

ONE COUNT FOR HER FATHER, ONE COUNT FOR HER STEP-MOTHER, AND A THIRD COUNT, CURIOUSLY, FOR BOTH TOGETHER!

LIZZIE WAS RETURNED TO TAUNTON TO AWAIT HER TRIAL — WHICH WAS SET FOR THE FOLLOWING SUMMER.

MISS RUSSELL'S REVELATION WAS ENOUGH TO SEVER ALL TIES OF FRIENDSHIP BETWEEN HERSELF AND THE BORDEN SISTERS FOREVER.

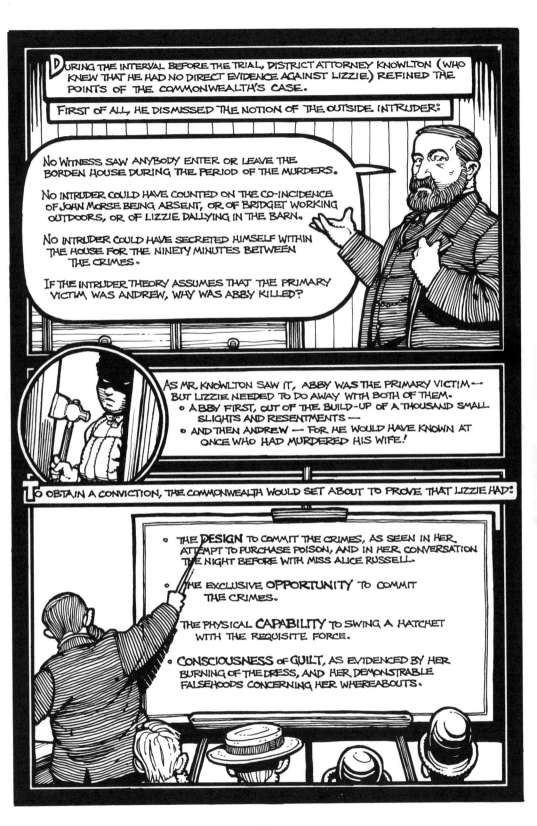

DURING THE INTERVAL BEFORE THE TRIAL, DISTRICT ATTORNEY KNOWLTON (WHO KNEW THAT HE HAD NO DIRECT EVIDENCE AGAINST LIZZIE) REFINED THE POINTS OF THE COMMONWEALTH'S CASE.

FIRST OF ALL, HE DISMISSED THE NOTION OF THE OUTSIDE INTRUDER:

NO WITNESS SAW ANYBODY ENTER OR LEAVE THE BORDEN HOUSE DURING THE PERIOD OF THE MURDERS.

NO INTRUDER COULD HAVE COUNTED ON THE CO-INCIDENCE OF JOHN MORSE BEING ABSENT, OR OF BRIDGET WORKING OUTDOORS, OR OF LIZZIE DALLYING IN THE BARN.

NO INTRUDER COULD HAVE SECRETED HIMSELF WITHIN THE HOUSE FOR THE NINETY MINUTES BETWEEN THE CRIMES.

IF THE INTRUDER THEORY ASSUMES THAT THE PRIMARY VICTIM WAS ANDREW, WHY WAS ABBY KILLED?

AS MR. KNOWLTON SAW IT, ABBY WAS THE PRIMARY VICTIM — BUT LIZZIE NEEDED TO DO AWAY WITH BOTH OF THEM.
- ABBY FIRST, OUT OF THE BUILD-UP OF A THOUSAND SMALL SLIGHTS AND RESENTMENTS —
- AND THEN ANDREW — FOR HE WOULD HAVE KNOWN AT ONCE WHO HAD MURDERED HIS WIFE!

TO OBTAIN A CONVICTION, THE COMMONWEALTH WOULD SET ABOUT TO PROVE THAT LIZZIE HAD:

- THE **DESIGN** TO COMMIT THE CRIMES, AS SEEN IN HER ATTEMPT TO PURCHASE POISON, AND IN HER CONVERSATION THE NIGHT BEFORE WITH MISS ALICE RUSSELL.

- THE EXCLUSIVE **OPPORTUNITY** TO COMMIT THE CRIMES.

- THE PHYSICAL **CAPABILITY** TO SWING A HATCHET WITH THE REQUISITE FORCE.

- **CONSCIOUSNESS** OF **GUILT**, AS EVIDENCED BY HER BURNING OF THE DRESS, AND HER DEMONSTRABLE FALSEHOODS CONCERNING HER WHEREABOUTS.

AS THE YEAR 1893 PROGRESSED, LIFE IN FALL RIVER BEGAN TO RESUME ITS NORMAL RHYTHM.

WHILE UP IN TAUNTON, LIZZIE WAS ALLOWED TO FURNISH HER CELL TO A RELATIVE COMFORT.

SHE HAD BECOME UNIVERSALLY CELEBRATED! EACH DAY'S MAIL BROUGHT GIFTS FROM WELL-WISHERS — AND EVEN PROPOSALS OF MARRIAGE.

ON MAY 31, ANOTHER HORRIBLE MURDER OCCURRED IN FALL RIVER.

A YOUNG WOMAN NAMED BERTHA MANCHESTER, AGED 22 YEARS, WAS CHOPPED TO PIECES IN HER HOME BY AN AXE-WIELDING INTRUDER.

THIS NEWS CAUSED MANY TO REVISE THEIR OPINION OF LIZZIE. THE VISION OF THE WANDERING MADMAN AGAIN INVADED THE PUBLIC MIND.

HOWEVER, IT MUST BE MENTIONED THAT THE MAN SUBSEQUENTLY ARRESTED — A DEVIANT PORTUGESE NAMED CORREIRO — HAD NOT YET ENTERED THE COUNTRY AT THE TIME OF THE BORDEN MURDERS.

AT LAST, LIZZIE'S TRIAL OPENED AT THE NEW BEDFORD COURT-HOUSE ON JUNE 5, 1893.

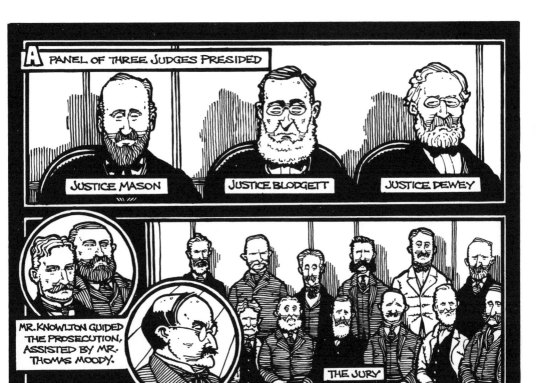

A PANEL OF THREE JUDGES PRESIDED

JUSTICE MASON

JUSTICE BLODGETT

JUSTICE DEWEY

MR. KNOWLTON GUIDED THE PROSECUTION, ASSISTED BY MR. THOMAS MOODY.

THE JURY

FOR THE DEFENSE, MR. JENNINGS ENLISTED THE AID OF MR. GEORGE ROBINSON, THE DISTINGUISHED FORMER GOVERNOR OF MASSACHUSETTS.

THE COMMONWEALTH CASE PROCEEDED FOR TEN DAYS.

THE TRIAL'S MOST DRAMATIC MOMENT CAME WHEN THE CLEANED AND BLANCHED SKULLS OF ANDREW AND ABBY BORDEN WERE EXHIBITED TO THE JURY.

LIZZIE, FEELING FAINT FROM THE SIGHT, HAD TO BE LED FROM THE ROOM.

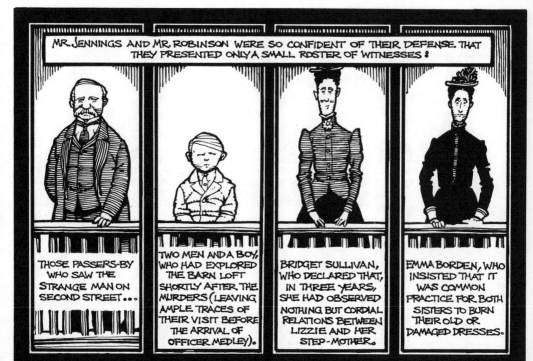

MR. JENNINGS AND MR. ROBINSON WERE SO CONFIDENT OF THEIR DEFENSE THAT THEY PRESENTED ONLY A SMALL ROSTER OF WITNESSES:

THOSE PASSERS-BY WHO SAW THE STRANGE MAN ON SECOND STREET...

TWO MEN AND A BOY, WHO HAD EXPLORED THE BARN LOFT SHORTLY AFTER THE MURDERS (LEAVING AMPLE TRACES OF THEIR VISIT BEFORE THE ARRIVAL OF OFFICER MEDLEY).

BRIDGET SULLIVAN, WHO DECLARED THAT, IN THREE YEARS, SHE HAD OBSERVED NOTHING BUT CORDIAL RELATIONS BETWEEN LIZZIE AND HER STEP-MOTHER.

EMMA BORDEN, WHO INSISTED THAT IT WAS COMMON PRACTICE FOR BOTH SISTERS TO BURN THEIR OLD OR DAMAGED DRESSES.

I WAS AMONG THE THRONG IN THE COURT-ROOM WHEN MR. KNOWLTON AND MR. ROBINSON DELIVERED THEIR IMPASSIONED SUMMATIONS.

WHAT IS THE ANSWER TO THIS ARRAY OF IMPREGNABLE FACTS? NOTHING; NOTHING!

TO FIND HER GUILTY, YOU MUST BELIEVE SHE IS A FIEND! DOES SHE LOOK IT?

ON JUNE 20, THE JURY AT LAST RETIRED FOR DELIBERATION.

NOT GUILTY.

THEY RETURNED IN A MERE ONE HOUR AND SIX MINUTES WITH A VERDICT THAT SURPRISED NO ONE.

LIZZIE SOBBED QUIETLY, AS THE COURT-ROOM ERUPTED IN HUZZAHS.

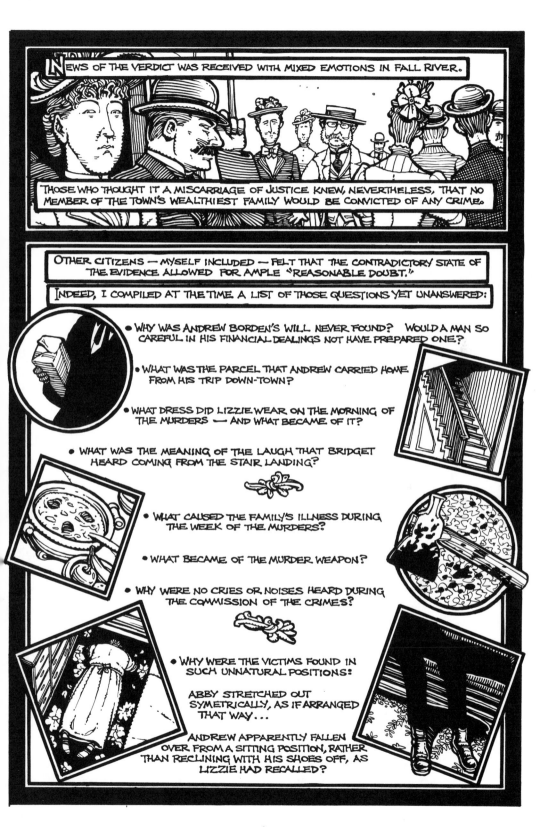

NEWS OF THE VERDICT WAS RECEIVED WITH MIXED EMOTIONS IN FALL RIVER.

THOSE WHO THOUGHT IT A MISCARRIAGE OF JUSTICE KNEW, NEVERTHELESS, THAT NO MEMBER OF THE TOWN'S WEALTHIEST FAMILY WOULD BE CONVICTED OF ANY CRIME.

OTHER CITIZENS — MYSELF INCLUDED — FELT THAT THE CONTRADICTORY STATE OF THE EVIDENCE ALLOWED FOR AMPLE "REASONABLE DOUBT."

INDEED, I COMPILED AT THE TIME A LIST OF THOSE QUESTIONS YET UNANSWERED:

- WHY WAS ANDREW BORDEN'S WILL NEVER FOUND? WOULD A MAN SO CAREFUL IN HIS FINANCIAL DEALINGS NOT HAVE PREPARED ONE?

- WHAT WAS THE PARCEL THAT ANDREW CARRIED HOME FROM HIS TRIP DOWN-TOWN?

- WHAT DRESS DID LIZZIE WEAR ON THE MORNING OF THE MURDERS — AND WHAT BECAME OF IT?

- WHAT WAS THE MEANING OF THE LAUGH THAT BRIDGET HEARD COMING FROM THE STAIR LANDING?

- WHAT CAUSED THE FAMILY'S ILLNESS DURING THE WEEK OF THE MURDERS?

- WHAT BECAME OF THE MURDER WEAPON?

- WHY WERE NO CRIES OR NOISES HEARD DURING THE COMMISSION OF THE CRIMES?

- WHY WERE THE VICTIMS FOUND IN SUCH UNNATURAL POSITIONS:

  ABBY STRETCHED OUT SYMETRICALLY, AS IF ARRANGED THAT WAY...

  ANDREW APPARENTLY FALLEN OVER FROM A SITTING POSITION, RATHER THAN RECLINING WITH HIS SHOES OFF, AS LIZZIE HAD RECALLED?

LIZZIE BORDEN RETURNED TO FALL RIVER A FREE WOMAN.

NEVERTHELESS, A CLOUD OF UNCERTAINTY HUNG OVER HER FOR MANY YEARS THEREAFTER.

THE BORDEN SISTERS SOLD THE HOUSE ON SECOND STREET AND PURCHASED AN ELEGANT MANSION ON "THE HILL," WHICH THEY CHRISTENED "MAPLECROFT."

A FALL RIVER JOURNALIST NAMED PORTER PRODUCED AN ACCOUNT OF THE CASE.

BUT WHEN IT APPEARED, LATE IN 1893, MOST OF THE EDITION WERE PURCHASED BY THE BORDENS AND DESTROYED.

DESPITE HER SOCIAL ISOLATION, LIZZIE USED HER NEW WEALTH TO ESTABLISH A COMFORTABLE LIFE FOR HERSELF.

AN ENTHUSIASTIC THEATRE-GOER, SHE SOUGHT THE COMPANY OF ARTISTES AND BOHEMIAN TYPES.

AT LAST, SOMETIME IN 1905, EMMA BORDEN MOVED FROM MAPLECROFT, AFTER A FINAL FALLING-OUT WITH HER SISTER.

PERHAPS THEIR MUTUAL SECRETS PROVED TOO MUCH OF A STRAIN BETWEEN THEM.

LIZZIE WAS LEFT TO LIVE OUT HER YEARS ALONE.

LIZZIE BORDEN REMAINED AN OBJECT OF CURIOSITY UNTIL HER DEATH AT 67 YEARS IN 1927.

EIGHT DAYS LATER, EMMA BORDEN, WHO HAD RELOCATED TO NEW HAMPSHIRE, PASSED AWAY AT AGE 77.

BRIDGET SULLIVAN LEFT FALL RIVER, AND SETTLED, YEARS LATER, IN MONTANA. SHE DIED THERE IN 1948, AT AGE 82.

JOHN V. MORSE RETURNED TO IOWA, WHERE HE DIED IN 1912.

MISS ALICE RUSSELL, HAVING RETURNED TO OBSCURITY, DIED AT FALL RIVER IN 1941.

THE BORDEN HOUSE STILL STANDS IN FALL RIVER TODAY.

A.J.BORDEN

ANDREW AND ABBY BORDEN — REUNITED WITH THEIR SKULLS — LIE AT PEACE IN OAK GROVE CEMETERY.

EMMA

LIZBETH

CLOSE BY LIE THEIR DAUGHTERS, EMMA AND LIZZIE.

The Borden Tragedy

———— ❧ ————

Press Clippings of the Time
⌒ and ⌒
Borden's Indictment

SHOCKING CRIME.

A Venerable Citizen and His Aged Wife

HACKED TO PIECES AT THEIR HOME.

Mr. and Mrs. Andrew Borden Lose Their Lives

AT THE HANDS OF A DRUNKEN FARM HAND.

Police Searching Actively for the Fiendish Murderer.

The community was terribly shocked this morning to hear that an aged man and his wife had fallen victims to the thirst of a murderer, and that an atrocious deed had been committed. The news spread like wildfire and hundreds poured into Second street. The deed was committed at No. 62 Second street, where for years Andrew J. Borden and his wife had lived in happiness.

It is supposed that an axe was the instrument used, as the bodies of the victims are hacked almost beyond recognition. Since the discovery of the deed the street in front of the house has been blocked by an anxious throng, eagerly waiting for the news of the awful tragedy and vowing vengeance on the assassin.

"FATHER IS STABBED."

The first intimation the neighbors had of the awful crime was a groaning followed by a cry of "murder!" Mrs. Adelaide Churchill, who lives next door to the Bordens, ran over and heard Miss Borden cry: "Father is stabbed; run for the police!"

Mrs. Churchill hurried across the way to the livery stable to get the people there to summon the police John Cunningham, who was passing, learned of the murder and telephoned to police headquarters, and Officer Allen was sent to investigate the case.

Meanwhile the story spread rapidly and a crowd gathered quickly. A HERALD reporter entered the house, and a terrible sight met his view. On the lounge in the cosy sitting room on the first floor of the building lay Andrew J. Borden, dead. His face presented a sickening sight. Over the left temple a wound six by four had been made as if the head had been pounded with the dull edge of an axe. The left eye had been dug out and a cut extended the length of the nose. The face

was hacked to pieces and the blood had covered the man's shirt and soaked into his clothing. Everything about the room was in order, and there were no signs of a scuffle of any kind.

SEVEN WOUNDS.

Upstairs in a neat chamber in the northwest corner of the house, another terrible sight met the view. On the floor between the bed and the dressing case lay Mrs. Borden, stretched full length, one arm extended and her face resting upon it. Over the left temple the skull was fractured and no less than seven wounds were found about the head. She had died, evidently where she had been struck, for her life blood formed a ghastly clot on the carpet.

Dr. Bowen was the first physician to arrive, but life was extinct, and from the nature of the wounds it is probable that the suffering of both victims was very short. The police were promptly on hand and strangers were kept at a distance. Miss Borden was so overcome by the awful circumstances that she could not be seen, and kind friends led her away and cared for her.

A squad of police who had arrived conducted a careful hunt over the premises for trace of the assailant. No weapon was found and there was nothing about the house to indicate who the murderer might have been. A clue was obtained, however. A Portuguese whose name nobody around the house seemed to know, has been employed on one of the Swansey farms owned by Mr. Borden. About 9 o'clock this man went to the house and asked to see Mr. Borden. He had a talk with his employer and asked for the wages due him. Mr. Borden told the man he had no money with him, to call later. If anything more passed between the men it cannot be learned. At length the Portuguese departed and Mr. Borden soon afterward started down town. His first call was to Peter Leduc's barber shop, where he was shaved about 9:30 o'clock. He then dropped into the Union bank to transact some business and talked with Mr. Hart, treasurer of the savings bank, of which Mr. Borden was president. As nearly as can be learned after that he went straight home. He took off his coat and composed himself comfortably on the lounge to sleep. It is presumed, from the easy attitude in which his body lay, that he was asleep when the deadly blow was struck. It is thought that Mrs. Borden was in the room at the time, but was so overcome by the assault that she had no strength to make an outcry. In her bewilderment, she rushed upstairs and went into her room. She must have been followed up the stairs by the murderer, and as she was retreating into the furthest corner of the room, she was felled by the deadly axe.

MISS BORDEN ATTRACTED.

The heavy fall and a subdued groaning attracted Miss Borden into the house. There the terrible sight which has been described met her gaze. She rushed to the staircase and called the servant, who was washing a window in her room on the third floor. So noiselessly had the deed been done that neither of them was aware of the bloody work going on so near them.

To a police officer, Miss Borden said she was at work in the barn about 10 o'clock. On her return she found her father in the sitting room with a horrible gash in the side of his head. He appeared at the time as though he had been hit while in a sitting posture. Giving the alarm, she rushed up stairs to find her mother, only to be more horrified to find that person lying between the dressing case and the bed

THE CROWD GATHERED AT 92 SECOND STREET

sweltering in a pool of blood. It appeared as though Mrs. Borden had seen the man enter, and the man, knowing that his dastardly crime would be discovered, had followed her upstairs and finished his fiendish work. It was a well known fact that Mrs. Borden always left the room when her husband was talking business with anyone. A person knowing this fact could easily spring upon his victim without giving her a chance to make an outcry. Miss Borden had seen no person enter or leave the place. The man who had charge of her father's farm was held in the highest respect by Mr. Borden. His name was Alfred Johnson, and he trusted his employer so much that he left his bank book at Mr. Borden's house for safe keeping. The young lady had not the slightest suspicion of his being connected with the crime. As far as the Portuguese suspected of the crime was concerned, she knew nothing of him, as he might have been a man who was employed by the day in the busy season. What his motive could have been it is hard to tell, as Mr. Borden had always been kind to his help.

Another statement made by the police, and which, though apparently light, would bear investigation, is the following: Some two weeks ago a man applied to Mr. Borden for the lease of a store on South Main street that was vacant. After a short time as Miss Borden was passing the room loud words were heard, her father making the remark. "I will not let it for that purpose." Quietness was restored in a short while, and when the man departed her father said: "When you come to town next time I will let you know." This was two weeks ago, but in the meantime the store has been let to another party, but why a person would commit such a brutal affair because of being refused the rental of a store is hard to see. Miss Borden thinks that the party wanted the store for the sale of liquor and her father refused. It was dark at the time of his calling and she did not recognize his features.

WENT TO SWANSEY.

At 12:45 o'clock Marshal Hilliard and Officers Doherty and Connors procured a carriage and drove over to the farm, hoping that the suspected man would return there in order to prove an alibi. The officers will arrive at the place some time before the man, as the distance is some ten miles, though it is hardly probable that he will return there. What makes it rather improbable that the man suspected is a Portuguese laborer is the statement of Charles Gifford of Swansey. Mr. Gifford says that the only Portuguese employed on the upper farm is Mr. Johnson, and he is confined to his bed by illness. Another man might be employed by Mr. Borden on the lower farm for a few days, but he does not believe it. An attempt was made to reach Swansey by telephone, but no answer was received.

A SIGNIFICANT INCIDENT.

Among the significant incidents revealed in the search through the premises was brought to light by John Donnelly, who with others searched through the barn to see if any trace of the fugitive could be found there. In the hay was seen the perfect outline of a man as if one had slept there over night. Besides this, it was evident that the sleeper was either restless or had been there before, because an imprint was found in another part of the hay that corresponded with the outlines of the first impression. Somebody may have been in the habit of going there for a nap, but the imprint was that of a person of about five feet six inches tall, and was shorter than Mr. Borden. This has given rise to the suspicion that the murderer may have slept about the place and waited for an opportunity to accomplish his deed.

ANOTHER STORY.

Another sensational story is being told in connection with the murder. It ap-

ANDREW JACKSON BORDEN

pears that the members of the family have been ill for some days and the symptoms were very similar to those of poison. In the light of subsequent events this sickness has been recalled. It has been the custom of the family to receive its supply of milk from the Swansey farm every morning, and the can was left out of doors until the servant opened the house in the morning. Ample opportunity wae afforded, therefore, for anybody who had a foul design to tamper with the milk, and this circumstance will be carefully investigated by the police.

Medical Examiner Dolan, who promptly responded to the call for his presence, made a careful examination of the victims and reached the conclusion that the wounds were inflicted by a heavy, sharp weapon like an axe or hatchet. He found the skull fractured in both instances and concluded that death was instantaneous. As to the blow which killed Mrs. Borden he thought that it had been delivered by a tall man, who struck the woman from behind.

A BOGUS LETTER.

It is reported that Mrs. Borden received a letter this morning announcing the illness of a very dear friend and was preparing to go to see her. This letter has turned out to be a bogus one, evidently intended to draw her away from home. In this case it would look as if the assault had been carefully planned. A suspicious

character was seen on Second street this morning who seemed to be on the lookout for somebody, and the police have a description of the man.

Marshal Hilliard, Officers Dowty and Connors went to Swansey this afternoon, but found the men at work on the upper farm who had been employed there of late. The lower farm will be visited at once. William Eddy has charge of this one.

At 2:15 o'clock a sturdy Portuguese named Antonio Auriel was arrested in a saloon on Columbia street and brought into the police station. The man protested his innocence and sent after Joseph Chaves, clerk for Talbot & Co., who recognized the man, and he was immediately released.

SKETCH OF MR. BORDEN.

Andrew J. Borden was born in this city 69 years ago. By perseverance and industry he accumulated a fortune. A short time since he boasted that he had yet to spend his first foolish dollar. Mr. Borden was married twice. His second wife was the daughter of Oliver Gray and was born on Rodman street. He had two children by his first wife, Emma and Elizabeth. The former is out of town on a visit and has not yet learned of the tragedy.

Mr. Borden was at the time of his death president of the Union saving's bank and director in the Durfee bank, Globe yarn, Merchants and Troy mill. He was interested in several big real estate deals, and was a very wealthy man.

ABBY DURFEE GRAY BORDEN

The Fall River Herald

SENSATIONS in this city always move in cycles. It has been so for fully a dozen years. It will be a fortunate thing if the Borden murder is not followed by another tale of bloodshed.

The Fall River Herald

THURSDAY'S AFFRAY

No Clue as Yet to its Perpetrator.

POLICE WORKING HARD TO REMOVE THE VEIL

Of Mystery That Envelops the Awful Tragedy.

A POSTAL CARD THAT WOULD SERVE AS A LINK.

Further investigation into the circumstances of the Borden murder shroud it with an impenetrable mystery. Nothing that has ever occurred in Fall River or vicinity has created such intense excitement. From the moment the story of the crime was first told to long after midnight Second street was crowded with curious people anxious to hear some particulars that had not been told before.

ANDREW J. BORDEN.

Theories were advanced, some of them plausible enough, but not one could be formed against which some objection could not be offered from the circumstances surrounding the case. Everybody agreed that money was at the bottom of the foul murder, but in what measure and concerning what person could not be conceived. That a bloody deed such as that perpetrated in broad daylight, in a house on one of the busiest streets could have been so quickly and noiselessly accomplished and the murderer escape from the house without attracting attention is wonderful to a degree. Nobody was seen to enter the house by any of the occupants, although all of them except Mr. Borden were busy about the rooms or in the yard.

WAS HE CONCEALED?

Could it be that the murderer was concealed inside the dwelling and had awaited a favorable moment to carry out his nefarious plans? The more the circumstances are considered, the more probable becomes this view of the case. People who have carefully examined the ground believe that Mr. Borden was the first victim, and that the killing of Mrs. Borden was by no means unpremeditated. Having accomplished the bloody work downstairs, the murderer slipped stealthily into the rooms above in search of the wife and, finding her in the northwest chamber walking across the floor to the dressing case, had crept up behind her without attracting her attention and delivered the fatal blow.

The plausibility of this view lies in the fact that the fall of Mrs. Borden, who weighed very nearly 200 pounds, would certainly have jarred the building and awakened her husband, who could only have been sleeping lightly on the lounge, as it was but a few moments after his daughter had seen him quietly reading there that the deed was done. Further investigation confirms the belief that Mrs. Borden was not chased upstairs by the murderer because she was so near the end of the room that she would have been forced to turn and face her pursuer, and the cuts on the head would have been of a different nature.

Twenty minutes were all the time the murderer had to finish his terrible work; conceal the weapon with which he accomplished his crime, and conceal it in such a way as to leave no traces of blood on the carpet or through the house that would reveal how he escaped; to pass out of the house by the side door within 15 feet of the barn where the daughter was engaged and a like distance from the Buffinton house on the north; pass the length of the house and disappear up or down Second street. John Cunningham was going down the street about that time, and he saw nobody pass him, and people who live below saw nobody.

TALKS WITH INMATES.

There are no new developments in the case to be gathered from the people in the house. Regarding the servant, Bridget Sullivan, a woman of about 25, it is pretty well established that at the time that Mr. Borden was assaulted she was in the attic of the house. Her statement to the police is as follows: "I was washing windows most all of the morning and passed in and out of the house continually. At the time Miss Lizzie came down stairs I went to one of the upper rooms to finish the window washing. I remained there until Lizzie's cries attracted my attention; then I came down and went for Dr. Bowen; I never saw any one enter or leave the house."

Miss Borden made the following statement to Officer Harrington as soon as she was sufficiently composed to talk coherently of the affair. It differs in only one particular from the one she told Dr. Bowen, namely, the time in which she was out of the house and in the barn. She said that she was absent 20 minutes, and, upon being requested to be particular, insisted that it was not more than 20 minutes or less than that time. She said that her father enjoyed the most perfect confidence and friendship of his workmen across the river, and that she was in a position to know this, unless something unusual had happened within a few days. She told the story of the angry tenant, saying that the man came to her father twice about the matter, and that he persistently refused to let the store which he wanted for the purpose desired. The only vacant property of Mr. Borden was the room recently vacated by Baker Gadsby, and it is thought that this is the place the man wanted to use. Mr. Borden told the man at the first visit to call again and he would let him know about the rental. It is supposed to be an out-of-town man and that he called and found that Jonathan Clegg had occupied the store. It is also thought that the tenant wanted to use the place as a rum shop; this Mr. Borden would not allow. It may be added that the police attach little importance to this latter matter.

MR. MORSE TALKS.

Visiting at the house on the day of the murder was John W. Morse, a brother of Mr. Borden's first wife. He is fully six feet in height with gray beard and hair. He was not averse to talking, and said in response to questions:

"My sister, Sarah A. Morse, married Andrew Borden in the city of Fall River when both were, as I remember, in their 22d year. That was 47 years ago. At that time Mr. Borden was in reduced circumstances and was just beginning to enter business. They lived for years on Ferry street. They had three children, one of whom died when he was but three or four years old. The others, both girls, grew to womanhood and are now living; they are Emma L., aged 37, and Lizzie A., aged 32.

"Mr. Borden first went into the furniture business on Anawan street, where he remained for 30 years or more. My sister died 28 years ago. At that time Mr. Borden was worth fully $150,000, which amount he had invested largely in mill stocks, which were highly paying securities. He told me on one occasion that he had $78,000 in mill stocks alone. He afterwards invested heavily in a horsecar line, but now I am ahead of my story.

"About 20 years ago I went out west, and settled at Hastings Mills, Ia. On the 14th of of April two years ago I returned home, and since last February I have been staying with a butcher by the name of Davis, in the little town of South Dartmouth, which is near New Bedford. Yes, I am a bachelor. I have a sister living in this city. She married Joseph Morse, a second cousin. I have also one brother whose name is William, who lives at Excelsior, Minn. He is 65 years of age.

"Wednesday I came here from New Bedford early in the afternoon. I left that city on the 12:35 train, which arrived here about 1:30 o'clock. I walked from the station up to the house and rang the front door bell. Mrs. Borden opened it. She welcomed me and I went in. Andrew was then reclining on the sofa in about the position he was found murdered. He looked up and laughed saying, 'Hullo, John, is that you? Have you been to dinner?' I replied in the negative. Mrs. Borden interrupted Mr. Borden, saying: 'Sit right down, we are just through and everything is hot on the stove. It won't cost us a mite of trouble.' They sat by my side through dinner, and then I told them I was going over to Kirby's stable and get a team to drive over to Luther's. I invited Andrew to go, but he declined, saying he didn't feel well enough. He asked me to bring him over

some eggs from his farm which is there located. I returned from the ride about 8:30 o'clock and we sat up until about 10 o'clock. Then Mr. Borden showed me to my room, his wife having previously retired, and bade me good night. That was the last I saw of him until Thursday morning.

"It was about 6 o'clock when I got up, and had breakfast about an hour later. Then Andrew and I read the papers, and we chatted until about 9 o'clock. I am not positive as to the exact time, and it may have been only 8:45 o'clock. While at the table I asked Andrew why he did not buy Gould's yacht for $200,000, at which price it was advertised, and he laughed, saying what little good it would do him if he really did have it. We also talked about business. I had come to Fall River, for one reason, to buy a pair of oxen for Butcher Davis, with whom I lived. He had wanted them, and I had agreed to take them on a certain day, but had not done so. Andrew told me when I was ready to go after them to write him at the farm, which would save him bothering in the matter. When I left the house I started for the postoffice. I walked down Second street, and, stopping in, got a postal card and wrote to William Vinnicum of South Swansey. I dropped it in the office and then went out at the north door of the building to Bedford street, and thence on to Third street, to Pleasant, to Weybosset street. I stopped there at the house of my cousin, Daniel Emery, No. 4; I went there to see my nephew and niece, the former of whom I found away. There I remained until 11:30 or 11:45 and then I started back to Borden's, as I had been asked there to dinner. I hailed a car going by and rode to Second street and thence I walked to the house.

"When I entered the premises I did not go by the front door. On the contrary, I walked around behind the house and picked some pears. Then I went in the back door. Bridget then told me that Mr. and Mrs. Borden had been murdered. I opened the sitting-room door and found a number of people, including the doctors. I entered, but only glanced once at the body. No, I did not look closely enough to be able to describe it. Then I went upstairs and took a similar hasty view of the dead woman. Everything is confusion, however, and I recall very little of what took place."

THE MEDICAL EXAMINER.

Dr. Dolan was called upon after the autopsy, but he had no further facts to disclose. He described the wounds and said that death must have been almost instantaneous in both cases after the first blow. Acting upon the rumor about the poisoned milk, the doctor took samples of it and saved the soft parts of the body for further analysis. He was of the opinion that the wounds were inflicted by a hatchet or a cleaver, and by a person who could strike a blow heavy enough to crush in the skull. In the autopsy, Drs. Coughlin, Dedrick, Leary, Gunning, Dutra, Tourtellot, Peckham and Bowen assisted.

NOTES.

John J. Maher was on a street car on New Boston road Thursday afternoon rather under the influence of liquor. He was telling that when a reward was offered for the man he could find him in 15 minutes. When questioned by an officer as to what he really knew, Maher said that a boy had seen a small man with a dark moustache come out of the house at the time of the murder and, going down Second street, had turned up Pleasant. Maher was locked up on a charge of drunkenness.

Officers Doherty and Harrington have been on continuous duty since the case was reported.

It was rather warm for the officers who were detailed to hunt for the murderer's weapon in the loft of the barn, but they thoroughly examined every corner for the article.

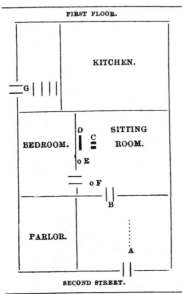

FIRST FLOOR.

KITCHEN.

G

BEDROOM.

D
C
E

SITTING ROOM.

o F

B

PARLOR.

A

SECOND STREET.

A—front door. B—door to room where murder was committed. C—where the body was found. D—the lounge where Mr. Borden was lying. E and F—blood spots. G—back stairs and door.

ROOM WHERE BODY OF MR. BORDEN WAS FOUND.

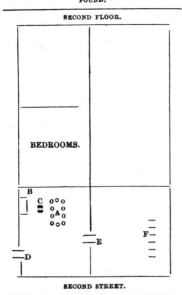

SECOND FLOOR.

BEDROOMS.

B
C

F

E

D

SECOND STREET.

A—the bed. B—dressing case. C—where body of Mrs. Borden was found. D—window. E—door to room. F—staircase.

WHERE BODY OF MRS. BORDEN WAS FOUND.

Officer Medley was one of the busiest men about town Wednesday night, and every remark or idea connected with the tragedy was thoroughly sifted by him.

When the news of the murder reached the people on the excursion it seemed too incredible, and a great many would not be convinced untill they reached home.

If interest and hard work in the case were to land the perpetrator of the crime into custody Assistant Marshal Fleet would have the man behind the bars long before now.

Every morning paper in Boston had a representative in this city Thursday night, and as a result the telegraph operators were kept busy into the small hours of the morning.

The excitement attending the tragedy continued at blood heat throughout the night, and it required a number of officers to keep the street clear in front of the house up to midnight.

Among the many articles secured on the premises is a crowbar over three feet long and weighing about nine pounds. It was found in the shed by one of the officers. It appeared, at first that there was blood on it, and a hasty investigation by two or three policemen convinced the finder that the substance with which it was spotted was blood. It was consequently brought to the police station, where it was found that the spots were nothing else than a few drops of paint and rust.

MORSE'S NIECE.

Mrs. Emery, upon whom Mr. Morse called, was disposed to talk freely to Officer Medley, who interviewed her Thursday night. She said in reply to questions that she had several callers during the day, and that one of them was John Morse.

"Was Morse the name we heard?" asked the officer of a companion.

"Yes," retorted Mrs. Emery quickly, "Morse was the man. He left here at 11:30 o'clock this morning."

"Then you noticed the time?" observed the officer.

"Oh, yes," was the reply, "I noticed the time.

"How did you fix it?" was the next question.

After some little hesitation, Mrs. Emery said that one of her family was sick, and that Dr. Bowen was her physician. "Dr. Bowen came in just as Mr. Morse left."

"Did they meet?" queried the officers.

"No, they did not," said Mrs. Emery.

At this point the niece in question entered the room and corroborated Mrs. Emery's statements, though both women finally fixed upon 11:20 as the exact time of Mr. Morse's departure.

Mrs. Emery volunteered information that Mr. Morse was well-to-do, at least she supposed he was comfortably off and that he had come east to spend his money. She was not positive on this point, however. Morse's niece was asked if she had ever seen her uncle before, and replied that she had. She had met him when she was five years old, and three weeks ago he had taken her from the cars at Warren to the Borden farm, Swansey.

THE OLDEST DAUGHTER.

Miss Emma Borden, who had been visiting in Fairhaven, returned home Thursday evening, having been summoned by the news of the crime. The details of the murder had not been told to her, and she was overcome by the recital. She is the oldest daughter of Andrew Borden by his first wife. All through the early hours of the evening the street was crowded with people, none of whom was admitted to the premises until they had disclosed the nature of their business.

A watch surrounded the house all night, and officers were on guard inside. No further developments were reported. The family retired soon after 10 o'clock and all was in darkness. Undertaker Winward had taken charge of the remains at the request of Miss Borden, and will prepare them for burial.

THE THEORIES DISCUSSED.

Today nothing but the murder was talked about on the streets, and the interest continues to be intense. The announcement that the family had offered a reward of $5000 for the detection of the murderers was the only new item to be discussed.

The theories which were advanced by those who have been closely connected with the case agree in one thing, and that is that the murderer knew his ground and carried out his bloodthirsty plan with a speed and surety that indicated a well matured plot. How quickly the report that was gathered about the premises five minutes after the deed was discovered that a Portuguese had done it was scattered abroad after the murder is looked on with suspicion.

Detective Seaver and other members of the state police force are assisting the local department in its work, and the office of the city marshal is the busiest place in town. New clues are being reported every hour and officers are busy tracking the stories to earth.

Mr. Morse, the guest of the Bordens, is well known in this city where he was born and lived many years. People recall that he went west quite early in life and engaged in raising horses in Iowa. He was said to have had considerable success with his stock and to have gathered together considerable property. Nothing definite about his affairs was known other than that he had told friends that he had brought a train load of horses with him from Iowa to sell, and they were now at Fairhaven.

SIGNIFICANT DISAPPEARANCE.

That letter of which mention was made Thursday as having been sent to Mrs. Borden, announcing that a friend was sick, has since disappeared. The explanation that was given out was that after reading its contents, Mrs. Borden tore it up and threw the pieces in the fire. Bits of charred paper were found in the grate, but not enough to give any idea of the nature of the note. Nobody about the house seems to know where the letter could have come from, and since publicity has been given and considerable importance attached to it, it is considered probable that the writer will inform the family of the circumstances and thus remove suspicions.

Various rumors have been started, one of which was that Miss Borden had assured a friend last winter after a mysterious robbery at the house that her father had an enemy somewhere. A HERALD reporter interviewed a lady to whom it was said this story had been told, but she denied any knowledge of it. Another was that the axe had been found in the yard, but the police have not heard of it.

A TENANT THEORY.

Causes for the murder are arising so fast at the present time that it is nearly impossible to investigate them. Hardly any of them are of sufficient weight to put a person under the ban of suspicion, but all are being thoroughly investigated. The latest story is about a former tenant named Ryan. According to the informant Ryan occupied the upper floor of a house belonging to Mr. Borden, and was so obnoxious that he ordered him to move. While notifying the people he was compelled to seek the lower floor to escape the torrent of abuse that was heaped on him, and when the family moved the remark was made that they would like to see him dead. There is nothing more than this in the matter, but as all acts or words in connection with Mr. Borden in the past are being looked into the affair was looked into and found to amount to nothing.

A MAN WITH A CLEAVER.

Griffiths Bros., the carpenters on Anawan street, tell a story which may have an important bearing upon the terrible tragedy. They were driving up Pleasant street about 10 o'clock Thursday morning, when their attention was drawn to a man who was proceeding rapidly along the sidewalk in front of Flint's building. Under his arm, with the handle down, he carried a cleaver entirely unlike anything they had ever seen. It was the size of the instrument that caused them to take more than a passing glance at it. To them it looked like a tool sometimes used by fish dealers. It had a rusty appearance, as if it had not been used for some time.

The man was dressed very poorly. He had no beard and was short in stature. As the weapon with which the deed was committed has not been found, the carpenters venture the opinion that the cleaver they saw was the means by which Mr. Borden and his wife were killed.

SOUTHARD H. MILLER,

one of the city's most venerable citizens, and Mr. Borden's intimate friends, was spoken to on the matter. He replied that as far as motive was concerned for the deed he could not answer. He had known Mr. Borden for over half a century, and his dealings were such that nobody could take offence with him. Having learned the cabinet making business, Mr. Borden applied to him in 1844, when the city-hall was building, for a situation as carpenter, work at cabinet making being dull. Mr. Borden continued in Mr. Miller's employ for about two years. He was a generous, plain and simple man. The reason he went into the bank business was so that he could more handily manage the property of Thomas Borden, his uncle.

The building in which Mr. Borden was killed had been erected by Mr. Miller, and throughout all their transactions he had found him to be a man of his word. As far as Mr. Morse was concerned, Mr. Miller had known him but for about a year, and in that time he had seen nothing that would prejudice him against the man. Mr. Borden's daughters were ladies who had always conducted themselves so that the breath of scandal could never reach them.

As the reporter was leaving Mr. Miller's parlor, Mrs. Miller who was present during the interview, said that she had lost, in Mrs. Borden, the best and most intimate neighbor she had ever met.

CONTEMPORARY EMPLOYMENT OPPORTUNITY

The Boston Daily Globe

DISCOVERY!

A Woman Inquired for Poison.

Said That Drug Clerk Identified Her.

Strange Story Told by Lizzie Borden.

Members of the Family Are Shadowed.

Stepmother the Cause of Trouble.

Reward of $5000 Has Been Offered.

[Associated Press.]

FALL RIVER, Mass., Aug. 5.—The Globe will publish the following tonight:

"At police headquarters, Thursday night at 7 o'clock, Capt. Desmond was posting himself on the murder by reading the papers and receiving reports.

"Marshal Hilliard was busy with his men, and inquiry for assistant Fleet revealed the fact that he had gone to supper. In a few minutes Mr. Fleet returned, and then a conversation took place between him and the marshal. Officers Harrington and Doherty were given instructions and passed out.

"Within 30 minutes after that the most important clue yet discovered was in their possession.

"The two officers made their discovery on Main st.

"At D. R. Smith's drug store they got the first important evidence.

"They approached the clerk, Eli Bence, and from him learned that Miss Borden had been in the store within 36 hours past and had inquired for a certain poison.

"The clerk was asked to accompany the officers and closely questioned as to the exact facts relative to the time, the girl's condition mentally, the amount and quality of the poison she had bought, or called for.

"The officers then led the drug clerk to a residence on 2d st. where Miss Lizzie was stopping for the time being. The young man was not previously well acquainted with the young woman, but he told them that he could identify her at sight.

"He did identify her, and in the presence of the police officers informed them that she was in his place of business and made inquiry for a bottle of poison.

"Miss Borden's reply to this accusation, as well as the exact language which was used at the time, is known only to the two policemen and herself.

"The statement above made is absolutely correct, and was verified in every particular by a GLOBE reporter last night within 10 minutes after it happened."

POLICE AT THE DOORS.

Shadowing Everybody Who Comes and Goes at House.

FALL RIVER, Mass., Aug. 5.—In the closely shuttered dining-room of the Borden residence on 2d st. are the bodies of the victims of yesterday's tragedy, which will tomorrow with brief burial services be consigned to the grave.

At the front door is a police officer whose instructions are to pass no one into the

80

ROOM WHERE A.J. BORDEN WAS MURDERED
At left is the sofa where he laid. The door next to that leads to the yard, and the right-hand door leads to the kitchen.

house, unless in authority, without the consent of the family.

A second officer stands in a sheltered nook at the rear of the premises, for what purpose cannot be said. The rear fence is fully 25 feet high, and it could scarcely be scaled with the aid of a ladder.

Still a third sentinel is at the outer gate, his duty is to keep the sidewalk clear and open for travel.

A crowd of men, women and children are braving a severe shower this forenoon for the privilege of lingering on the street and watching the scene of the tragedy.

Among them are officers in citizens' clothes, who are instructed to shadow and follow closely any member of the household who may go out.

Very little of importance has transpired around the house this morning. The family were astir at 6.30 o'clock, and about an hour later breakfast was served. There were the Misses Borden, Mr. Morse and a lady friend of the daughters present, and from the statements of the servant girl, Bridget Sullivan, they ate but little and talked less.

Miss Emma Borden, who was absent from home at the time of the tragedy, returned late yesterday afternoon. She appears very calm and self-possessed, and was seen this morning and interviewed by officers in the case. Miss Lizzie has not yet decided to speak

for publication, and has denied all press visitors an interview. The city marshal will call on her today and take her statement, together with that of the servant.

The details of the funeral have not been arranged as yet, but will be before the day ends.

It is becoming well settled that there was

Not Perfect Harmony

in the Borden household.

It is said Lizzie and her stepmother never got along together peacefully, and that for a considerable time back they have not spoken.

When seen this morning, however, Mr. Morse denied the story, saying Lizzie and Mrs. Borden were always friendly.

Mr. Morse made his first appearance about 8 o'clock. He had a basket in his hand, and was evidently on his way to a store. He walked down 2d st. with a policeman at his heels, and soon after returned and went indoors.

He came out later on another errand, and again was trailed by the sleuth-hound of the law.

Then he stayed indoors until noon.

The writer has the assurance of the chief of police that no move will be made by his department until after the funeral tomorrow. Then the procedure will depend upon a combination of circumstances that are now being investigated.

The New York Herald

LIZZIE BORDEN UNDER ARREST.

Fall River Police Take Her in Custody, Charged with the Murder of Her Father and Stepmother.

UTTER COLLAPSE OF THE PRISONER.

When the Warrant Was Shown Her the Accused Woman Lost Her Nerve and Was Taken to the Matron's Room Instead of a Cell.

REFUSED TO MAKE EXPLANATIONS.

Confronted by Witnesses Who Told Damaging Stories About Her She Declined to Say Anything Further—To Be Taken Into Court To-Day.

[BY TELEGRAPH TO THE HERALD.]

FALL RIVER, Mass., August 11, 1892.—Lizzie A. Borden, the younger daughter of Andrew J. Borden, was arrested at ten minutes past seven o'clock to-night charged with the murder and inhuman butchery of her father and mother.

This long expected and much predicted climax in the strange Borden mystery occurred in the courtroom over the central police station, where all the afternoon the inquiry into the murder had gone on with Lizzie Borden as the leading witness.

The wonderful courage and self-possession that have sustained this extraordinary woman abandoned her in her chief hour of need. Very likely she had not been without some expectation that possibly such a fate was in store for her, yet at the reading of the warrant she fell into a fit of abject and pitiable terror. A fit of violent trembling seized her, and so complete was the collapse of her physical system, weakened, no doubt, by the prolonged and terrible strain, that instead of the cell that had been prepared for her the matron's room in the central station was made her prison.

She is there now under close guard and lock and key. Ten minutes after the poor trembling, half fainting creature had been almost carried into these quarters she could hear the newsboys in the streets crying the news of her arrest, and the solution of the mystery and the clattering feet of the people who thronged to the station house with the hope of catching a glimpse of her.

THE NEXT STEP.

The next step in the procedure will be to bring her before the committing magistrate, who, in this case, is Judge Blaisdell. Under the Massachusetts law, either side has in such cases opportunity to move for a continuance of the hearing to any date within two weeks. In this case the State will undoubtedly ask for such a continuance, which will be granted, and in the meantime Lizzie Borden will be a close prisoner in the matron's room, if her condition demands it.

The arrest had been expected all day. Lizzie Borden and her sister were brought down to the inquest again to continue their testimony. Instead of arrest what was wanted of her just then was to give her a last chance to explain some of the circumstances that look so black against her and the discrepancies in her statement.

She found there Bridget Sullivan, Eli Bence, the clerk from Smith's drug store, from whom she tried to buy poison; another drug clerk, Frank Kilroy by name, and Medical Student Fred Hart.

SHE SAID NOTHING.

Lizzie did not say anything, and still paid no heed to what was going on about her. Emma Borden looked into her sister's face, and the tears began to run down her face, but she did not say anything. Mr. Jennings addressed a few words of hope and comfort to his unfortunate client and bade her goodby. Emma Borden went with her. She did not kiss her sister or even bid her goodby, but went crying down stairs and through the police guard room filled with curious people.

I don't think she saw any of them, hard as they stared at her. Then, still accompanied by Mr. Jennings and Mrs. Brigham, she went home, where she is now save one the only inmate of the household who was there eight days ago.

During the afternoon by the Chief's orders one of the matrons had fitted up one of the cells down stairs for Lizzie's reception, but as the Chief stood and looked at her, after the serving of the warrant, he concluded that a cell was no place for a human being so crushed and broken. He gave orders instead that she should occupy the matron's sleeping room, a large, well furnished apartment on the second floor.

Matron Russell had been summoned as soon as the arrest was made. She now led Lizzie into the room which is to be her prison quarters.

Up to this time the girl had not said a word nor indicated in any way a consciousness of her position. She arose and, the matron taking her arm, they walked away together. She was taken ill and the matron placed her upon a couch.

After a time she recovered some of that impenetrable bearing she had shown, though she was far from the Lizzie Borden of old. She would not converse much with the good hearted matron and soon went to bed.

PRELIMINARY EXAMINATION.

To-morrow she is to be arraigned before Judge Blaisdell for examination to determine whether there is evidence enough to have her committed to the Grand Jury.

The law in this State allows a wide latitude for preliminary examinations. The State is probably not well prepared to go ahead. Mr. Borden's safe has not been opened yet. No doubt there is other evidence the authorities will want to develop. District Attorney Knowlton will probably ask for a continuance for ten days or two weeks, which will be granted, and the prisoner will be remanded without bail.

If, when examination takes place, Judge Blaisdell does not think there is enough evidence against her to warrant the Grand Jury's investigation, he will discharge her. In that case she will have no ground for action against Hillyard nor anybody else. If the action of the Grand Jury is invoked she may be indicted in September and come to trial during the winter.

Her counsel, Mr. Jennings, refuses to give any opinion about the turn the case has taken, nor will he offer any reply to the charges against his client.

INDICTMENT.

COMMONWEALTH
VS.
LIZZIE ANDREW BORDEN.

MURDER.

Commonwealth of Massachusetts.

BRISTOL SS. At the Superior Court begun and holden at Taunton within and for said County of Bristol, on the first Monday of November, in the year of our Lord one thousand eight hundred and ninety-two.

The Jurors for the said Commonwealth, on their oath present,—That Lizzie Andrew Borden of Fall River in the County of Bristol, at Fall River in the County of Bristol, on the fourth day of August in the year eighteen hundred and ninety-two, in and upon one Andrew Jackson Borden, feloniously, wilfully and of her malice aforethought, an assault did make, and with a certain weapon, to wit, a sharp cutting instrument, the name and a more particular description of which is to the Jurors unknown, him, the said Andrew Jackson Borden feloniously, wilfully and of her malice aforethought, did strike, cut, beat and bruise, in and upon the head of him, the said Andrew Jackson Borden, giving to him, the said Andrew Jackson Borden, by the said striking, cutting, beating and bruising, in and upon the head of him, the said Andrew Jackson Borden, divers, to wit, ten mortal wounds, of which said mortal wounds the said Andrew Jackson Borden then and there instantly died.

And so the Jurors aforesaid, upon their oath aforesaid, do say, that the said Lizzie Andrew Borden, the said Andrew Jackson Borden, in manner and form aforesaid, then and there feloniously, wilfully and of her malice aforethought did kill and murder; against the peace of said Commonwealth and contrary to the form of the statute in such case made and provided.

A true bill.

HENRY A. BODMAN,

HOSEA M. KNOWLTON, Foreman of the Grand Jury.

District Attorney.

Bristol ss. On this second day of December, in the year eighteen hundred and ninety-two, this indictment was returned and presented to said Superior Court by the Grand Jury, ordered to be filed, and filed; and it was further ordered by the Court that notice be given to said Lizzie Andrew Borden that said indictment will be entered forthwith upon the docket of the Superior Court in said County.

Attest:—

SIMEON BORDEN, Jr.,
Asst. Clerk.

A true copy.
Attest: *Simeon Borden* Clerk.

LIZZIE BORDEN GOES FREE.

THE JURY NOT LONG IN REACHING A VERDICT.

A Scene of Tremendous Excitement in the Court Room When the Verdict Was Announced — Cheers and Waving of Handkerchiefs —Tears Mingled With Joy.

United Press Dispatch to the REPORT.

NEW BEDFORD, June 20.— District Attorney Knowlton resumed his argument this morning in the Borden trial, and made rather a strong presentation of detailed circumstances to sustain his contention that Lizzie Borden first murdered her step-mother, as a result of hatred and jealousy, then murdered her father when he come home, because he knew too much about family relations, and she did not dare to let him live.

The prisoner watched Mr. Knowltan fixedly during his long argument. In concluding, Knowlton claimed the defence amounted to nothing. He closed at 12:05 with an eloquent appeal to the jury to decide as their consciences should decide.

Court then took a recess till 1.45.

LIZZIE SAYS "I AM INNOCENT."

At 1.45 the court resumed its session, and the defendant was given an opportunity to speak.

She said, "I am innocent, but I will leave my case in your hands and with my counsel."

Justice Dewey then charged the jury. He told them to disregard previous hearings and defined the different degrees of murder. He stated the presumption of innocence, which was increased by defendant's character. There must be a real and operative motive.

The judge concluded his charge at 3:09, and the jury retired.

NEW BEDFORD, Mass., June 21.—Lizzie Borden was yesterday afternoon at 5 o'clock acquitted of the murder of her father and step-mother.

The jury filed into their seats after being out about one hour and a half, and were polled on their return. Miss Borden was asked to stand up and the foreman was asked to return the verdict, upon which he announced "Not guilty."

After the verdict had been received, the district attorney moved that the other cases against Miss Borden be nolle prossed, and the order of the court was to that effect.

Justice Mason gracefully thanked the jurors in appreciation of their work and faithful service, and reminded them that the precautions taken with them, which may have seemed irksome at the time, were solely in the interest of justice, a fact which they undoubtedly realized now. The jury was then dismissed and court adjourned.

THE VERDICT RECEIVED WITH CHEERS.

The closing scene in the trial was in direct contrast with those which had preceded it. Heretofore all had been decorous and in keeping with the dignity of the most dignified court in the country. But when the verdict of not guilty was returned a cheer went up which might have been heard half a mile away, and no attempt made to check it. The stately judges looked straight ahead at the bare walls. Sheriff Wright was powerless, and not once during the tremendous excitement, which lasted fully a minute, did he make the slightest sign of having heard it. He never saw the people rising in their seats and waving their handkerchiefs in unison with their voices, because his eyes were full of tears and completely blinded for the time. Miss Borden's head went down upon the rail in front of her and tears came where they had refused to come for many a long day, as she heard the sweetest words ever poured into her willing ears, the words "not guilty."

"THANK GOD," SAID MR. JENNINGS.

Mr. Jennings was almost crying, and his voice broke as he put his hand out to Mr. Adams, who sat next to him, and said, "Thank God," while Mr. Adams returned the pressure of the hand and seemed incapable of speech. Governor Robinson turned to the rapidly dissolving jury as they filed out of their seats and glanced on them with a fatherly interest in his kindly eyes, and stood up as Mr. Knowlton and Mr. Moody came over to shake hands with counsel for the defense. When the spectators had finally gone, Miss Borden was taken to the room of the justices and allowed to recover her composure. At the expiration of an hour, she was placed in a carriage and driven to the station, where she took a train for Fall River, her home no longer probably, but still the only objective point for the immediate present.

The Mystery of Mary Rogers

A Chronicle of
The Disappearance and Murder of
"The Beautiful Segar Girl"
in July, 1841 ~

A Crime Which
Was Never Solved ~

BROADWAY

THE NEW JERSEY
SHORE

And Which Inspired The
Sensational Tale By
Edgar A. Poe

Compiled and Illustrated by
RICK GEARY

BIBLIOGRAPHY

Burroughs, Edwin G. and Mike Wallace, *Gotham, A History of New York City to 1898.* (New York, Oxford University Press, 1999)

Byrnes, Thomas, *1886 Professional Criminals of America.* (New York, Chelsea House, 1969)

Cohen, Paul E. and Robert T. Augustyn, *Manhattan in Maps 1527-1995.* (New York, Rizzoli, 1997)

Homberger, Eric, *The Historical Atlas of New York City.* (New York, Henry Holt and Co., 1994)

Paul, Raymond, *Who Murdered Mary Rogers?* (Englewood Cliffs, NJ, Prentice Hall, 1971)

Poe, Edgar Allan, "The Mystery of Marie Roget," reprinted in *Great Tales and Poems of Edgar Allan Poe.* (New York, Pocket Books, 1951)

Silverman, Kenneth, *Edgar Allan Poe, Mournul and Never-Ending Remembrance.* (New York, Harper Collins, 1992)

Srebnick, Amy Gilman, *The Mysterious Death of Mary Rogers.* (New York, Oxford University Press, 1995)

Wallace, Irving, "The Real Marie Roget," reprinted in *The Mammoth Book of Unsolved Crimes.* (New York, Carroll & Graf Publishers, Inc., 1999)

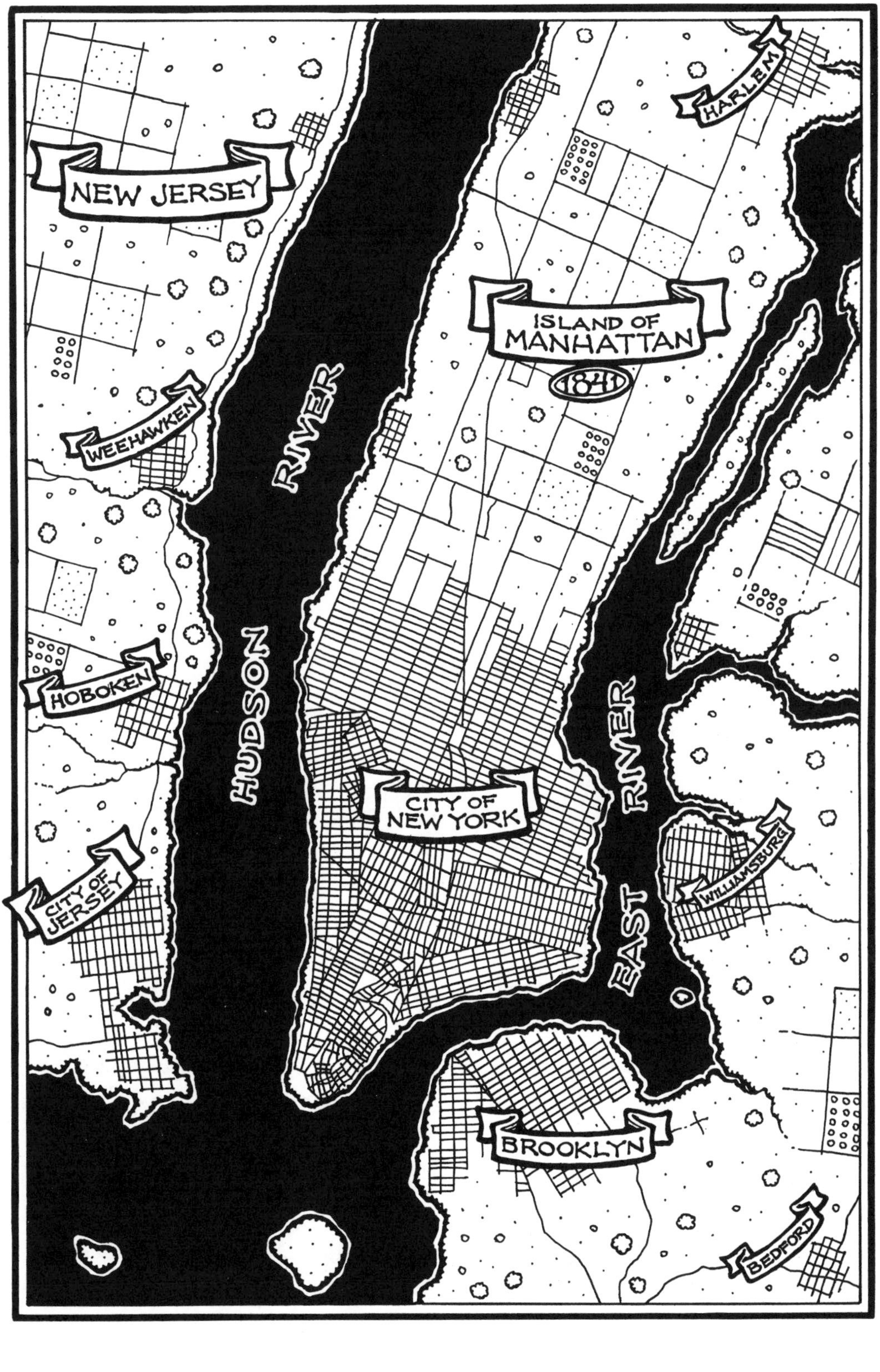
NEW JERSEY
HARLEM
ISLAND OF MANHATTAN
1841
WEEHAWKEN
HUDSON RIVER
HOBOKEN
CITY OF NEW YORK
EAST RIVER
CITY OF JERSEY
WILLIAMSBURG
BROOKLYN
BEDFORD

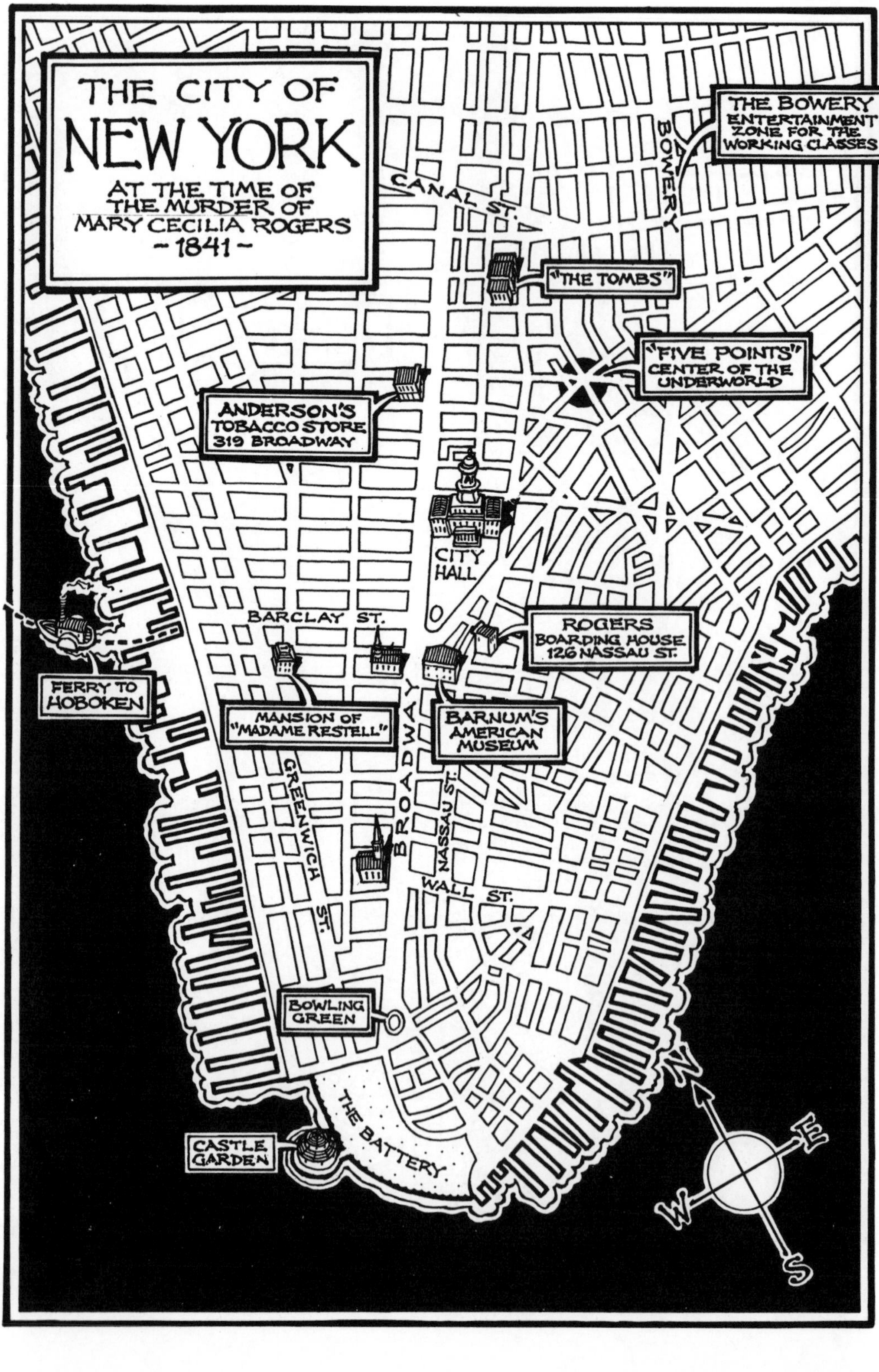
THE CITY OF
NEW YORK
AT THE TIME OF
THE MURDER OF
MARY CECILIA ROGERS
-1841-
THE BOWERY
ENTERTAINMENT ZONE FOR THE WORKING CLASSES
BOWERY
CANAL ST.
"THE TOMBS"
"FIVE POINTS"
CENTER OF THE UNDERWORLD
ANDERSON'S
TOBACCO STORE
319 BROADWAY
CITY HALL
BARCLAY ST.
ROGERS
BOARDING HOUSE
126 NASSAU ST.
FERRY TO HOBOKEN
MANSION OF
"MADAME RESTELL"
BARNUM'S
AMERICAN
MUSEUM
GREENWICH ST.
BROADWAY
NASSAU ST.
WALL ST.
BOWLING GREEN
CASTLE GARDEN
THE BATTERY
N
E
W
S

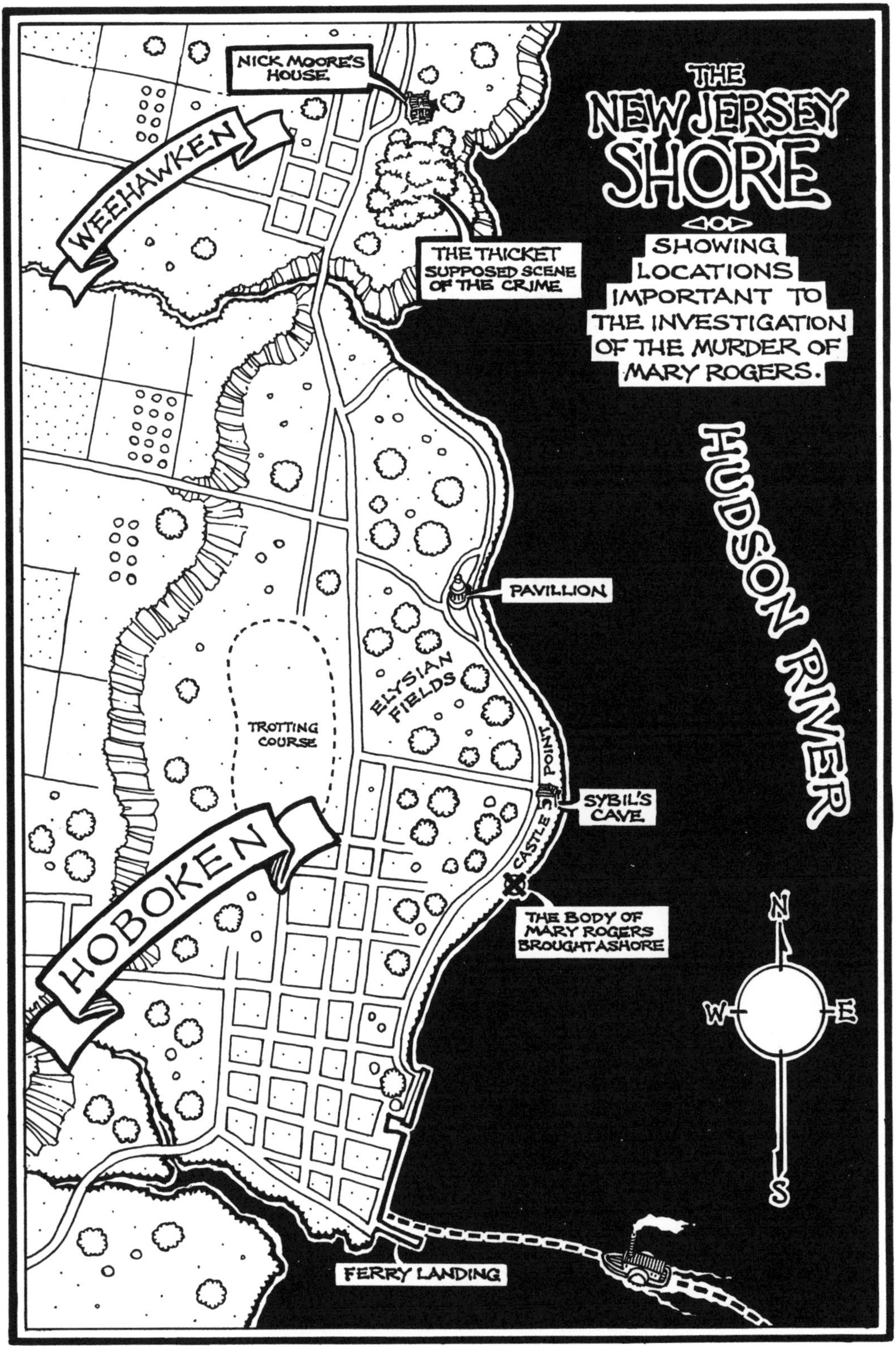
THE NEW JERSEY SHORE
SHOWING LOCATIONS IMPORTANT TO THE INVESTIGATION OF THE MURDER OF MARY ROGERS.
NICK MOORE'S HOUSE
WEEHAWKEN
THE THICKET SUPPOSED SCENE OF THE CRIME
HUDSON RIVER
PAVILLION
ELYSIAN FIELDS
TROTTING COURSE
CASTLE POINT
SYBIL'S CAVE
THE BODY OF MARY ROGERS BROUGHT ASHORE
HOBOKEN
N
W
E
S
FERRY LANDING

PART I.

A BODY IN THE RIVER

WEDNESDAY, JULY 28, 1841
ON THIS SWELTERING DAY, NEW YORKERS IN DROVES
SOUGHT TO ESCAPE THE FOUL AIR OF THE CITY...

AND ENJOY THE WOODED GLADES AND COOL
BREEZES OF THE NEW JERSEY SHORE.

THEY ARRIVED AT
HOBOKEN...

STROLLED THROUGH
THE "ELYSIAN FIELDS..."

AND WOULD PERHAPS TARRY
AT THE "SYBIL'S CAVE," WHERE
FRESH SPRING WATER COULD
BE HAD FOR A PENNY A GLASS.

AT ABOUT 3:00 PM, FIVE SUCH YOUNG GENTLEMEN WALKED NORTHWARD FROM THE FERRY LANDING ...

ALONG THE SHORE TOWARD CASTLE POINT.

SUDDENLY, THEIR ATTENTION WAS DISTRACTED BY SHOUTS FROM THE RIVER.

HO!

TWO BOYS IN A ROW-BOAT ~

THERE'S A DEAD BODY!

INDEED, WHAT APPEARED TO BE A HUMAN FORM COULD BE SEEN DRIFTING IN THE TIDES OF THE HUDSON.

THREE OF THE MEN — HENRY MALLIN, JAMES BOULARD, AND H.G. LUTHER — RAN TO A NEARBY PAVILLION AND HIRED A BOAT.

WHAT THEY FOUND WAS THE FULLY-CLOTHED BODY OF A YOUNG WOMAN.

BRUISED AND WATER-LOGGED... BUT THE LINEAMENTS OF HER BEAUTY WERE STILL PERCEPTIBLE.

WITH GREAT DIFFICULTY, THE MEN SECURED THE CORPSE, AND BROUGHT IT IN TO LIE UPON THE SHORE...

AS A SUBSTANTIAL CROWD ACCUMULATED.

BEFORE LONG, TWO YOUNG MEN EMERGED FROM THE CROWD TO EXAMINE THE REMAINS CLOSELY.

DEAR GOD...

THEY KNEW THE UNFORTUNATE YOUNG LADY.

THIS IS MARY ROGERS!

OH GOD — THE NEWS MAY KILL HER MOTHER!

THE CORPSE LAY ON THE SHORE INTO THE LATE AFTERNOON, BLOATING AND BLACKENING IN THE SUN...

UNTIL THE ARRIVAL OF HUDSON COUNTY AUTHORITIES, IN THE PERSONS OF:

GILBERT C. MERRITT, JUSTICE OF THE PEACE.

AND THE CORONER, DR. RICHARD F. COOK.

THE TWO MEN WHO IDENTIFIED THE REMAINS — MR. CROMMELIN AND MR. PADLEY — WERE DETAINED WITH OTHER WITNESSES...

WHILE THE BODY WAS REMOVED TO A BUILDING IN HOBOKEN FOR A SOMEWHAT HASTY POST-MORTEM.

THE CORONER'S INQUEST, WHICH CONVENED AT 7:00 PM, WAS SIMILARLY HURRIED.

IN TOTAL, ONLY FIVE WITNESSES WERE CALLED:

BEGINNING WITH TWO GENTLEMEN...

WHO HAD STOOD ON SHORE AND WATCHED THE RECOVERY OF THE BODY...

WHILE, CURIOUSLY, THE THREE MEN WHO HAD MADE THE ACTUAL RECOVERY WERE NOT SWORN.

THE THIRD WITNESS TO TESTIFY WAS MR. ALFRED CROMMELIN, WHO CLAIMED TO BE A FRIEND OF THE DECEASED.

HE IDENTIFIED HER AS MARY CECILIA ROGERS, AGED ABOUT TWENTY...

WHO HAD LEFT HER HOME ON NASSAU ST. IN NEW YORK CITY ON THE PREVIOUS SUNDAY...

AND, DESPITE A VIGOROUS SEARCH, HAD NOT BEEN SEEN SINCE.

HE RECOGNIZED THE REMAINS, HE SAID, NOT SO MUCH BY THE DISCOLORED FACE...

AS BY THE TINY FEET, AND THE DISTINCTIVE PATTERN OF HAIR ON THE ARMS.

HE WENT ON TO STATE THAT SHE WAS WELL-KNOWN IN THE CITY, DUE TO HER FORMER EMPLOYMENT AT A POPULAR BROADWAY TOBACCO STORE.

NEVERTHELESS, HER MORAL CHARACTER WAS OF THE HIGHEST ORDER.

TRUTHFULNESS, MODESTY, DISCRETION...

MR. ARCHIBALD PADLEY, NEXT TO TESTIFY, DID NOT KNOW THE DECEASED SO WELL AS HIS FRIEND, BUT AGREED WITH HIM ON ALL POINTS.

FINALLY, DR. COOK PRESENTED THE FINDINGS OF HIS POST-MORTEM:

THE YOUNG WOMAN, HE CONCLUDED, WAS MOST CERTAINLY THE VICTIM OF A VIOLENT ABDUCTION AND MURDER.

BRUISES ABOUT THE FACE AND NECK INDICATED BEATING AND CHOKING.

IN ADDITION, A STRIP OF LACE FROM HER OWN PETTICOAT WAS TIED AROUND HER NECK, SO TIGHTLY AS TO BE EMBEDDED IN THE FLESH.

HER FLOWERED BONNET WAS TIED SECURELY TO HER HEAD BY A KIND OF HITCH THE CORONER CALLED A "SAILOR'S KNOT."

ANOTHER STRIP OF CLOTH WAS SECURED ABOUT HER WAIST BY THE SAME KIND OF KNOT — AS IF USED TO DRAG THE BODY.

HER WRISTS, CROSSED STIFFLY AT THE CHEST, BORE THE IMPRINT OF THE CORDS USED TO BIND THEM.

ABRASIONS AND EXCORIATIONS ABOUT THE BODY INDICATED THAT SHE HAD BEEN HELD DOWN AND VIOLATED — MOST LIKELY BY TWO OR THREE MEN!

THE JURY QUICKLY CAME TO ITS VERDICT: "DEATH DUE TO VIOLENCE COMMITTED BY SOME PERSON OR PERSONS."

AFTER THE INQUEST ADJOURNED, IT WAS THOUGHT BEST, DUE TO THE INTENSE HEAT, TO GIVE THE REMAINS AN IMMEDIATE, IF TEMPORARY, BURIAL.

MARY ROGERS WAS THEREFORE QUICKLY INTERRED—TWO FEET BENEATH THE EARTH IN A DOUBLE-LINED COFFIN.

CROMMELIN AND PADLEY, HAVING MISSED THE LAST FERRY BACK TO NEW YORK, SPENT THE NIGHT AT A HOTEL IN JERSEY CITY.

IN THE MEANTIME, THE MEN WHO HAD RECOVERED THE BODY—HAVING BEEN INFORMED THAT THEIR 'TESTIMONY' WOULD NOT BE NEEDED—RETURNED TO THE CITY AT ABOUT 7:00 P.M.

ONE OF THEIR NUMBER—MR. H.G. LUTHER—TOOK IT UPON HIMSELF TO VISIT THE HOME OF THE DECEASED: A BOARDING HOUSE WHICH SHE MANAGED WITH HER MOTHER AT 126 NASSAU ST.

HE IMPARTED THE GRIM NEWS TO THE AGED LADY... AND TO A YOUNG MAN NAMED PAYNE, A RESIDENT OF THE HOUSE, WHO CLAIMED TO BE THE FIANCÉ OF THE DEAD GIRL.

NEITHER OF THEM SEEMED, TO HIM, PARTICULARLY SURPRISED OR SHOCKED.

ALTHOUGH THE HOUR WAS STILL EARLY, MR. PAYNE DECLINED TO GO TO HOBOKEN THAT EVENING, A LACK OF ACTION THAT WOULD REFLECT POORLY UPON HIM IN THE WEEKS TO COME.

THURSDAY, JULY 29 —
ON THAT MORNING, CROMMELIN AND PADLEY RETURNED TO THE CITY AND PAID A CALL UPON THE GRIEVING MRS. ROGERS.

THEY DISPLAYED FOR HER AN ARRAY OF IDENTIFYING ITEMS GIVEN THEM BY THE CORONER...

INCLUDING EVEN A LOCK OF MARY'S HAIR—

IN THE DAYS THAT FOLLOWED, ANY KIND OF OFFICIAL INVESTIGATION WAS FRUSTRATED BY A JURISDICTIONAL DISPUTE:

THE NEW YORK AUTHORITIES DECLARED IT A NEW JERSEY CASE...

WHILE NEW JERSEY OFFICIALS FELT THAT, SINCE THE VICTIM WAS A CITY RESIDENT, THE CASE SHOULD BE NEW YORK'S. (AFTER ALL, WERE NOT THE VICTIMS OF THE CITY'S CRIMES CONSTANTLY WASHING UP ON THE SHORES OF NEW JERSEY?)

FRIDAY, JULY 30— ON THAT MORNING, WORD WAS ABROAD OF THE MURDER OF THE "BEAUTIFUL SEGAR GIRL."

SUNDAY, AUGUST 1— SAW THE FIRST NEWSPAPER NOTICE— IN THE SUNDAY MERCURY...

AND BY THE NEXT MORNING, THE CRIME WAS FEATURED IN EACH OF THE CITY'S NUMEROUS DAILY JOURNALS.

PROVING ESPECIALLY DILIGENT IN ITS COVERAGE WAS THE HERALD, PUBLISHED BY JAMES GORDON BENNET...

WHO WAS NOT ABOVE EXPLOITING THE MURDER IN HIS ONGOING CRUSADE AGAINST CERTAIN CITY ADMINISTRATORS.

EQUALLY ASSIDUOUS WERE: THE SUN, EDITED BY MOSES BEACH...

BENJAMIN DAY'S EVENING TATTLER...

AND ITS SUNDAY COUNTERPART, BROTHER JONATHAN, WHICH UNFOLDED INTO A SINGLE MAMMOTH SHEET.

THE MORE TRADITIONAL JOURNALS, SUCH AS WILLIAM CULLEN BRYANT'S EVENING POST AND HORACE GREELEY'S TRIBUNE, COULD DO NAUGHT BUT FOLLOW SUIT—

FOR THESE PUBLICATIONS, EVEN IN THE LEAST EVENTFUL OF TIMES, ENGAGED IN A DEADLY COMPETITION.

AT THAT TIME, THE CITY OF NEW YORK WAS ALL-TOO-EAGER TO FOLLOW SUCH A SENSATIONAL STORY.

IT WAS A BOISTEROUS, BURGEONING COMMERCIAL CENTER WITH AN EXPLODING POPULATION (THEN ABOUT 500,000) ...

EXTENDING IN RESIDENTIAL AREA AS FAR NORTHWARD AS 35TH STREET.

THE ECONOMIC DEPRESSION OF 1837 HAD FORCED COUNTLESS COUNTRY-DWELLERS INTO THE CITY.

IMMIGRANTS FROM IRELAND AND GERMANY AND OTHER STRIFE-TORN NATIONS STREAMED ASHORE TO MAKE NEW LIVES IN AMERICA.

MANY OF THEM MOVED ON TO THE INTERIOR....

BUT AS MANY REMAINED, ENTICED BY THE FREEDOM, THE OPPORTUNITY, AND THE ANONYMITY OF CITY LIFE.

LARGE NUMBERS OF THE NEWCOMERS WERE UNATTACHED YOUNG MEN AND WOMEN...

FOR WHOM THE CITY OFFERED UNHEARD-OF DELIGHTS AND DANGERS...

A NEW SOCIAL ORDER, A MORE RELAXED MORAL CODE...

LEADING OFTEN TO CONFUSION, AND EVEN TO TRAGEDY.

THE BOWERY WAS THE CITY'S FORBIDDEN RECREATIONAL AVENUE, OFFERING TEMPTATIONS FOR ALL TASTES.

IN 1841, PHINEAS T. BARNUM OPENED HIS AMERICAN MUSEUM ON BROADWAY, BRINGING A TASTE OF THE BOWERY TO THE ELITE DISTRICT AROUND CITY HALL PARK.

THE CITY'S GROWING POPULATION BROUGHT NEW AND UNFORTUNATE LEVELS OF POVERTY AND CRIME.

A VAST AREA NORTH OF THE CITY HALL HAD BECOME A SINK-HOLE FOR SOCIETY'S REFUSE.

THE NEIGHBORHOOD OF FIVE-POINTS, WITH ITS NOTORIOUS "OLD BREWERY" WAS THE CENTER OF DEPRAVITY.

THE NIGHT WAS RULED BY GANGS OF ROUGH YOUNG MEN WHO HAD NO FEAR OF THE LAW.

"FIRE-ROWDIES, SOAPLOCKERS AND BUTCHER-BOYS," AS THEY WERE DUBBED BY THE HERALD...

WITH SUCH NAMES AS: "FORTY THIEVES"

"THE PLUG-UGLIES"

"THE DEAD RABBITS"

"THE SHIRT-TAILS"

"HUDSON DUSTERS"

"THE ROACH GUARDS"

"GOPHERS"

THESE GANGS GREW SO LARGE AND POWERFUL THAT THEY OFTEN ALLIED THEMSELVES WITH FACTIONS OF THE CITY'S POLITICAL MACHINERY.

AT THAT TIME, OF COURSE, NEW YORK'S POLICE FORCE WAS UTTERLY INADEQUATE TO THE CRIME PROBLEM.

THE CITY, IN FACT, HAD NO FULL-TIME PROFESSIONAL LAW ENFORCEMENT.

WHAT IT DID HAVE CONSISTED OF VARIOUS UNSALARIED MARSHALS AND CONSTABLES . . .

WHO LIVED UPON COURT FEES AND PRIVATE REWARDS.

THE NIGHT FORCE WAS MADE UP OF WATCHMEN —— OFTEN RETIREES OR MOONLIGHTERS . . .

CALLED "LEATHERHEADS" BECAUSE OF THEIR AWKWARD HELMETS.

REGRETTABLY, THESE GUARDIANS FAILED TO RETAIN THE RESPECT OF EITHER THE GENERAL PUBLIC OR THE CRIMINAL CLASSES.

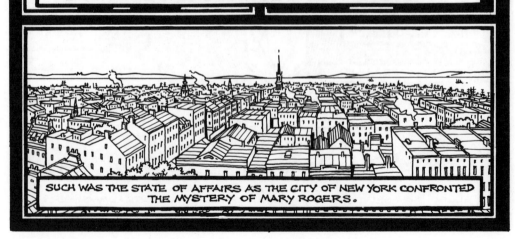

SUCH WAS THE STATE OF AFFAIRS AS THE CITY OF NEW YORK CONFRONTED THE MYSTERY OF MARY ROGERS.

PART II.

THE HISTORY OF MARY CECILIA ROGERS, AND THE DAYS THAT LED TO HER MURDER.

So far as can be determined, the forebears of Mary Rogers settled in the country around Lyme, Connecticut, where she was born in 1820.

Her mother, the former Phoebe Wait, had already borne five children...

By her earlier marriage to Daniel Mather, who had died in 1808.

In 1814, Phoebe married Daniel Rogers, who hailed from a ship-building family.

Six years later, Mary Cecilia was born — their only child.

Note —

Because of the mother's advanced age of 42, some have speculated that Mary was actually the illegitimate child of Phoebe's own daughter, then age 19. However, for purposes of this narrative, Mrs. Rogers will be referred to as Mary's "mother."

Daniel Rogers perished in a steamship explosion in 1834...

And in 1837, widow and daughter moved to New York City, as part of the massive migration triggered by hard economic times.

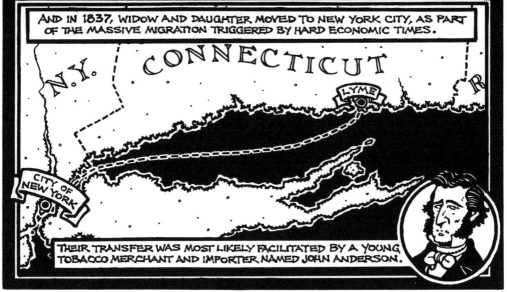

Their transfer was most likely facilitated by a young tobacco merchant and importer named John Anderson.

109

MRS. ROGERS AND MARY AT FIRST LIVED IN THE HOME OF MR. ANDERSON ON DUANE STREET— PERHAPS IN EXCHANGE FOR HOUSEKEEPING.

IN 1838, THEY MOVED INTO THE HOME OF MRS. ROGERS' COUSIN, MRS. HAYES, AT 114 PITT STREET.

AT THAT TIME, JOHN ANDERSON HAD THE INSPIRATION TO HIRE MARY ROGERS . . .

TO SERVE BEHIND THE COUNTER OF HIS TOBACCO STORE AT 319 BROADWAY . . .

AS WAS THEN THE FASHION IN ENGLAND AND ON THE CONTINENT.

WITH HER NATURAL VIVACITY AND WARMTH—AND HER "DARK SMILE"— SHE PROVED AN IMMEDIATE FAVORITE WITH THE CUSTOMERS.

ANDERSON'S TOBACCO STORE WAS A POPULAR GATHERING SPOT FOR NEW YORK'S MEN OF POWER AND POTENTIAL.

GOVERNMENT LEADERS FROM CITY HALL MINGLED WITH EDITORS AND REPORTERS FROM ALL OF THE CITY'S JOURNALS.

SUCH RENOWNED WRITERS AS:

JAMES FENIMORE COOPER...

AND WASHINGTON IRVING...

HELD FORTH WITH TALES AND LORE.

THE YOUNG POET EDGAR A. POE, BRIEFLY RESIDENT IN THE CITY...

TOOK IT ALL IN.

STORE "REGULARS" ALSO INCLUDED THE YOUNG GAMBLERS AND SPORTY BACHELORS OF THE BOULEVARD...

AS WELL AS ROUGH-AND-TUMBLE ORGANIZERS FROM TAMMANY HALL.

THE AIR WAS FILLED WITH IDEAS, ORATIONS, RUMORS AND CURSES...

AND MARY HEARD THEM ALL...

ENSURING FOR HERSELF AN EDUCATION AND A SOPHISTICATION FAR BEYOND HER YEARS.

DID MARY SUCCUMB TO THE ADVANCES OF ANY OF ANDERSON'S CUSTOMERS?

NO ONE TODAY CAN SAY FOR CERTAIN.

WHAT WE DO KNOW IS THAT SHE VANISHED FROM HER HOME AND FROM HER DUTIES AT THE STORE FOR A PERIOD IN THE AUTUMN OF 1838.

ON THE MORNING OF OCTOBER 4 (SO THE STORY WENT) MRS. ROGERS FOUND WHAT APPEARED TO BE A SUICIDE NOTE.

WHICH SHE TOOK TO THE POLICE.

THIS LED TO A BRIEF NOTICE PUBLISHED IN THE JOURNAL OF COMMERCE.

THE NEWS EXCITED QUITE A STIR AMONG THE BROADWAY CROWD THAT KNEW MARY.

IN THE DAYS THAT FOLLOWED, HOWEVER, SHE WAS REPORTED TO BE IN FINE HEALTH AND MERELY VISITING RELATIONS IN BROOKLYN.

LESS CHARITABLE OBSERVERS SUGGESTED THAT THE ENTIRE EPISODE WAS STAGED BY JOHN ANDERSON AS PROMOTION FOR HIS STORE.

IN ANY CASE, MARY RETURNED THE FOLLOWING WEEK, OFFERING NO EXPLANATION FOR HER ACTIONS.

ON HER FIRST DAY BACK AT WORK, A CURIOUS THRONG PACKED THE TOBACCO STORE.

HORRIFIED AND EMBARRASSED BY THE ATTENTION, SHE FELL IN A FAINT — AND REMAINED HOME FOR FIVE DAYS.

MARY'S GROWING NOTORIETY WAS NO DOUBT A FACTOR IN HER DECISION TO QUIT THE STORE SOMETIME IN THE SUMMER OF 1839...

DESPITE AN OFFER FROM ANDERSON OF A GENEROUS RAISE IN SALARY.

AT THAT TIME, MARY AND HER MOTHER TOOK OVER THE OPERATION OF THE BOARDING HOUSE AT 126 NASSAU STREET...

LOCATED IN THE VERY HEART OF THE CITY'S BUSTLING COMMERCIAL ACTIVITY.

MRS. ROGERS BEING THEN ABOUT AGE 60, THE BULK OF THE HOUSEKEEPING DUTIES FELL TO MARY AND THE SINGLE NEGRO MAID.

THE BOARDING HOUSE WAS HOME TO SINGLE YOUNG MEN OF ALL TYPES, MAKING THEIR WAY IN THE WORLD:

CLERKS AND LABORERS ...

PEDDLERS, ARTISANS AND SEA-MEN.

MARY'S PRESENCE WAS CERTAINLY AN ATTRACTION.

IN FACT, SHE WAS NEVER AT A LOSS FOR ESCORTS AND SUITORS.

THE COMPETITION, AT TIMES, TURNED UGLY.

STILL, SHE DECLINED ALL OFFERS OF MARRIAGE.

ONE PARTICULARLY ARDENT SUITOR WAS THE YOUNG LAW CLERK ALFRED CROMMELIN, WHO MOVED INTO THE HOUSE IN DECEMBER OF 1840.

IN MARY, HE SAW THE EMBODIMENT OF EVERY FEMININE IDEAL.

SHE APPEARED TO FIND HIM AN AGREEABLE COMPANION, YET SHE CONTINUED TO RESIST HIS MOST HEART-FELT ENTREATIES.

HER ATTENTION WAS CLEARLY DISTRACTED BY ANOTHER BOARDER: DANIEL PAYNE, A CORK-CUTTER BY TRADE.

OUT-GOING AND CONVIVIAL, HE AFFECTED THE MANNER OF A BROADWAY DANDY...

AND WAS VICTIM TO AN UNFORTUNATE WEAKNESS FOR SPIRITS.

THE TWO MEN, FROM THE BEGINNING, LOATHED EACH OTHER INTENSELY.

WE ARRIVE NOW AT THE TERRIBLE SUMMER OF 1841.

IN JUNE, THE SITUATION IN THE BOARDING HOUSE CAME TO A HEAD WHEN MARY AND PAYNE ANNOUNCED THEIR BETROTHAL.

BOTH CROMMELIN AND MRS. ROGERS WERE ADAMANTLY OPPOSED TO THE IDEA.

ONE AFTERNOON, THERE WAS A FURIOUS SCENE IN THE PARLOR...

AFTER WHICH CROMMELIN—ALONG WITH HIS FRIEND PADLEY—MOVED FROM THE HOUSE.

HE TOLD MARY THAT, NEVERTHELESS, HE WOULD EVER BE AT HER SERVICE.

THE TWO MEN FOUND ROOMS NEARBY, IN A HOUSE AT 19 JOHN ST.

HALL PARK

BROADWAY

JOHN ST.

NASSAU ST.

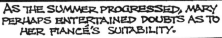
AS THE SUMMER PROGRESSED, MARY PERHAPS ENTERTAINED DOUBTS AS TO HER FIANCÉ'S SUITABILITY.

ON FRIDAY, JULY 23, MRS. ROGERS WAS OVERHEARD BY THE MAID TO EXACT A PROMISE FROM HER DAUGHTER: THAT SHE WOULD NOT MARRY DANIEL PAYNE.

LATER THAT DAY, ALFRED CROMMELIN FOUND A NOTE SLIPPED UNDER HIS DOOR. WRITTEN IN MARY'S HAND, IT URGED HIM TO CALL UPON NASSAU STREET AT HIS EARLIEST CONVENIENCE.

BUT, STILL HURTING FROM REJECTION, HE DECLINED TO PAY THE CALL.

ON THE FOLLOWING DAY— SATURDAY, JULY 24—HE FOUND A SIMILAR NOTE AT HIS PLACE OF BUSINESS— ACCOMPANIED BY A SINGLE ROSE.

WHY DID MARY WISH TO SEE HER FORMER SUITOR?

(WAS IT MERELY TO BORROW MONEY, AS HER MOTHER LATER SUGGESTED?)

IN ANY CASE, CROMMELIN DID NOT RESPOND TO THIS SECOND PLEA—A DECISION THAT WOULD CAUSE HIM GREAT ANGUISH IN THE DAYS TO COME.

SUNDAY, JULY 25: THE MORNING OF MARY'S DISAPPEARANCE DAWNED CLEAR, HOT AND HUMID.

AT ABOUT 10:00 AM, ACCORDING TO DANIEL PAYNE, SHE APPEARED AT HIS DOOR.

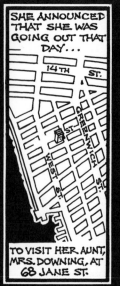
SHE ANNOUNCED THAT SHE WAS GOING OUT THAT DAY...

TO VISIT HER AUNT, MRS. DOWNING, AT 68 JANE ST.

SHE REQUESTED THAT HE MEET HER THAT EVENING, AS HE OFTEN DID, AT THE OMNIBUS STOP ON THE CORNER OF BROADWAY AND ANN STREET — IN FRONT OF BARNUM'S MUSEUM.

MARY THEN WENT CHEERFULLY ON HER WAY, NEVER TO BE SEEN ALIVE BY PAYNE AGAIN.

THAT EVENING, A HEAVY RAIN-STORM STRUCK THE CITY, AND HE FAILED TO KEEP THEIR APPOINTMENT, ASSUMING THAT SHE WOULD STAY THE NIGHT WITH HER AUNT.

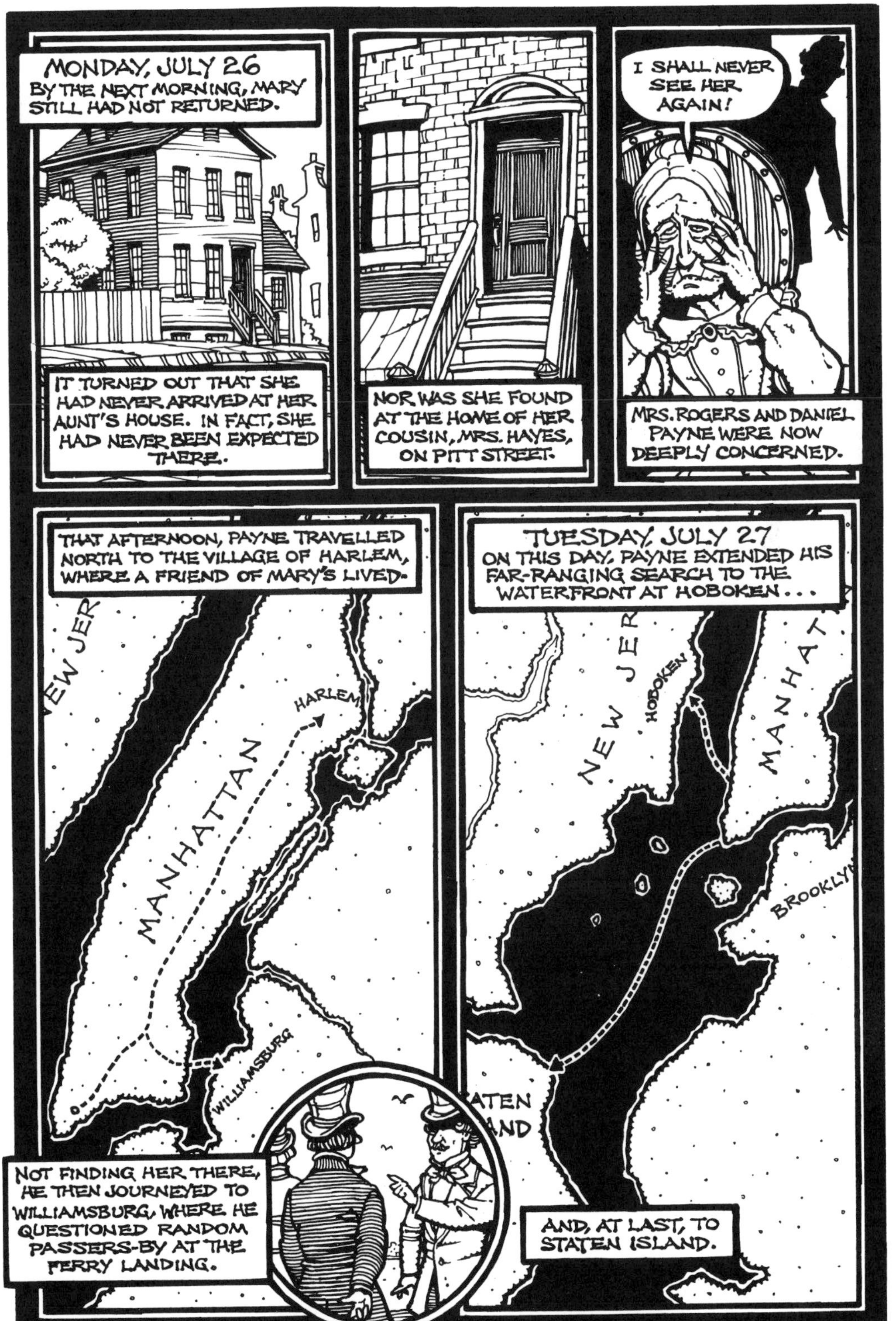
MONDAY, JULY 26
BY THE NEXT MORNING, MARY STILL HAD NOT RETURNED.
IT TURNED OUT THAT SHE HAD NEVER ARRIVED AT HER AUNT'S HOUSE. IN FACT, SHE HAD NEVER BEEN EXPECTED THERE.
NOR WAS SHE FOUND AT THE HOME OF HER COUSIN, MRS. HAYES, ON PITT STREET.
I SHALL NEVER SEE HER AGAIN!
MRS. ROGERS AND DANIEL PAYNE WERE NOW DEEPLY CONCERNED.
THAT AFTERNOON, PAYNE TRAVELLED NORTH TO THE VILLAGE OF HARLEM, WHERE A FRIEND OF MARY'S LIVED.
NEW JER
HARLEM
MANHATTAN
WILLIAMSBURG
NOT FINDING HER THERE, HE THEN JOURNEYED TO WILLIAMSBURG, WHERE HE QUESTIONED RANDOM PASSERS-BY AT THE FERRY LANDING.
TUESDAY, JULY 27
ON THIS DAY, PAYNE EXTENDED HIS FAR-RANGING SEARCH TO THE WATERFRONT AT HOBOKEN...
NEW JER
HOBOKEN
MANHAT
BROOKLY
ATEN
AND
AND, AT LAST, TO STATEN ISLAND.

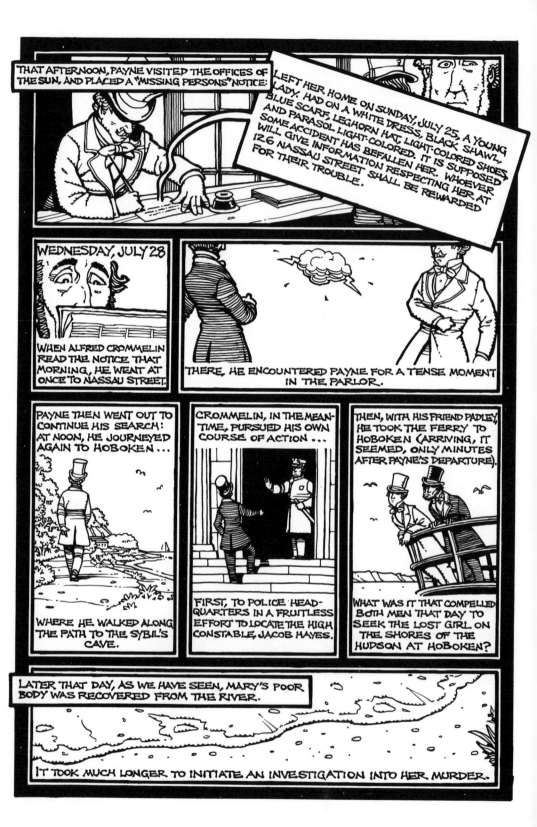

THAT AFTERNOON, PAYNE VISITED THE OFFICES OF THE SUN, AND PLACED A "MISSING PERSONS" NOTICE:

LEFT HER HOME ON SUNDAY, JULY 25, A YOUNG LADY. HAD ON A WHITE DRESS, BLACK SHAWL, BLUE SCARF, LEGHORN HAT, LIGHT-COLORED SHOES AND PARASOL LIGHT-COLORED. IT IS SUPPOSED SOME ACCIDENT HAS BEFALLEN HER. WHOEVER WILL GIVE INFORMATION RESPECTING HER AT 126 NASSAU STREET SHALL BE REWARDED FOR THEIR TROUBLE.

WEDNESDAY, JULY 28

WHEN ALFRED CROMMELIN READ THE NOTICE THAT MORNING, HE WENT AT ONCE TO NASSAU STREET.

THERE, HE ENCOUNTERED PAYNE FOR A TENSE MOMENT IN THE PARLOR.

PAYNE THEN WENT OUT TO CONTINUE HIS SEARCH: AT NOON, HE JOURNEYED AGAIN TO HOBOKEN ...

WHERE HE WALKED ALONG THE PATH TO THE SYBIL'S CAVE.

CROMMELIN, IN THE MEAN-TIME, PURSUED HIS OWN COURSE OF ACTION ...

FIRST, TO POLICE HEAD-QUARTERS IN A FRUITLESS EFFORT TO LOCATE THE HIGH CONSTABLE, JACOB HAYES.

THEN, WITH HIS FRIEND PADLEY, HE TOOK THE FERRY TO HOBOKEN (ARRIVING, IT SEEMED, ONLY MINUTES AFTER PAYNE'S DEPARTURE).

WHAT WAS IT THAT COMPELLED BOTH MEN THAT DAY TO SEEK THE LOST GIRL ON THE SHORES OF THE HUDSON AT HOBOKEN?

LATER THAT DAY, AS WE HAVE SEEN, MARY'S POOR BODY WAS RECOVERED FROM THE RIVER.

IT TOOK MUCH LONGER TO INITIATE AN INVESTIGATION INTO HER MURDER.

PART III.

THE INVESTIGATION

WEDNESDAY, AUGUST 11, 1841
A FULL, TWO WEEKS AFTER THE RECOVERY OF THE BODY, A GROUP OF INFLUENTIAL CITIZENS, IMPATIENT WITH THE INACTION OF THE POLICE FORCE, MET TO PUT FORWARD A MONETARY REWARD FOR THE CAPTURE OF MARY'S KILLER OR KILLERS.

OVER 300 DOLLARS WAS PLEDGED.

(THE TOTAL WOULD EVENTUALLY RISE TO OVER 1,350 DOLLARS.)

ON THE SAME DAY, GOADED BY THE PRESS, THE CITY OF NEW YORK AT LAST TOOK ON THE INVESTIGATION.

(BY A RELUCTANT ORDER FROM THE ACTING MAYOR, JOSIAH PURDY.)

THE DEATH OF MARY ROGERS WAS OFFICIALLY REGISTERED...

HER REMAINS DISINTERRED FROM THEIR SITE IN HOBOKEN...

AND BROUGHT TO THE DEAD HOUSE IN CITY HALL PARK.

THE REPORT OF NEW YORK'S CORONER GENERALLY CONFIRMED THE FINDINGS OF DR. COOK IN HOBOKEN.

THURSDAY, AUGUST 12 DANIEL PAYNE, ALONG WITH MRS. ROGERS, MRS. HAYES, AND A GIRL-FRIEND OF MARY'S, WERE BROUGHT IN TO MAKE THE OFFICIAL IDENTIFICATION.

OUT OF DELICACY, ONLY PAYNE WAS ALLOWED TO VIEW THE DECOMPOSED CORPSE.

SADLY, HE RECOGNIZED THE FORM OF HIS DEPARTED LOVE.

THE LADIES, FOR THEIR PART, IDENTIFIED FURTHER ARTICLES OF APPAREL.

LATER THAT DAY, PAYNE WAS QUESTIONED BY POLICE SERGEANT McARDLE AS TO HIS MOVEMENTS ON THE SUNDAY OF MARY'S DISAPPEARANCE.

THIS WAS HIS STATEMENT:

AFTER BIDDING MARY GOODBYE AT 10:00 AM, HE COMPLETED HIS TOILET, CONSUMED BREAKFAST AND LEFT THE HOUSE AT 11:00 AM.

HE WALKED TO THE HOME OF HIS BROTHER, JOHN PAYNE AT 33 WARREN ST.

THE TWO OF THEM STROLLED DOWN BROADWAY, AND BROWSED AT SCOTT'S BAZAAR ON DEY STREET.

THEY PARTED IN FRONT OF ST. PAUL'S CHAPEL.

DANIEL PAYNE INDULGED HIMSELF TO A DRINK AT BICKFORD'S TAVERN ON JAMES STREET...

AND DINED AT GOSLIN'S RESTAURANT ON FULTON STREET.

HE THEN RETURNED TO THE BOARDING HOUSE FOR A THREE-HOUR SLUMBER.

IN THE LATE AFTERNOON (HIS STATEMENT CONTINUED) PAYNE AGAIN EMERGED FROM THE HOUSE, THIS TIME ARRAYED IN HIS FINEST...

AND WALKED DOWN TO THE BATTERY FOR A DRINK.

HE THEN MINGLED WITH THE FASHIONABLE CROWD ALONG BROADWAY...

ALL THE WHILE WATCHING THE SKY GROW HEAVIER WITH THE APPROACHING STORM.

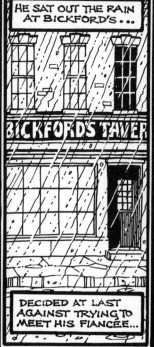

HE SAT OUT THE RAIN AT BICKFORD'S...

BICKFORD'S TAVERN

DECIDED AT LAST AGAINST TRYING TO MEET HIS FIANCÉE...

AND RETURNED HOME AT ABOUT 9:00 P.M.

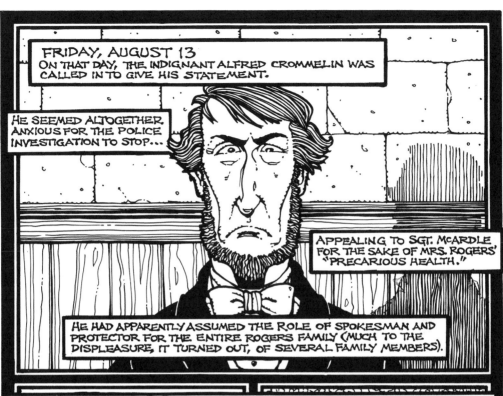

FRIDAY, AUGUST 13
ON THAT DAY, THE INDIGNANT ALFRED CROMMELIN WAS CALLED INTO GIVE HIS STATEMENT.

HE SEEMED ALTOGETHER ANXIOUS FOR THE POLICE INVESTIGATION TO STOP...

APPEALING TO SGT. McARDLE FOR THE SAKE OF MRS. ROGERS' "PRECARIOUS HEALTH."

HE HAD APPARENTLY ASSUMED THE ROLE OF SPOKESMAN AND PROTECTOR FOR THE ENTIRE ROGERS FAMILY (MUCH TO THE DISPLEASURE, IT TURNED OUT, OF SEVERAL FAMILY MEMBERS).

AS TO HIS ACTIVITIES ON SUNDAY, JULY 25, THIS WAS HIS SIMPLE STATEMENT:

THAT AFTER MARY'S MESSAGES OF FRIDAY AND SATURDAY, HE DECLINED AGAIN TO CALL UPON 126 NASSAU ST.

AND SPENT THE DAY, HE CLAIMED, IN HIS ROOMS ON JOHN STREET.

MR. CROMMELIN REMAINED UNDER SUSPICION.

OVER THE ENSUING DAYS, VARIOUS CITIZENS CAME FORWARD WHO CLAIMED TO HAVE SEEN MARY — OR SOMEONE WHO RESEMBLED HER — ON THE SUNDAY OF HER DISAPPEARANCE:

MEETING WITH A MAN SHE SEEMED TO KNOW IN THEATRE ALLEY...

ARGUING WITH A MAN ON THE OPEN STREET...

WALKING WITH A MAN WESTWARD ON BARCLAY STREET.

BARCLAY STREET WAS, OF COURSE, THE AVENUE TO THE FERRY LANDING.

BUT IT ALSO LED, AS MANY KNEW, TO THE MANSION OF "MADAME RESTELL," THE NOTORIOUS ABORTIONIST...

146 GREENWICH ST.

THE ALL-TOO-FREQUENT DESTINATION, IN THOSE DAYS, OF YOUNG LADIES "IN TROUBLE."

THE QUESTION WOULD NOT GO AWAY: COULD MARY HAVE BEEN THE VICTIM OF A FAILED ATTEMPT TO TERMINATE A PREGNANCY?

TWO MEN — MR. FANSHAW AND MR. THOMAS — AT THIS POINT CAME FORWARD WITH AN INTRIGUING STORY:

ON SUNDAY, JULY 25 (THEY SAID), THEY HAD BEEN STROLLING ALONG THE HOBOKEN SHORE, NEAR THE SYBIL'S CAVE...

WHEN A ROWBOAT LANDED, AND SIX YOUNG MEN JUMPED OUT.

WITH THEM WAS A GIRL, WHOM THEY CARRIED, TO ALL APPEARANCES AGAINST HER WILL, INTO THE WOODS.

FOR A FEW DAYS, THIS ACCOUNT LENT SUPPORT TO SPECULATION THAT A ROWDY GANG HAD COMMITTED THE MURDER...

UNTIL THE YOUNG LADY IN QUESTION CAME FORWARD.

SHE HAD BEEN ON AN OUTING WITH HER FAMILY THAT DAY (SHE SAID) AND HAD INDEED BEEN ABDUCTED BY A GROUP OF YOUTHS.

SHE WAS LATER RELEASED UNHARMED.

APPARENTLY, THE EPISODE WAS ONE OF INNOCENT HIGH SPIRITS.

ALSO AT THIS TIME, A YOUNG SAILOR NAMED WILLIAM KIEKUK WAS REMOVED FROM HIS SHIP, THE NORTH CAROLINA, AND PLACED UNDER ARREST.

HE HAD ROOMED AT THE ROGERS HOUSE DURING DIFFERENT PERIODS IN 1840...

AND HAD BEEN OBSERVED BOARDING THE SHIP ON THE NIGHT OF SUNDAY, JULY 25, LATE AND IN A GREAT HURRY.

IN ADDITION, DARK STAINS COULD BE SEEN IN PLACES ON HIS TROUSERS.

(THESE TURNED OUT TO BE QUITE INNOCENT.)

KIEKUK ADMITTED HAVING KNOWN MARY, BUT HAD NOT BEEN ONE OF HER SUITORS.

HE HAD LAST SEEN HER, HE SAID, ON JULY 3.

IN ANY CASE, HE HAD SPENT THE SUNDAY IN QUESTION IN THE COMPANY OF FRIENDS AND RELATIONS WHO COULD AMPLY ACCOUNT FOR HIS MOVEMENTS.

NEVERTHELESS, HE REMAINED UNDER SUSPICION...

NORTH CAROLIN[A]

AND WAS REMOVED FROM HIS SHIP THREE MORE TIMES OVER THE ENSUING WEEKS FOR FURTHER INTERROGATION.

IN MID-AUGUST, ATTENTION FELL UPON MR. JOSEPH MORSE...

A FINE WOOD ENGRAVER WHO KEPT A SHOP AT 120 NASSAU STREET.

APPARENTLY, HE HAD BEEN MISSING FROM HIS HOME OVER THE NIGHT OF SUNDAY, JULY 25.

RETURNING ON MONDAY EVENING, HE INITIATED A FURIOUS BATTLE WITH HIS WIFE...

WHICH SPILLED INTO THE STREET OUTSIDE THEIR HOME AT THE CORNER OF BROOME AND GREENE STREETS.

ON THE FOLLOWING DAY, MRS. MORSE (NOT FOR THE FIRST TIME) SWORE A COMPLAINT AGAINST HER HUSBAND...

ALTHOUGH BY THAT TIME HE HAD FLED THE CITY.

OFFICER HILLIKER OF NEW YORK AT LAST FOUND HIM HIDING IN HOLDEN, MASSACHUSETTS.

MORSE WAS ARRESTED AND BROUGHT TO THE CITY ON SUNDAY, AUGUST 15.

AN ANGRY CROWD SOON GATHERED OUTSIDE "THE TOMBS."

THE STATEMENT OF JOSEPH MORSE:

POSSESSED OF A SELF-ACKNOWLEDGED WEAKNESS FOR THE TENDER SEX, HE HAD SPENT THE SUNDAY IN QUESTION WITH A YOUNG LADY HE HAD MET OUTSIDE HIS SHOP.

HE PERSUADED HER INTO AN EXCURSION WITH HIM TO STATEN ISLAND.

THEY TOOK REFRESHMENT AT A PAVILLION THERE.

IN A CLEVER SUBTERFUGE, HE SET HIS WATCH BACK BY ONE HOUR...

THUS ENSURING THAT THEY MISS THE LAST FERRY BACK.

AS THE RAINSTORM ERUPTED, HE ENTREATED HER TO A HOTEL ROOM...

WHERE THEY LAY IN THE SAME BED, FULLY-CLOTHED...

AND SHE REPELLED HIS ADVANCES FOR THE REMAINDER OF THE NIGHT

THEY RETURNED TOGETHER ON MONDAY MORNING.

AT LENGTH, THE YOUNG LADY CAME FORWARD TO CONFIRM THE STORY, AS DID SEVERAL WITNESSES FROM STATEN ISLAND.

CLOSED

AND JOSEPH MORSE WAS NEVER HEARD FROM AGAIN.

FRIDAY, AUGUST 27
THE UNFORTUNATE ARCHIBALD PADLEY WAS PLACED UNDER ARREST...

AND HELD IN "THE TOMBS" FOR THREE ENTIRE DAYS OF QUESTIONING.

HE INSISTED THAT HE WAS NEVER A SUITOR OF MARY'S AND HAD NO KNOWLEDGE OF HER ASSOCIATES.

VICTIM OF ILL-LUCK AND CIRCUMSTANCE, PADLEY WAS AT LAST RELEASED.

YET HE REMAINED UNDER SUSPICION—AS DID EVERY MAN KNOWN TO HAVE COME INTO CONTACT WITH THE DECEASED YOUNG LADY.

EVEN MARY'S EARLY BENEFACTOR, JOHN ANDERSON, FELL UNDER OFFICIAL SCRUTINY.

WHAT WAS THE TRUE NATURE OF THEIR RELATIONSHIP?

HE WAS INTERROGATED AND BRIEFLY PLACED UNDER ARREST...

ALL OF IT QUITE EMBARRASSING FOR A YOUNG ENTREPRENEUR, WITH WIFE AND CHILDREN AND AMBITION FOR A POLITICAL CAREER.

IN LATE AUGUST—AS THE INVESTIGATION RAN OUT OF PATHS TO FOLLOW AND PUBLIC INTEREST WANED—MARY'S REMAINS WERE AT LAST REMOVED FROM THE DEAD HOUSE...

AND LAID TO REST, AT THE CITY'S EXPENSE, IN THE YARD OF A SMALL CHURCH ON CARMINE STREET.

NONE OF HER FAMILY OR FRIENDS ATTENDED THE BRIEF SERVICE...

SAVE A SINGLE UNKNOWN GENTLEMAN.

NO STONE WOULD EVER MARK THE SPOT.

134

THURSDAY, SEPTEMBER 2, 1841
ON THIS DAY, A DISCOVERY WAS REVEALED WHICH SET THE POLICE INQUIRY INTO MOTION AGAIN — AND EXCITED FRESH PUBLIC SPECULATION.

ON AUGUST 25 (IT WAS ANNOUNCED), IN THE WOODS NEAR WEEHAWKEN (ABOUT ONE MILE ABOVE THE SPOT WHERE MARY'S BODY WAS RECOVERED)...

TWO LOCAL BOYS HAD COME UPON AN OPENING IN A THICKET.

INSIDE, THE BRANCHES FORMED A KIND OF "CAVE" — BARELY HIGH ENOUGH FOR A MAN TO STAND ERECT.

ON THE GROUND, LARGE STONES FORMED A NATURAL "CHAIR" AND "FOOT-STOOL."

STREWN ON THE GROUND AND IMPALED UPON BRANCHES WERE SEVERAL ARTICLES OF LADIES' CLOTHING.

THE SCENE WAS HEAVILY TRAMPLED WITH MENS' BOOT TRACKS...

WHICH LED DOWN A PATH TO THE RIVER BANK — ALONG WITH THE MARKS OF A BUNDLE BEING DRAGGED.

THE TWO BOYS, CHARLES KELLENBARACK, AGE 16 ...

AND HIS BROTHER OSSIAN, AGE 12 ...

WERE THE YOUNGER SONS OF MRS. FREDERICA LOSS, A GERMAN WIDOW ...

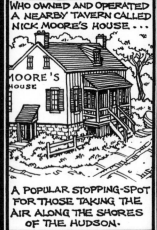

WHO OWNED AND OPERATED A NEARBY TAVERN CALLED NICK MOORE'S HOUSE ...

A POPULAR STOPPING-SPOT FOR THOSE TAKING THE AIR ALONG THE SHORES OF THE HUDSON.

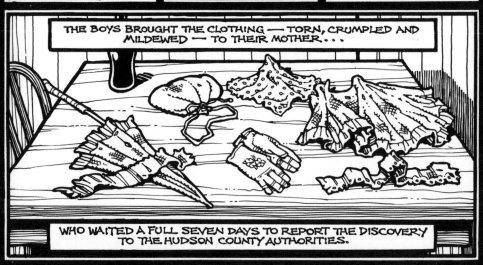

THE BOYS BROUGHT THE CLOTHING — TORN, CRUMPLED AND MILDEWED — TO THEIR MOTHER ...

WHO WAITED A FULL SEVEN DAYS TO REPORT THE DISCOVERY TO THE HUDSON COUNTY AUTHORITIES.

IN DUE COURSE, MRS. ROGERS IDENTIFIED THE ARTICLES AS HAVING BELONGED TO HER DAUGHTER ...

AND THE AREA AROUND WEEHAWKEN SWARMED WITH POLICE AND JOURNALISTS.

MRS. LOSS HAD A STORY READY FOR THEM.

THE STATEMENT OF MRS. FREDERICA LOSS:

ON SUNDAY, AUGUST 25, SHE NOTICED A YOUNG LADY THAT COULD HAVE BEEN MARY ROGERS ENTER HER ESTABLISHMENT IN THE COMPANY OF A "SWARTHY" MAN.

THEY SAT WITH OTHER MERRY YOUNG COUPLES, CONSUMING DRINKS AND CAKES...

THE GIRL ATTRACTING HER NOTICE BY ORDERING ONLY LEMONADE.

AFTERWARD, THEY ALL ROMPED OFF INTO THE WOODS.

SOMEWHAT LATER, MRS. LOSS HEARD A SCREAM FROM THAT DIRECTION, BUT THOUGHT NOTHING OF IT.

FOR ON WEEKENDS, THE WOODS WERE ALWAYS FILLED WITH EXUBERANT YOUNG PEOPLE.

HER TALE WAS SUPPORTED BY A HOBOKEN CARRIAGE DRIVER NAMED ADAM WALL.

HE RECALLED HAVING SEEN, ON THAT SUNDAY, A BEAUTIFUL YOUNG LADY, ACCOMPANIED BY A SWARTHY MAN, ALIGHT FROM THE FERRY — AND WALK UP THE SHORE TOWARD WEEHAWKEN.

THE DISCOVERY OF THE SUPPOSED MURDER SCENE GAVE FURTHER CREDENCE TO THE THEORY CHAMPIONED BY THE *HERALD*: THAT A MURDEROUS GANG OF YOUNG TOUGHS HAD PERPETRATED THE CRIME.

IT WAS A KNOWN FACT THAT ON THAT PARTICULAR WEEKEND, TWO BOAT-LOADS OF RUFFIANS HAD COME OVER FROM MANHATTAN...

TO DRINK AND ROISTER AT A CERTAIN "RUM-HOLE" ON THE SHORE...

AFTER WHICH THEY ROAMED THE AREA WITH CLUBS AND KNIVES...

TERRORIZING INNOCENT YOUNG COUPLES.

IF MARY HAD BEEN ACCOMPANIED BY A MAN —SO THE THEORY WENT— HE WAS MOST LIKELY ALSO MURDERED BY THESE THUGS.

(NO CORRESPONDING MALE BODY, HOWEVER, WAS EVER RECOVERED.)

JUSTICE GILBERT MERRITT, WHO HAD TAKEN MRS. LOSS'S STATEMENT, HAD HIS OWN THEORY OF THE CASE:

MISS ROGERS HAD PERISHED FROM A FAILED ATTEMPT AT ABORTION...

"PERFORMED IN A 'SECRET ROOM' UNDER THE ROOF OF MRS. LOSS...

EITHER BY THE LADY HERSELF OR BY A PHYSICIAN IN HER SERVICE.

THUS, THE MAN SEEN WITH MARY WAS THAT VERY PHYSICIAN...

OR PERHAPS HER LOVER.

THIS MAN, ALONG WITH MRS. LOSS'S ELDEST SON OSCAR, THEN CONSIGNED THE BODY TO THE RIVER.

AND, LATER, THEY ARRANGED THE SCENE IN THE THICKET TO POINT TOWARD A VIOLENT ASSAULT.

THE INN-KEEPER AND HER SONS WERE INTERROGATED AT LENGTH BUT DIVULGED NOTHING INCRIMINATING.

WITHOUT SOLID EVIDENCE, THE COUNTY COULD HARDLY PROCEED WITH A PROSECUTION.

139

JUSTICE MERRITT'S THEORY WAS THOROUGHLY DISPUTED IN THE PRESS:

HAD NOT THE POST-MORTEM FOUND EVIDENCE ON THE BODY OF BEATING, STRANGULATION, AND SEXUAL ASSAULT?

AND WHY WOULD MRS. LOSS AND HER SONS RETAIN ARTICLES OF MARY'S CLOTHING AND PLANT THEM NEARBY...

THUS DRAWING SUSPICION UPON THEMSELVES, WHERE ABSOLUTELY NONE HAD EXISTED BEFORE?

YET ANOTHER THEORY WAS PROMOTED BY BENJAMIN DAY'S **TATTLER** AND ITS SUNDAY COUNTERPART, BROTHER JONATHAN:

THE REMAINS RECOVERED WERE **NOT** THOSE OF MARY ROGERS —

FIRST OF ALL, NO CORPSE CAN FLOAT AFTER A MERE THREE DAYS IN THE WATER. THIS ONE WAS SO DECOMPOSED AS TO HAVE BEEN SUBMERGED MUCH LONGER.

ALFRED CROMMELIN, BY HIS OWN ADMISSION, COULD NOT IDENTIFY THE DECEASED BY HER FACE.

LIKEWISE, DANIEL PAYNE'S IDENTIFICATION CAN BE DISCOUNTED BECAUSE OF THE EXTREME DECAY THAT HAD BY THEN SET IN.

THE VICTIM WAS MOST LIKELY ONE OF THE MANY NAMELESS GIRLS WHO MET AN UNLUCKY END IN THE CITY AT THAT TIME.

FURTHER, THE SCENE IN THE THICKET WAS OBVIOUSLY STAGED LATER BY PERSONS UNKNOWN, TO RE-INFORCE A DECEPTION.

◉

IF ALL OF THIS WAS TRUE — WHERE WAS MARY ROGERS? DID SHE ENGINEER HER OWN DISAPPEARANCE?

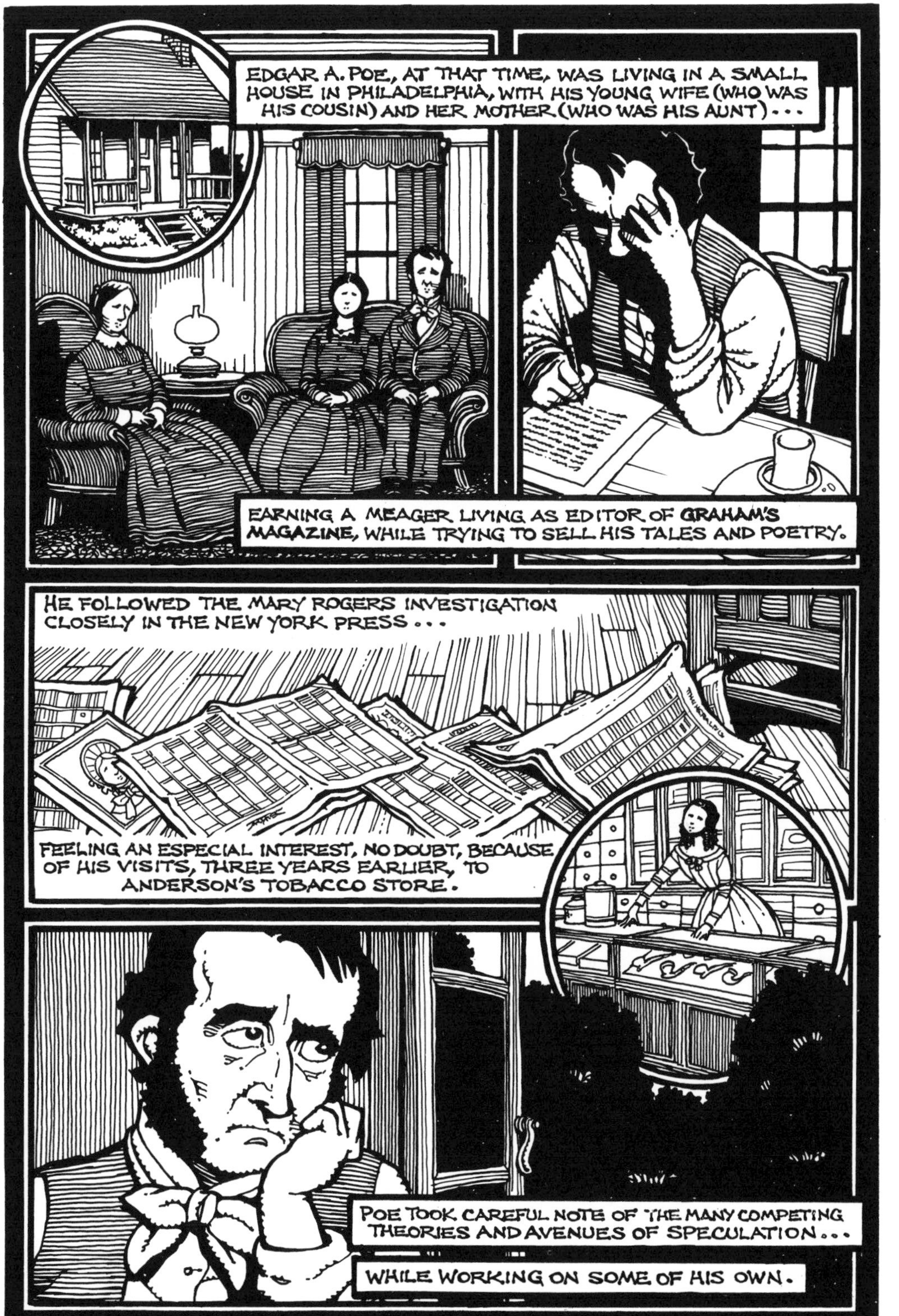
EDGAR A. POE, AT THAT TIME, WAS LIVING IN A SMALL HOUSE IN PHILADELPHIA, WITH HIS YOUNG WIFE (WHO WAS HIS COUSIN) AND HER MOTHER (WHO WAS HIS AUNT) . . .
EARNING A MEAGER LIVING AS EDITOR OF GRAHAM'S MAGAZINE, WHILE TRYING TO SELL HIS TALES AND POETRY.
HE FOLLOWED THE MARY ROGERS INVESTIGATION CLOSELY IN THE NEW YORK PRESS . . .
FEELING AN ESPECIAL INTEREST, NO DOUBT, BECAUSE OF HIS VISITS, THREE YEARS EARLIER, TO ANDERSON'S TOBACCO STORE.
POE TOOK CAREFUL NOTE OF THE MANY COMPETING THEORIES AND AVENUES OF SPECULATION . . .
WHILE WORKING ON SOME OF HIS OWN.

IN OCTOBER, THE LAST SAD CHAPTER IN THE TRAGEDY OF MARY ROGERS WAS ENACTED ON THE NEW JERSEY SHORE.

DANIEL PAYNE, WHO HAD REPORTEDLY EXISTED ON A DIET OF RUM SINCE HIS FIANCEE'S DEATH, WAS TORMENTED AT NIGHT BY VISIONS OF HER RESTLESS SPIRIT.

ON THURSDAY, OCTOBER 7, HE TOOK THE FERRY TO HOBOKEN AND WALKED NORTHWARD.

HE STOPPED TO DRINK AT NICK MOORE'S HOUSE AND ASKED TO BE SHOWN TO THE NOTORIOUS THICKET.

HE WAS LATER SEEN SITTING AT ITS ENTRANCE, APPARENTLY WRITING A LETTER.

AT SOME POINT, HE CONSUMED A QUANTITY OF LAUDANUM, FOR THE EMPTY PHIAL WAS FOUND ON THE SPOT.

AT ABOUT 10:00 PM, HE APPEARED AT THE BAR OF THE PHOENIX HOTEL IN HOBOKEN.

I'M A MAN OF A GOOD DEAL OF TROUBLE.

THE NEXT MORNING, PAYNE WAS SEEN LYING IN A PATCH OF WEEDS AT THE CENTER OF TOWN.

LATER, HE WANDERED THE WOODS BLINDLY, AS THE DRUG TOOK ITS DEADLY EFFECT.

AT LAST, HIS LIFELESS FORM WAS FOUND BESIDE THE PATH TO THE SIBYL'S CAVE, LOOKING OUT TOWARD THE RIVER.

AMONG THE PAPERS RECOVERED FROM HIS PERSON WAS A HAND-WRITTEN NOTE—

TO THE WORLD— HERE I AM ON THE VERY SPOT. MAY GOD FORGIVE ME FOR MY MISSPENT LIFE.

THE CORONER'S INQUEST, PRESIDED OVER BY JUSTICE MERRITT, CONCLUDED THAT PAYNE HAD EXPIRED FROM...

SUICIDE, BROUGHT ON BY CONGESTION OF THE BRAIN, EXPOSURE, ABERRATION OF THE MIND, AND IRREGULARITY OF LIVING.

THE OTHER PAPERS FOUND IN HIS POCKETS WERE HELD TO BE OF LITTLE INTEREST AND NOT RELEASED TO THE PUBLIC.

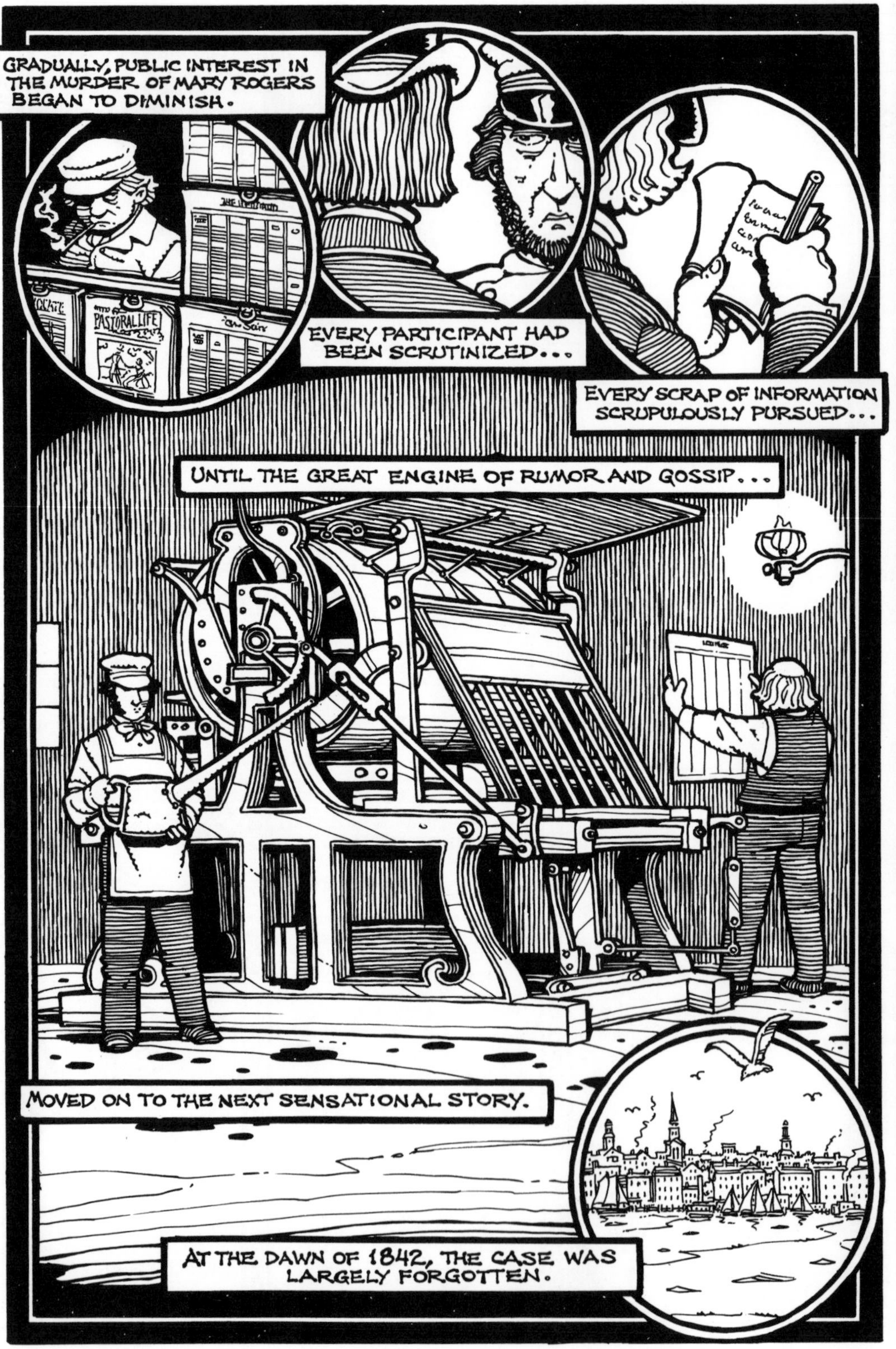
GRADUALLY, PUBLIC INTEREST IN THE MURDER OF MARY ROGERS BEGAN TO DIMINISH.
PASTORAL LIFE
EVERY PARTICIPANT HAD BEEN SCRUTINIZED...
EVERY SCRAP OF INFORMATION SCRUPULOUSLY PURSUED...
UNTIL THE GREAT ENGINE OF RUMOR AND GOSSIP...
MOVED ON TO THE NEXT SENSATIONAL STORY.
AT THE DAWN OF 1842, THE CASE WAS LARGELY FORGOTTEN.

PART IV.
EDGAR A. POE.

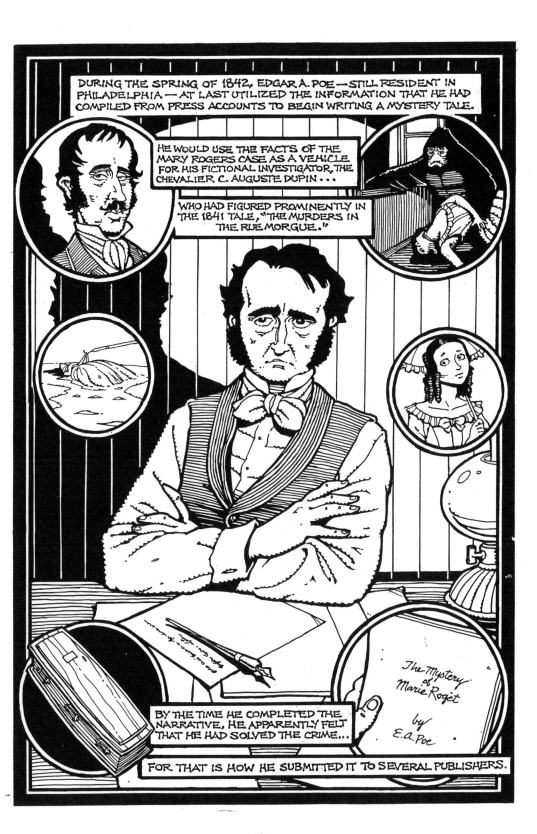

DURING THE SPRING OF 1842, EDGAR A. POE — STILL RESIDENT IN PHILADELPHIA — AT LAST UTILIZED THE INFORMATION THAT HE HAD COMPILED FROM PRESS ACCOUNTS TO BEGIN WRITING A MYSTERY TALE.

HE WOULD USE THE FACTS OF THE MARY ROGERS CASE AS A VEHICLE FOR HIS FICTIONAL INVESTIGATOR, THE CHEVALIER C. AUGUSTE DUPIN ...

WHO HAD FIGURED PROMINENTLY IN THE 1841 TALE, "THE MURDERS IN THE RUE MORGUE."

BY THE TIME HE COMPLETED THE NARRATIVE, HE APPARENTLY FELT THAT HE HAD SOLVED THE CRIME...

The Mystery of Marie Roget

by E.a.Poe.

FOR THAT IS HOW HE SUBMITTED IT TO SEVERAL PUBLISHERS.

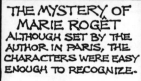

THE MYSTERY OF MARIE ROGÊT ALTHOUGH SET BY THE AUTHOR IN PARIS, THE CHARACTERS WERE EASY ENOUGH TO RECOGNIZE.

BEAUTIFUL MARIE IS THE DAUGHTER OF MME. ESTELLE ROGÊT...

WHO KEEPS A PENSION IN THE RUE PAVÉE SAINT ANDRÉE

SHE WORKS AT THE SHOP OF A PARFUMIER, M. LE BLANC...

WHERE SHE IS SURROUNDED BY ADMIRERS.

A PARTICULARLY ARDENT SUITOR IS THE GALLANT M. BEAUVAIS.

BUT MARIE BECOMES ENGAGED TO THE DISSIPATED M. EUSTACHE.

SHE LEAVES HOME ONE MORNING, TO VISIT AN AUNT IN THE RUE DES DRÔMES.

THREE DAYS LATER, HER CORPSE IS FOUND DRIFTING IN THE SEINE, BEATEN AND STRANGLED.

THE SO-CALLED MURDER SCENE IS DISCOVERED IN THE WOODS OF THE BARRIÈRE DU ROULE...

NEAR THE PUBLIC HOUSE OF MME. DULAC...

WHO CLAIMS TO HAVE SEEN THE VICTIM IN THE COMPANY OF A "SWARTHY MAN."

WITH ONLY NEWSPAPER ACCOUNTS TO GUIDE HIM, DUPIN TAKES ON THE MYSTERY.

POE (IN THE VOICE OF DUPIN) SPENDS MANY PAGES DISPUTING THE SEVERAL THEORIES THAT WERE ABOUT — BEGINNING WITH THAT WHICH PROMOTED A GANG OF YOUNG RUFFIANS:

• THE SCENE IN THE THICKET WAS TOO CRAMPED AND DISPLAYED **TOO MUCH** STRUGGLE FOR A GANG OF MEN TO HAVE SUBDUED A SINGLE FRAIL GIRL.

• LIKEWISE, A GROUP OF MEN WOULD HAVE **CARRIED** THE BODY TO THE RIVER — NOT LEAVING THE DRAG MARKS THAT WERE FOUND.

• MOST INDICATIVE: GIVEN THE LARGE REWARD, A THUG WOULD HAVE INFORMED UPON HIS FELLOWS BEFORE LONG.

THE DETECTIVE ALSO DISMISSES THE NOTION THAT THE BODY WAS NOT "MARIE'S."

• THE CORPSE COULD INDEED HAVE RISEN TO THE SURFACE WITHIN THREE DAYS.

• THE IDENTIFICATION AT THE INQUEST BY "BEAUVAIS" WAS CERTAIN, BASED AS IT WAS UPON SUCH **INTIMATE** DETAIL AS HER TINY FEET AND THE HAIR OF HER ARM.

DUPIN CONCLUDES THAT THE SCENE IN THE THICKET WAS STAGED AT A LATER DATE (OTHERWISE IT WOULD SURELY HAVE BEEN DISCOVERED EARLIER)...

ALTHOUGH HE DOES NOT RULE OUT THAT LOCATION AS THE ACTUAL MURDER SCENE...

NOR THE "SWARTHY MAN" AS A PARTICIPANT IN THE CRIME.

"MARIE" WAS MURDERED BY A FORMER LOVER, MOST LIKELY THE MAN BEHIND HER BRIEF DISAPPEARANCE OF TWO YEARS EARLIER.

THE SWARTHY COMPLEXION INDICATES A SEAMAN — AS DOES THE "SAILOR'S KNOT" AROUND THE VICTIM'S NECK.

SAILORS OFTEN RESIDE AT MME. ROGET'S PENSION, AND THE PERIOD BETWEEN THE TWO DISAPPEARANCES IS ABOUT THE DURATION OF A NAVAL VOYAGE.

THIS LOVER NO DOUBT RETURNED TO RESUME HIS ATTENTIONS UPON THE GIRL.

HE LURED HER TO THE WOODS — BUT SHE RESISTED HIM...

PROVOKING A FURIOUS ATTACK.

HE THEN ROWED THE BODY TO THE MIDDLE OF THE RIVER — THE DERELICT BOAT BEING FOUND THE NEXT DAY — AND MADE HIS ESCAPE.

(NO SUCH BOAT WAS EVER FOUND; A DETAIL FABRICATED BY THE AUTHOR.)

"THE MYSTERY OF MARIE ROGÊT" WAS AT LAST PURCHASED BY A RELATIVELY SEDATE PERIODICAL, SNOWDEN'S LADIES' COMPANION ...

SNOWDEN'S LADIES' COMPANION

AND WAS PUBLISHED IN THREE PARTS — IN THEIR ISSUES OF NOVEMBER AND DECEMBER, 1842, AND FEBRUARY, 1843.

PART V.

THE MYSTERY OF
MARY ROGERS.

BEFORE POE'S STORY WENT TO PRESS, A GRIM CODA TO THE MARY ROGERS CASE OCCURRED, WHICH WOULD ALTER PUBLIC PERCEPTION THEREAFTER.

OCTOBER 25, 1842
ON THAT DAY, MRS. FREDERICA LOSS WAS SHOT IN THE KNEE...

WHEN A PISTOL THAT HER SON WAS HANDLING ACCIDENTALLY DISCHARGED.

SHE FELL INTO A FEVER AND LINGERED FOR TWO WEEKS — EXPIRING ON NOVEMBER 9.

DURING THAT INTERVAL, SHE DRIFTED IN AND OUT OF LUCIDITY, SPEAKING IN BOTH ENGLISH AND GERMAN.

IN HER DELIRIUM, SHE MENTIONED A "FAMILY SECRET," AND TOLD OF BEING TORMENTED BY A FEMALE "SPIRIT."

JUSTICE MERRITT WAS SUMMONED TO THE DEATH-BED FOR A FINAL STATEMENT.

AFTER MRS. LOSS'S DEMISE, THE NORMALLY DIGNIFIED NEW YORK TRIBUNE REPORTED THAT SHE HAD MADE A STARTLING CONFESSION:

MARY ROGERS, SHE ADMITTED, HAD INDEED PERISHED UNDER HER ROOF— OF AN UNSUCCESSFUL ATTEMPT AT ABORTION.

THE UNNAMED PHYSICIAN, WHO HAD ACCOMPANIED MARY TO THE TAVERN, HELPED TO PLACE HER PARTIALLY-CLOTHED BODY IN THE RIVER.

THE REMAINING ARTICLES OF CLOTHING WERE SUNK INTO THE POND OF A NEARBY PROPERTY.

LATER, HOWEVER, THEY WERE REMOVED, FOR FEAR OF DISCOVERY, AND ARRANGED IN THE THICKET.

PUBLIC INTEREST IN THE CASE IGNITED ANEW...

AND THE WOODS, ONCE AGAIN, OVER-RUN WITH CURIOUS SIGHT-SEERS.

154

THE "CONFESSION" OF MRS. LOSS WAS SOON DISCREDITED BY THE TRIBUNE'S COMPETING JOURNALS:

HOW DOES IT EXPLAIN THE EVIDENCE ON THE BODY OF BEATING AND STRANGULATION?

WHY WOULD MRS. LOSS AND HER SONS ONLY PARTLY RECLOTHE THE BODY AND SAVE THE REMAINING ARTICLES?

WHY WOULD THEY LATER PLANT THE ARTICLES, ONLY TO "DISCOVER" THEM THEMSELVES?

IN ANY CASE, WITNESSES TO THE INNKEEPER'S LAST DAYS TESTIFIED AS TO HER COMPLETE INSENSIBILITY.

IN THE END, THE TRIBUNE, UNABLE TO CONFIRM ITS SOURCES, WAS FORCED TO WITHDRAW THE STORY.

NEVERTHELESS, THE IDEA OF THE FAILED ABORTION HAD CAUGHT ON IN THE PUBLIC MIND...

AND BECAME THE GENERALLY-ACCEPTED "SOLUTION" TO THE MYSTERY.

FOR THOSE STILL IN SEARCH OF A SOLUTION, CERTAIN QUESTIONS PERSISTED:

- WHY DID MRS. ROGERS AND DANIEL PAYNE APPEAR UNSURPRISED WHEN TOLD OF MARY'S DEATH?

- WHY DID ALFRED CROMMELIN SEEK TO STOP THE POLICE INVESTIGATION? WHY DID MARY WISH TO SEE HIM IN THE DAYS BEFORE HER DISAPPEARANCE?

- ON WHAT EVIDENCE DID JUSTICE MERRITT BELIEVE MARY THE VICTIM OF AN ABORTION AT MRS. LOSS'S TAVERN?

- IF SUCH WAS THE CASE, WHY, AND HOW, WAS SHE CHOKED AND BEATEN?

- WHAT WAS THE SIGNIFICANCE OF THE "SAILOR'S KNOTS" USED BY THE KILLER?

- WAS THERE A "SWARTHY MAN?" IF SO, WHO WAS HE?

- COULD THE ITEMS OF CLOTHING FOUND IN THE THICKET HAVE LAIN UNDISCOVERED FOR OVER A MONTH?

- IF THEY WERE ARRANGED THERE LATER, WHY? AND BY WHOM?

ONE PERSUASIVE THEORY ANSWERED MANY OF THE AFOREMENTIONED QUESTIONS...

PLACING THE MURDER SQUARELY ON THE SHOULDERS OF MARY'S PATHETIC FIANCÉ, DANIEL PAYNE!

THE THEORY WAS INSPIRED BY TWO INTERESTING FACTS:

DR. COOK'S POST-MORTEM FOUND MARY'S ARMS CROSSED STIFFLY AT HER CHEST — INDICATING THE ONSET OF RIGOR MORTIS.

THUS, SHE COULD ONLY HAVE BEEN IN THE RIVER FOR A SHORT TIME — PERHAPS LESS THAN ONE DAY!

A PAIR OF GLOVES WAS AMONG THE ITEMS FOUND IN THE THICKET — ALTHOUGH THE BODY TAKEN FROM THE RIVER ALSO WORE GLOVES!

THEREFORE, THE CLOTHING COULD ONLY HAVE BEEN PLANTED BY SOMEBODY WITH ACCESS TO MARY'S WARDROBE!

IN THIS SCENARIO, PAYNE, HAVING IMPREGNATED HIS BELOVED, ARRANGES FOR HER TO VISIT THE ESTABLISHMENT OF MRS. LOSS.

(WELL KNOWN FOR HER "SERVICES.")

TOGETHER, THEY CONCOCT THE STORY OF A TRIP TO HER AUNT ON JANE ST.

BY THIS TIME, HOWEVER, MARY IS COOLING IN HER AFFECTIONS FOR HIM.

ON SUNDAY, JULY 25, SHE UNDERGOES A SUCCESSFUL ABORTION AT THE WEEHAWKEN TAVERN...

AND REMAINS THERE, IN RECOVERY, FOR TWO MORE DAYS.

ON TUESDAY, JULY 27, PAYNE MEETS HER THERE...

AND, AS THEY WALK IN THE WOODS, MARY REVEALS HER INTENTION TO BREAK THEIR ENGAGEMENT.

IN RAGE AND ANGUISH, HE DRAGS HER INTO THE UNDERBRUSH, VIOLATES AND KILLS HER.

(THIS CERTAINLY ACCOUNTS FOR HIS LACK OF SURPRISE WHEN INFORMED OF HER DEATH THE NEXT EVENING.)

IN THE WEEKS THAT FOLLOW, PAYNE DRINKS HEAVILY AND IS CONSUMED BY GUILT.

HE ARRANGES PIECES OF MARY'S CLOTHING IN THE THICKET, TO CALL ATTENTION TO THE ACTUAL MURDER SCENE.

ANOTHER THEORY— WITH CERTAIN SIMILARITIES— HAD A HAPPIER OUTCOME:

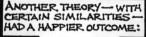

IN THIS VARIATION, MRS. ROGERS, TO OFFSET THE MEAGER LIVING FROM THE BOARDING HOUSE—AND WITH THE PROBABLE COLLUSION OF DANIEL PAYNE—HAS FORCED HER DAUGHTER INTO A CAREER OF PROSTITUTION.

FINDING HERSELF WITH CHILD, MARY PLOTS TO ESCAPE HER SITUATION...

WITH THE HELP OF ALFRED CROMMELIN, WHO HAD EARLIER PLEDGED HIS FRIENDSHIP AND PROTECTION.

AT HER BIDDING, HE ENLISTS THE "SERVICES" OF MRS. LOSS.

MARY UNDERGOES THE FORBIDDEN OPERATION AND REMAINS THERE — OR IN SOME OTHER SAFE PLACE— FOR THREE MORE DAYS...

DURING WHICH TIME, CROMMELIN, PERHAPS WITH THE ASSIST OF HIS COHORT PADLEY, ARRANGES FOR HER PASSAGE OUT OF THE CITY.

CROMMELIN AND PADLEY COME TO MEET MARY ON WEDNESDAY...

WHEN, BY GRIM HAPPENSTANCE, THE BODY OF AN UNKNOWN YOUNG WOMAN IS PULLED FROM THE RIVER (AN ALL-TOO-FREQUENT OCCURRENCE IN THOSE DAYS).

CROMMELIN SEIZES THE OPPORTUNITY TO "IDENTIFY" THE DISFIGURED CORPSE AS THE MISSING MARY ROGERS.

PADLEY FOLLOWS SUIT.

THAT EVENING, MARY MEETS THE TWO MEN AT THEIR HOTEL IN JERSEY CITY.

SHE GIVES THEM CERTAIN ITEMS OF HER CLOTHING TO SHOW TO HER MOTHER.

THE NEXT DAY, MARY DEPARTS FOR A PLACE UNKNOWN :

UP THE HUDSON? INTO THE WEST? ACROSS THE SEA?

TO REINFORCE THE IDEA OF HER MURDER, CROMMELIN PLACES FURTHER ARTICLES OF MARY'S CLOTHING IN THE WOODS NEAR WEEHAWKEN...

ARTISTICALLY CONSTRUCTING THE "CRIME SCENE."

EVEN EDGAR A. POE HAS NOT BEEN FREE OF ACCUSATION BY THEORISTS OF LATER YEARS.

HE HAD BEEN, AFTER ALL, ACQUAINTED WITH MARY ROGERS, AND, THOUGH RESIDENT IN PHILADELPHIA, HAD AMPLE OPPORTUNITY TO VISIT NEW YORK.

SHE COULD HAVE TAKEN PITY UPON HIS SORROWING SOUL AND ALLOWED HIM TO LURE HER TO A TRYST ON THE NEW JERSEY SHORE.

WELL KNOWN WAS HIS WEAKNESS FOR ALCOHOL—WHICH WOULD DRIVE HIM OCCASIONALLY TO GIVE WAY TO A MAD IMPULSE.

AS THINGS ACTUALLY HAPPENED, POE MOVED HIS FAMILY TO NEW YORK CITY IN 1845...

WHERE HE AT LAST GAINED A MEASURE OF FAME WITH THE PUBLICATION OF HIS POEM "THE RAVEN,"

HIS COLLECTED TALES, ALSO PUBLISHED THAT YEAR, CONTAINED A REVISED VERSION OF "THE MYSTERY OF MARIE ROGÊT."

BY THAT TIME, THE "SOLUTION" OF THE FAILED ABORTION WAS FIRMLY ENTRENCHED IN THE PUBLIC MIND...

AND SO POE HAD CLEVERLY ALTERED A FEW SENTENCES TO ALLOW FOR THAT CONCLUSION.

THE FINAL EPISODE IN THE MYSTERY CAME IN 1881, WITH THE DEATH OF JOHN ANDERSON.

NEVER COMPLETELY FREE OF SUSPICION, HE HAD ALWAYS CITED HIS INVOLVEMENT IN THE ROGERS CASE AS CAUSE FOR HIS FAILED POLITICAL ASPIRATIONS.

HE DIED A WEALTHY MAN IN PARIS, YET APPARENTLY OUT OF HIS SENSES.

DURING HIS LAST HOURS, HE CLAIMED TO BE VISITED BY THE MOURNFUL AND RESTIVE SPIRIT OF MARY ROGERS.

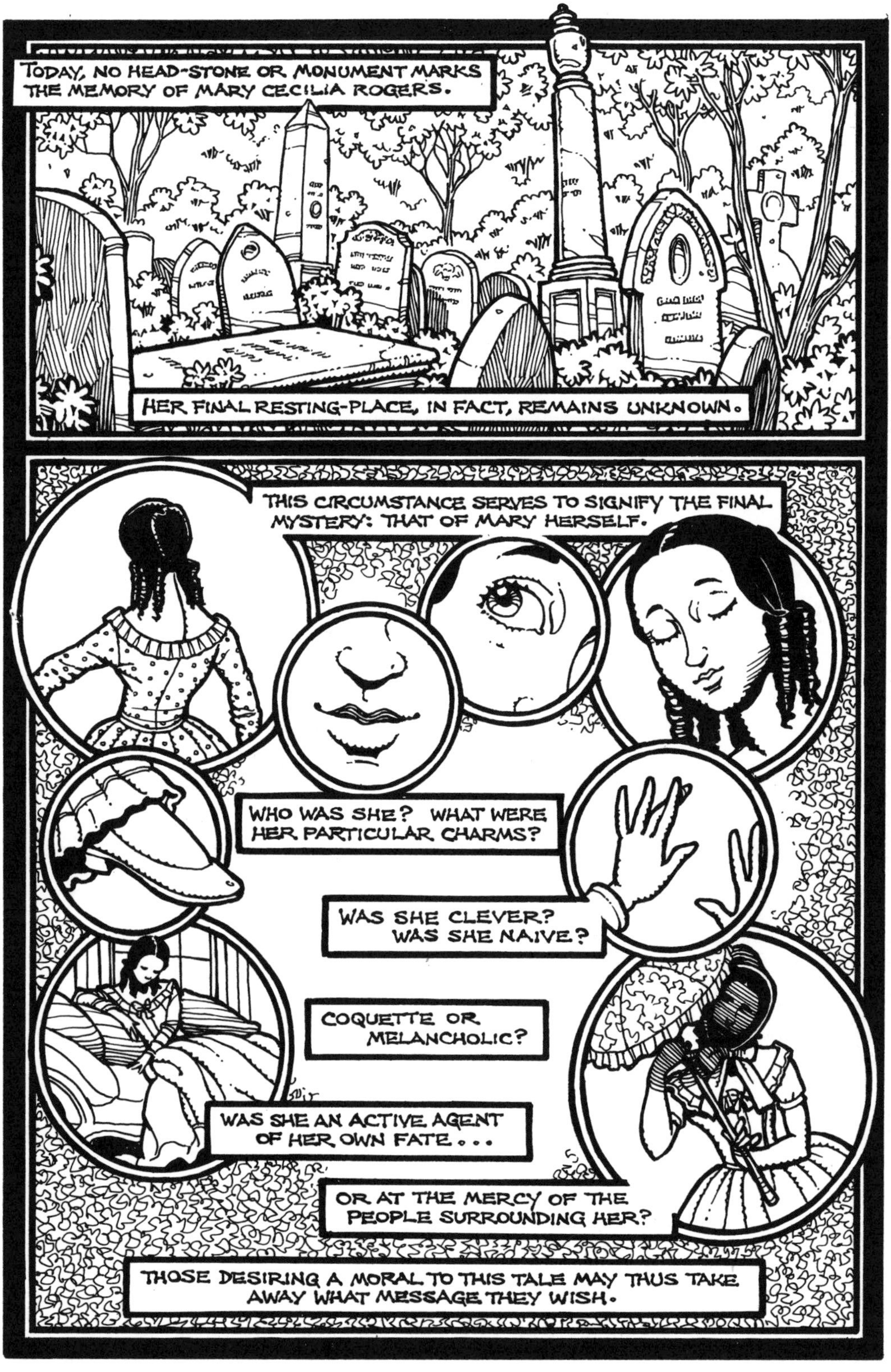
TODAY, NO HEAD-STONE OR MONUMENT MARKS THE MEMORY OF MARY CECILIA ROGERS.
HER FINAL RESTING-PLACE, IN FACT, REMAINS UNKNOWN.
THIS CIRCUMSTANCE SERVES TO SIGNIFY THE FINAL MYSTERY: THAT OF MARY HERSELF.
WHO WAS SHE? WHAT WERE HER PARTICULAR CHARMS?
WAS SHE CLEVER? WAS SHE NAIVE?
COQUETTE OR MELANCHOLIC?
WAS SHE AN ACTIVE AGENT OF HER OWN FATE . . .
OR AT THE MERCY OF THE PEOPLE SURROUNDING HER?
THOSE DESIRING A MORAL TO THIS TALE MAY THUS TAKE AWAY WHAT MESSAGE THEY WISH.

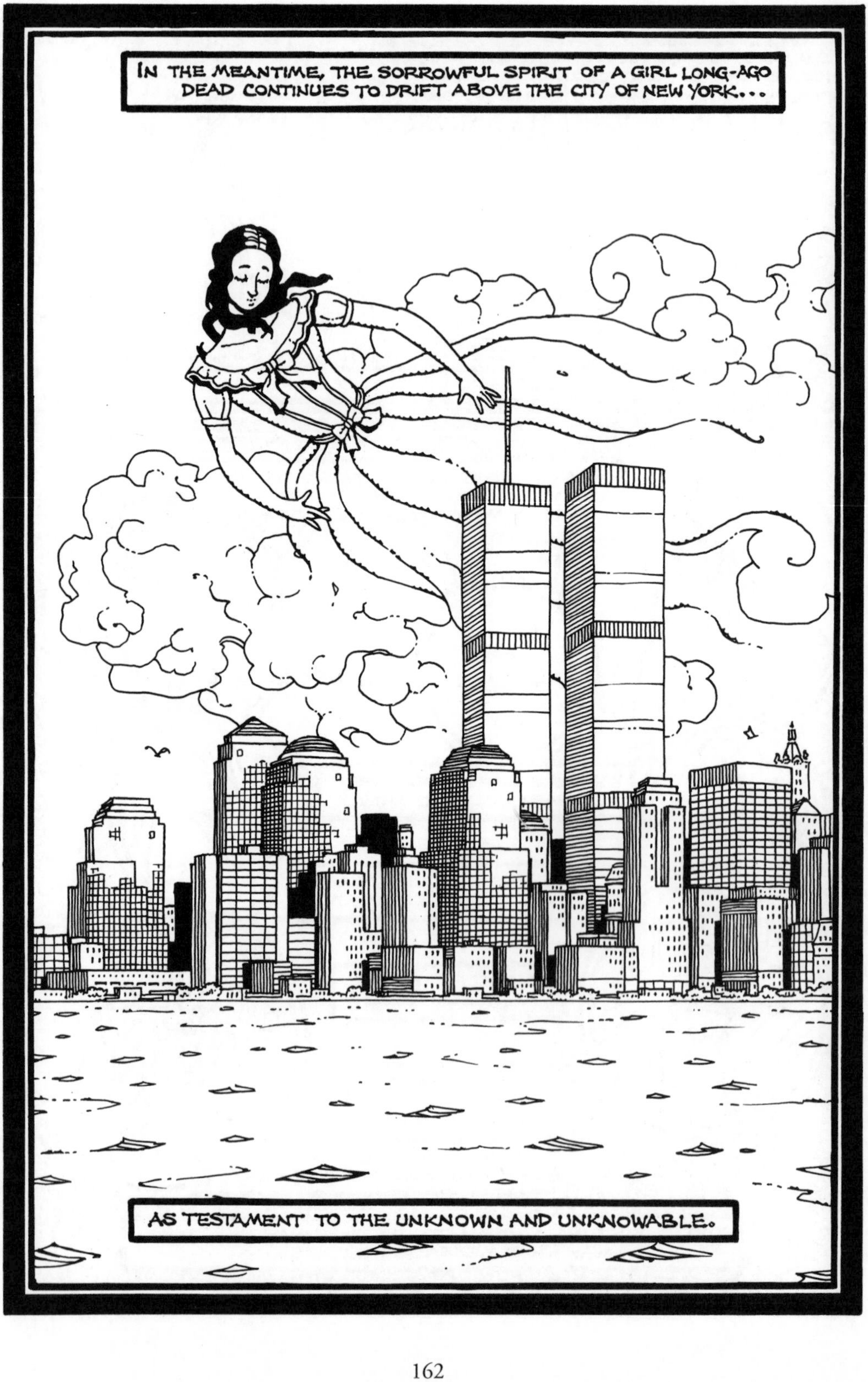
IN THE MEANTIME, THE SORROWFUL SPIRIT OF A GIRL LONG-AGO DEAD CONTINUES TO DRIFT ABOVE THE CITY OF NEW YORK...
AS TESTAMENT TO THE UNKNOWN AND UNKNOWABLE.

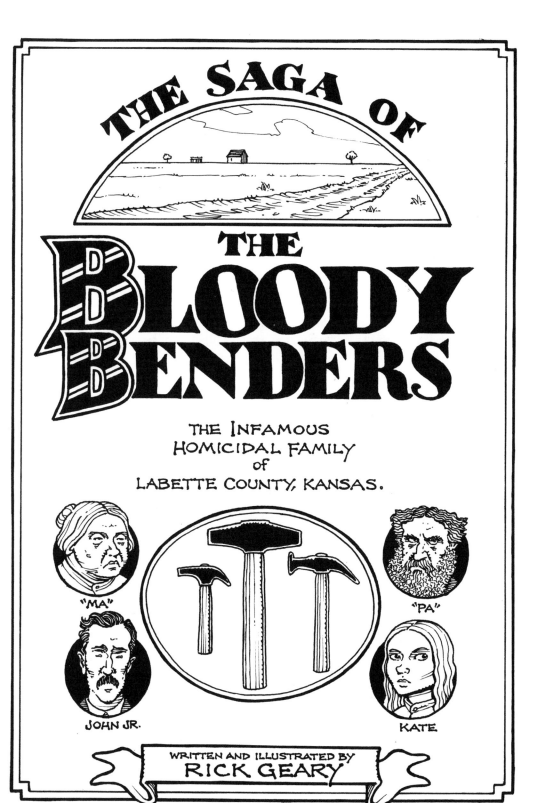

THE SAGA OF THE BLOODY BENDERS

THE INFAMOUS HOMICIDAL FAMILY of LABETTE COUNTY, KANSAS.

"MA"

"PA"

JOHN JR.

KATE

WRITTEN AND ILLUSTRATED BY
RICK GEARY

BIBLIOGRAPHY

Adleman, Robert H., *The Bloody Benders*. (New York, Stein and Day, 1970)

Dick, Leroy (as told to Jean McEwen), "The Bender Hills Mystery." Reprinted in The Little Balkans Review (Pittsburgh, KS, Little Balkans Press, Inc., Spring 1983, Summer 1983, Fall 1983, Winter 1983-84, Spring 1984, Summer 1984, Fall-Winter 1984-85, Winter 1988-89)

Lee, Wayne C., *Deadly Days in Kansas*. (Caldwell ID, The Caxton Printers, Ltd, 1997)

Socolofsky, Homer E. and Huber Self, *Historical Atlas of Kansas*. (Norman, OK, University of Oklahoma Press, second edition, 1988)

Wood, Fern Morrow, *The Benders, Keepers of the Devil's Inn*. (Chelsea, MI, BookCrafters, 1992)

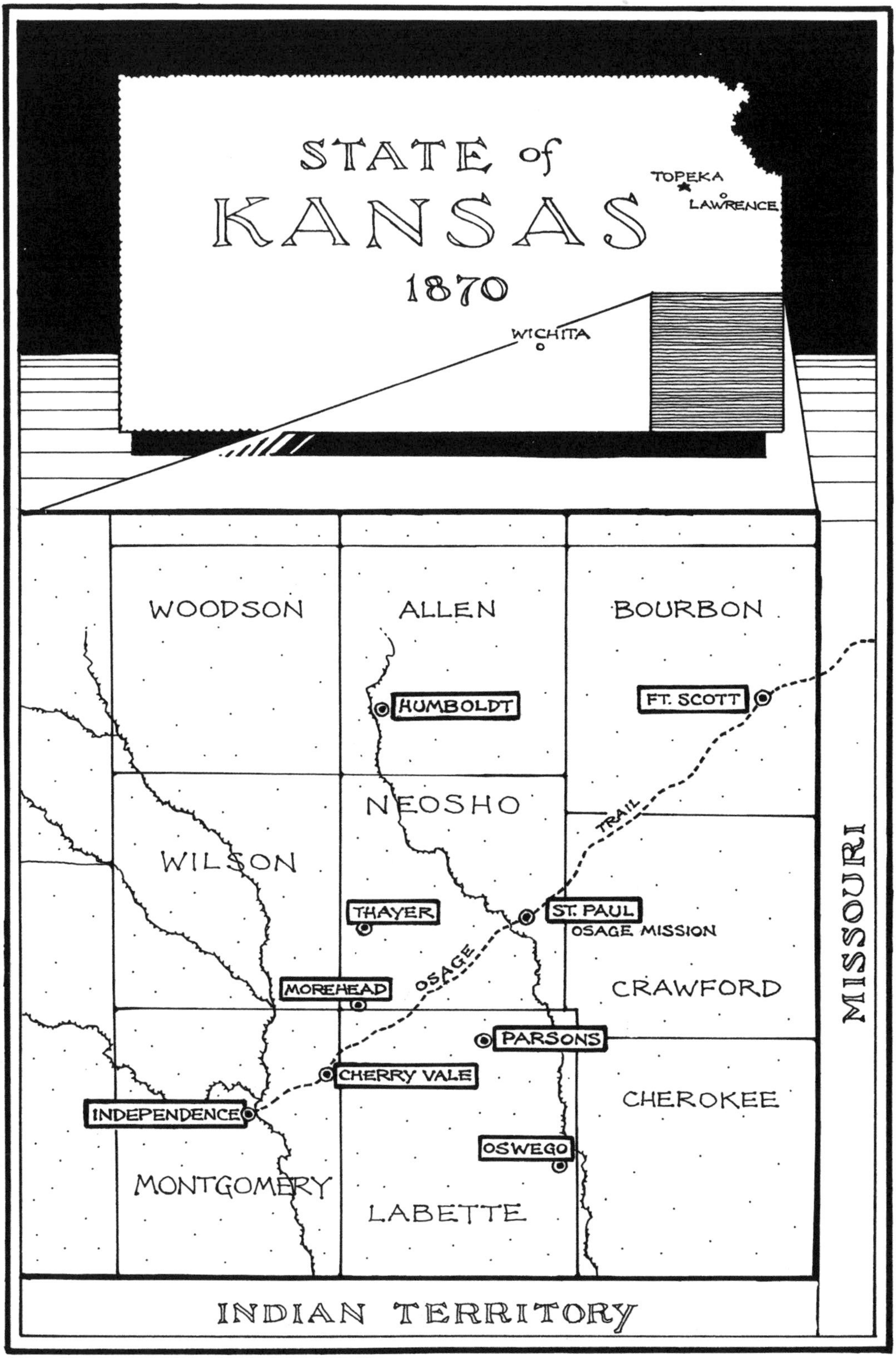
STATE of
KANSAS
1870
TOPEKA
LAWRENCE
WICHITA
WOODSON
ALLEN
BOURBON
HUMBOLDT
FT. SCOTT
NEOSHO
TRAIL
WILSON
THAYER
ST. PAUL
OSAGE MISSION
OSAGE
MOREHEAD
CRAWFORD
MISSOURI
PARSONS
CHERRY VALE
INDEPENDENCE
CHEROKEE
OSWEGO
MONTGOMERY
LABETTE
INDIAN TERRITORY

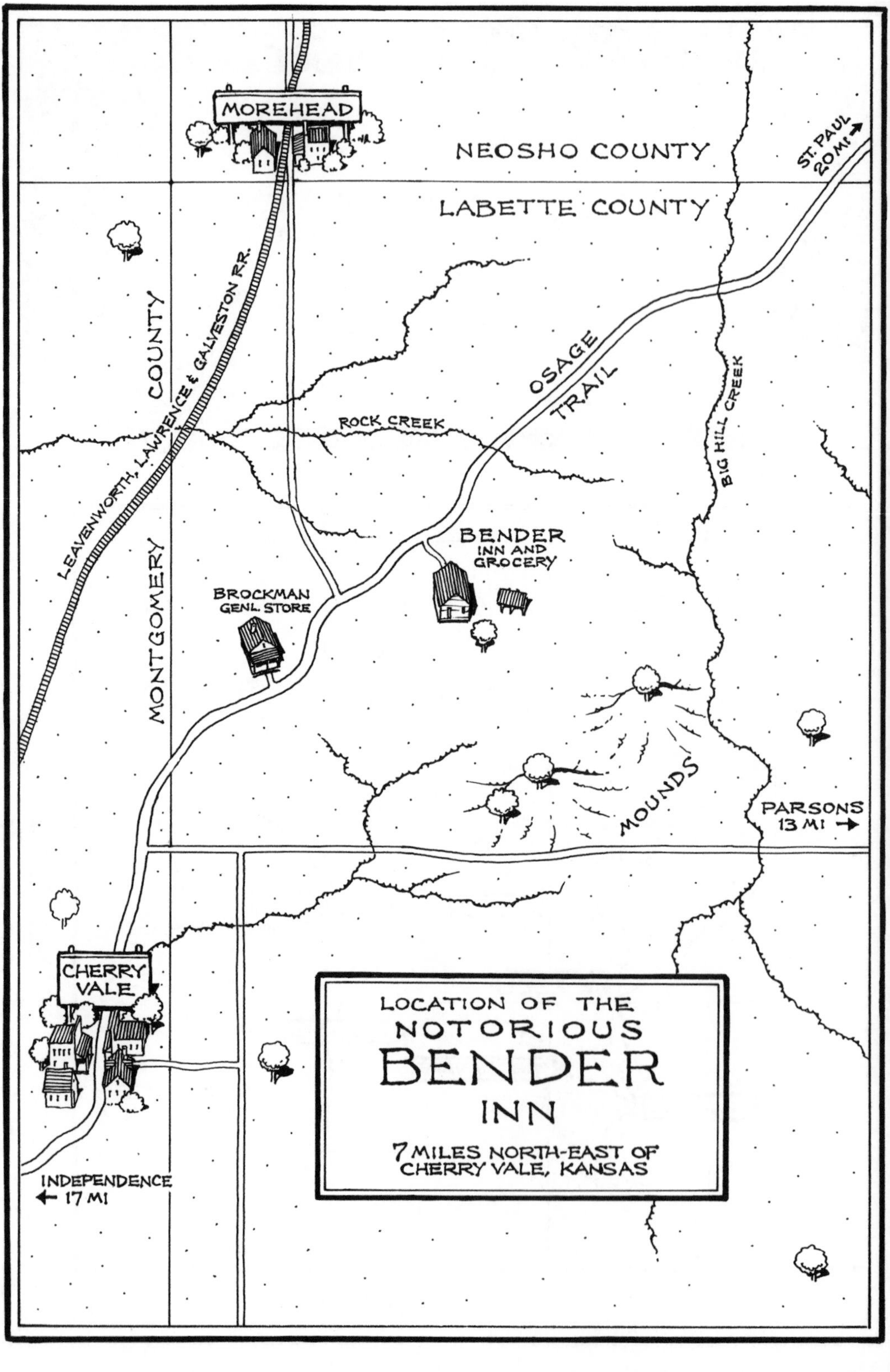
MOREHEAD
NEOSHO COUNTY
LABETTE COUNTY
ST. PAUL 20 MI.
LEAVENWORTH, LAWRENCE & GALVESTON RR.
MONTGOMERY COUNTY
OSAGE TRAIL
ROCK CREEK
BIG HILL CREEK
BENDER INN AND GROCERY
BROCKMAN GENL. STORE
MOUNDS
PARSONS 13 MI
CHERRY VALE
INDEPENDENCE 17 MI
LOCATION OF THE NOTORIOUS BENDER INN
7 MILES NORTH-EAST OF CHERRY VALE, KANSAS

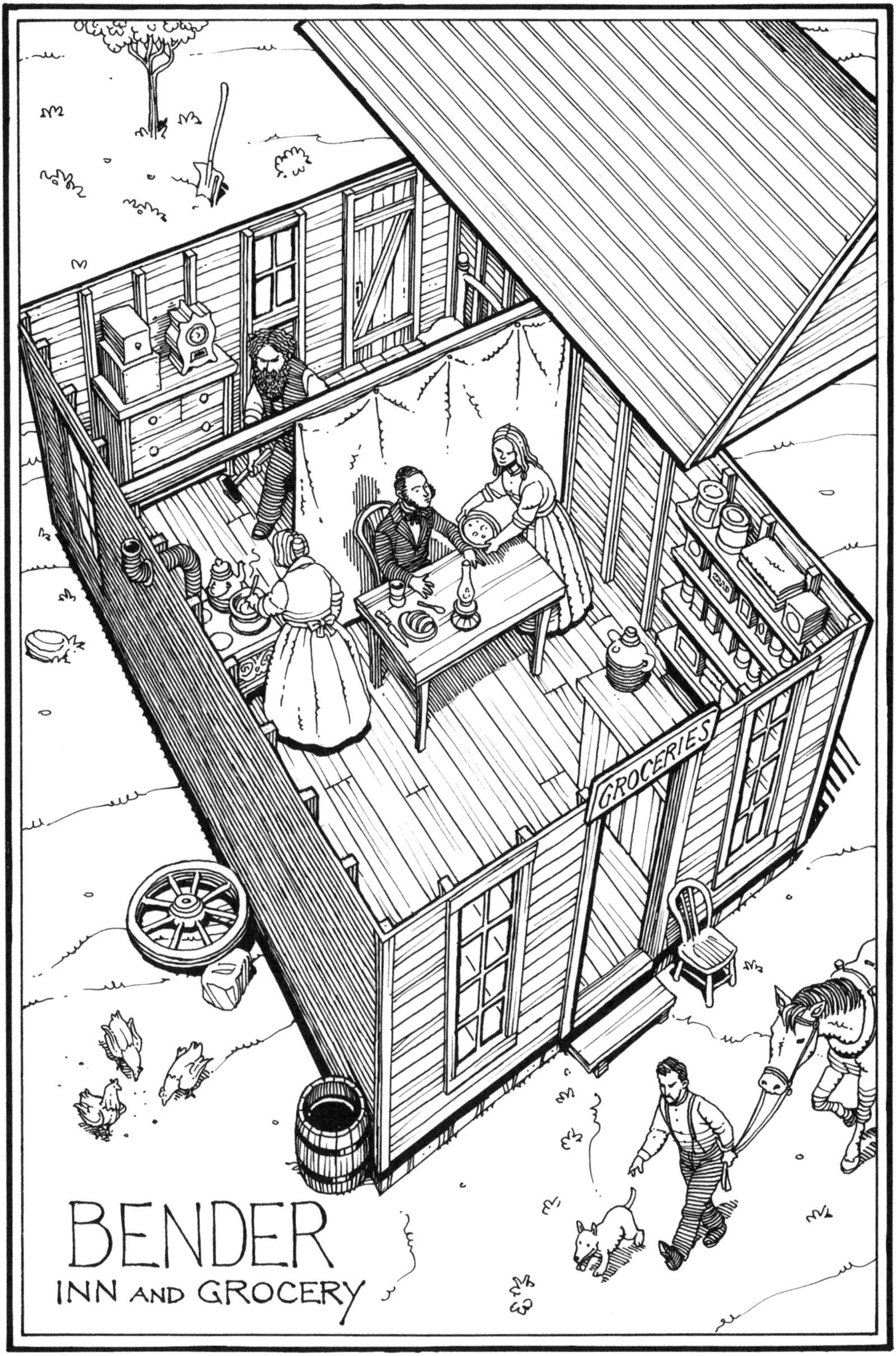
GROCERIES
BENDER
INN AND GROCERY

PART I
THE PRAIRIE

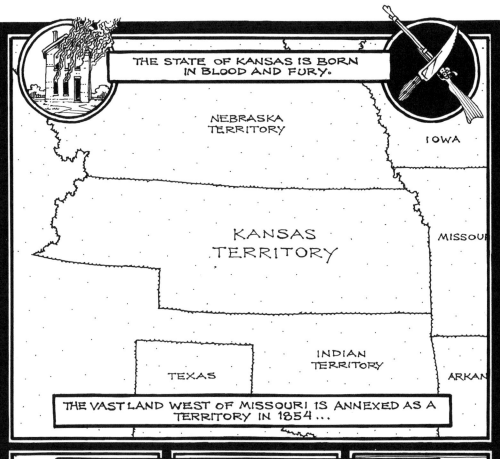

THE STATE OF KANSAS IS BORN IN BLOOD AND FURY.

NEBRASKA TERRITORY

IOWA

KANSAS TERRITORY

MISSOUI

TEXAS

INDIAN TERRITORY

ARKAN

THE VAST LAND WEST OF MISSOURI IS ANNEXED AS A TERRITORY IN 1854...

AND "BLEEDING KANSAS" BECOMES A CAULDRON OF THE SLAVERY ISSUE.

OF THE STAT
AD ASTRA PER ASPERA
JANUARY 29, 1861

NORTHERN AND SOUTHERN INTERESTS CLASH IN A FIERCE BORDER WAR THAT PRESAGES THE LARGER CONFLICT TO COME.

THE ABOLITIONIST JOHN BROWN AND HIS SONS PERPETRATE THE POTTAWATOMIE MASSACRE OF 1856.

AT LAST, ON JANUARY 29, 1861, KANSAS ENTERS THE UNION AS A FREE STATE.

WITH THE END OF THE CIVIL WAR, SETTLERS BEGIN TO ARRIVE IN LARGE NUMBERS.

THE HOMESTEAD ACT OF 1862 PROVIDES 160 ACRES FOR A SMALL REGISTRATION FEE AND FIVE YEARS OF HARD WORK.

THE SOUTHEASTERN REGION OF THE STATE, WITH ITS RICH, ROLLING PRAIRIE LAND, IS ESPECIALLY ATTRACTIVE.

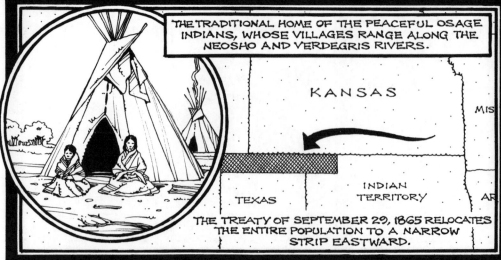

THE TRADITIONAL HOME OF THE PEACEFUL OSAGE INDIANS, WHOSE VILLAGES RANGE ALONG THE NEOSHO AND VERDEGRIS RIVERS.

KANSAS

MIS

INDIAN TERRITORY

TEXAS

AR

THE TREATY OF SEPTEMBER 29, 1865 RELOCATES THE ENTIRE POPULATION TO A NARROW STRIP EASTWARD.

MANY OF THE FAMILIES THAT STREAM INTO "THE OSAGE" ARE OF NORTHERN EUROPEAN ORIGIN...

RUSSIA

GERMANY

AUSTRIA-HUNGARY

FRANCE

GERMANY, HOLLAND AND THE REGION OF ALSACE-LORRAINE.

THEY STAKE OUT CLAIMS ALONG THE FERTILE RIVER BOTTOMS OF LABETTE, NEOSHO, WILSON AND MONTGOMERY COUNTIES. THEY CREATE THRIVING TOWNS.

FREDONIA

THAYER

ST. PAUL

WILSON

NEOSHO

NEODESHA

MOREHEAD

MONTGOMERY

PARSONS

CHERRYVALE

INDEPENDENCE LABETTE

OSWEGO

VERDEGRIS CITY

INDIAN TERRITORY

THE HOMESTEADERS ARE A HARDY BREED. THEY BUILD THEIR HOMES FROM THE NATIVE LIMESTONE, OR FROM THE SOD OF THE PRAIRIE ITSELF.

FAMILIES ARE LARGE, TO PROVIDE MANY HANDS...

PARENTS CAN RELY UPON SEVERAL OF THEIR OFFSPRING PERISHING FROM A VARIETY OF UNKNOWN DISEASES.

IN THE SPRING, DRENCHING RAIN, BATTERING HAIL, DEADLY CYCLONES...

IN THE SUMMER, STIFLING HEAT, INSECT SWARMS, PRAIRIE FIRES...

THE PARALYZING COLD OF WINTER.

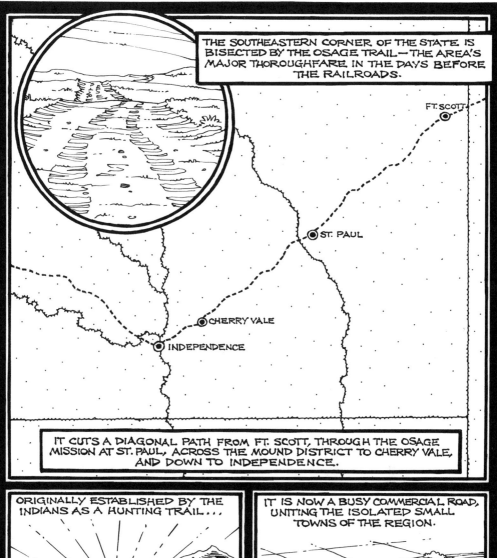

THE SOUTHEASTERN CORNER OF THE STATE IS BISECTED BY THE OSAGE TRAIL—THE AREA'S MAJOR THOROUGHFARE IN THE DAYS BEFORE THE RAILROADS.

FT. SCOTT

ST. PAUL

CHERRY VALE

INDEPENDENCE

IT CUTS A DIAGONAL PATH FROM FT. SCOTT, THROUGH THE OSAGE MISSION AT ST. PAUL, ACROSS THE MOUND DISTRICT TO CHERRY VALE, AND DOWN TO INDEPENDENCE.

ORIGINALLY ESTABLISHED BY THE INDIANS AS A HUNTING TRAIL....

AND USED BY TRAPPERS AND EXPLORERS VENTURING FROM MISSOURI TO THE ARKANSAS RIVER—AND THENCE TO THE FAR WEST!

IT IS NOW A BUSY COMMERCIAL ROAD, UNITING THE ISOLATED SMALL TOWNS OF THE REGION.

IN THE YEAR 1871, THE HONEST, HARDWORKING PEOPLE OF SOUTHEASTERN KANSAS FIND THEMSELVES THE SUBJECT OF SEVERAL DISTURBING INQUIRIES FROM THE EAST.

LOCAL OFFICIALS RECEIVE LETTERS ASKING AFTER RELATIVES WHO HAVE JOURNEYED TO THE OSAGE TRAIL AREA AND MYSTERIOUSLY VANISHED.

REPORTS ARE PUBLISHED IN NEWSPAPERS AS FAR DISTANT AS KANSAS CITY AND ST. LOUIS.

BUSINESS TRAVELLERS RIDING SOUTH FROM FT. SCOTT — SOME CARRYING LARGE AMOUNTS OF CASH...

ARE NEVER HEARD FROM AGAIN...

AS IF THE PRAIRIE HAS SIMPLY SWALLOWED THEM UP.

PART II

THE BENDERS
ARRIVE

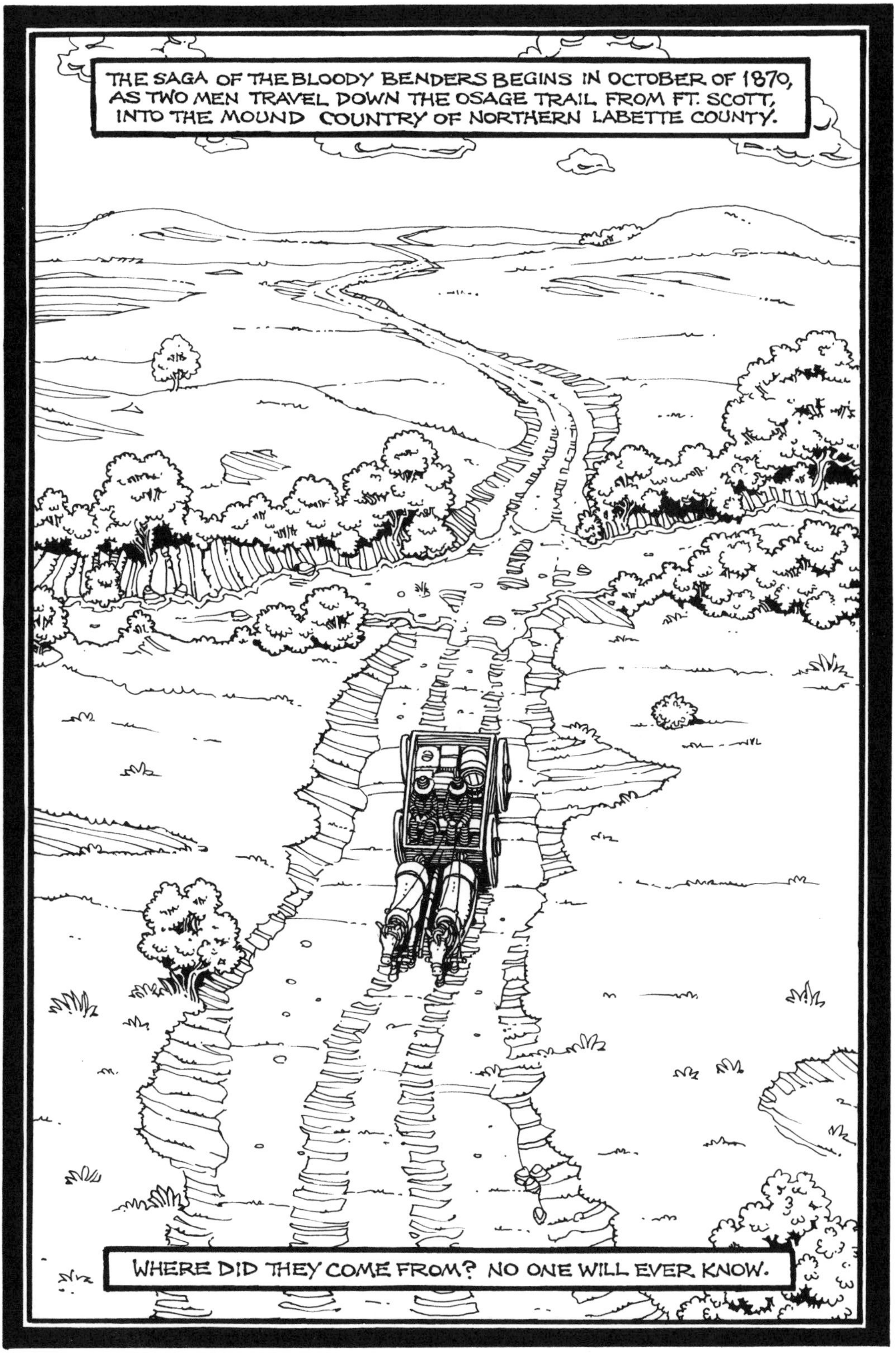
THE SAGA OF THE BLOODY BENDERS BEGINS IN OCTOBER OF 1870, AS TWO MEN TRAVEL DOWN THE OSAGE TRAIL FROM FT. SCOTT, INTO THE MOUND COUNTRY OF NORTHERN LABETTE COUNTY.
WHERE DID THEY COME FROM? NO ONE WILL EVER KNOW.

AT ABOUT NOON ONE DAY, THEY ARRIVE AT THE GENERAL STORE AND TRADING POST RUN BY RUDOLPH BROCKMAN AND AUGUST ERN — TWO GERMAN IMMIGRANTS.

BROCKMAN ERN

THE TWO STRANGERS INTRODUCE THEMSELVES AS JOHN BENDER, SENIOR AND JUNIOR, BOTH ALSO FROM GERMANY.

THE OLD MAN IS TACITURN AND SPEAKS LITTLE ENGLISH. THE YOUNGER, PROBABLY IN HIS MID-20'S, IS MORE TALKATIVE.

HE ANNOUNCES THEIR INTENTION TO STAKE A CLAIM IN THE AREA AND SETTLE DOWN.

ON THE FIRST NIGHT, THE PAIR CAMP IN THEIR WAGON BESIDE THE TRADING POST.

THE NEXT MORNING, THEY ARE GUIDED BY AUGUST ERN TO THE AVAILABLE LAND IN THE VICINITY...

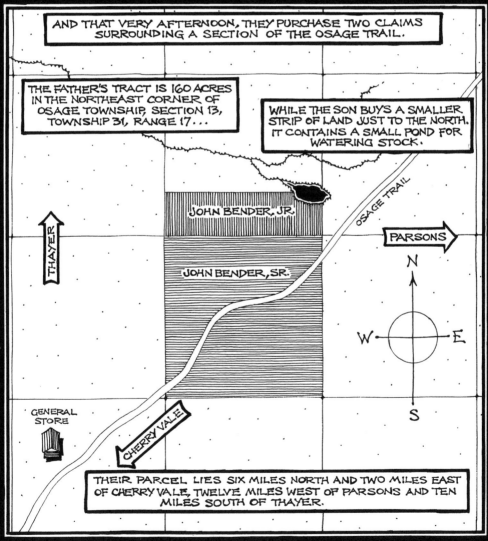

AND THAT VERY AFTERNOON, THEY PURCHASE TWO CLAIMS SURROUNDING A SECTION OF THE OSAGE TRAIL.

THE FATHER'S TRACT IS 160 ACRES IN THE NORTHEAST CORNER OF OSAGE TOWNSHIP, SECTION 13, TOWNSHIP 31, RANGE 17...

WHILE THE SON BUYS A SMALLER STRIP OF LAND JUST TO THE NORTH. IT CONTAINS A SMALL POND FOR WATERING STOCK.

JOHN BENDER, JR.

JOHN BENDER, SR.

THAYER

PARSONS

OSAGE TRAIL

N
W — E
S

GENERAL STORE

CHERRY VALE

THEIR PARCEL LIES SIX MILES NORTH AND TWO MILES EAST OF CHERRY VALE, TWELVE MILES WEST OF PARSONS AND TEN MILES SOUTH OF THAYER.

THE TWO MEN SET TO THE CONSTRUCTION OF A HOUSE UPON THEIR LAND.

THEY PURCHASE SANDSTONE BLOCKS FOR THE FOUNDATION FROM MR. HEIRONYMOUS NEAR THE MOUNDS...

INCLUDING A HUGE SLAB THREE INCHES THICK AND SEVEN FEET SQUARE FOR THE FLOOR OF THE CELLAR.

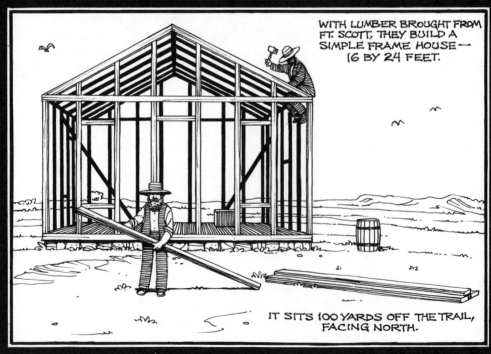

WITH LUMBER BROUGHT FROM FT. SCOTT, THEY BUILD A SIMPLE FRAME HOUSE — 16 BY 24 FEET.

IT SITS 100 YARDS OFF THE TRAIL, FACING NORTH.

ALSO ON THE PROPERTY, THEY DIG A WELL...

AND BUILD A SMALL STABLE FROM STOUT POLES AND THATCH MADE FROM HAY AND PRAIRIE GRASS.

BESIDE IT, A CORRAL, AND PENS FOR CHICKENS, CATTLE AND SWINE.

AS A FINAL TOUCH, THEY PLACE OVER THE FRONT DOOR A CRUDELY-LETTERED SIGN:

GROCRY

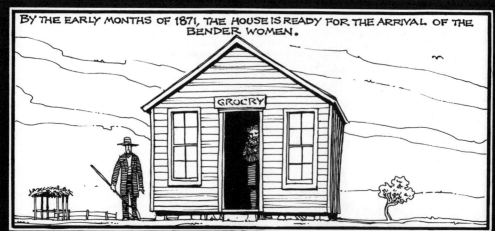

BY THE EARLY MONTHS OF 1871, THE HOUSE IS READY FOR THE ARRIVAL OF THE BENDER WOMEN.

THE MEN TRAVEL 108 MILES TO MEET THE TRAIN IN THE TOWN OF OTTAWA...

AND BRING THE TWO LADIES BACK TO THEIR NEW HOME.

"MA," ABOUT FIFTY, WHO WILL NEVER BE KNOWN BY ANY OTHER APELLATION...

AND THE DAUGHTER KATE, A YOUNG WOMAN OF ABOUT TWENTY.

AS THE WORST DAYS OF WINTER COME ON, THE FAMILY SETS TO MAKING LIVEABLE THEIR RUDE HOME.

A CAST-IRON STOVE, PURCHASED IN OTTAWA...

AN EIGHT-DAY CLOCK...

(RELIC OF THE OLD COUNTRY)...

EVEN A ROCKER!

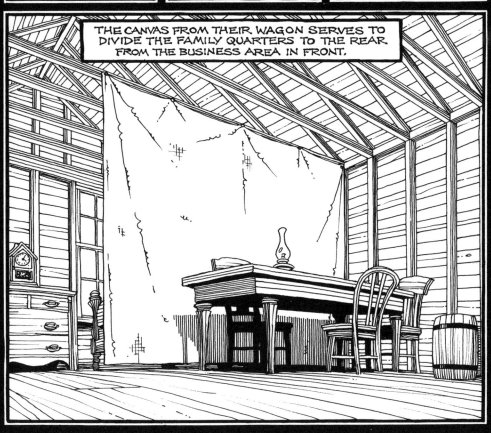

THE CANVAS FROM THEIR WAGON SERVES TO DIVIDE THE FAMILY QUARTERS TO THE REAR FROM THE BUSINESS AREA IN FRONT.

KATE LETTERS A MORE PRESENTABLE SIGN TO ANNOUNCE THE FAMILY'S BUSINESS...

GROCERIES

FROM A COUNTER BESIDE THE FRONT DOOR, THE PASSING TRAVELLER IS PROVISIONED.

SUCH NECESSITIES AS: TOBACCO, COFFEE, SARDINES, CRACKERS, SOAP, BLANKETS, AMMUNITION, ETC.

THE HOUSE BEING SITUATED UPON A SLIGHT RISE IN THE LAND, ANY APPROACHING RIDER CAN BE SEEN FOR MILES ALONG THE TRAIL.

THE OLD MAN KEEPS A LOOK-OUT, AS HE READS HIS GERMAN BIBLE.

THE TRAVELLER CAN ALSO BE SERVED A MEAL, PREPARED BY THE MOTHER.

CORNBREAD, BISCUITS, OR "FRIED BREAD." FOR MEAT THERE IS GREASY BACON, BUT MORE OFTEN, JACKRABBIT.

SEATED AT THE DINING TABLE, THE VISITOR IS WAITED UPON BY THE VOLUPTUOUS KATE.

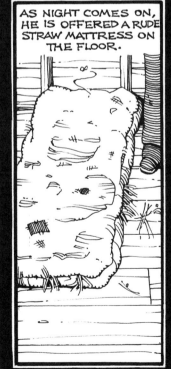

AS NIGHT COMES ON, HE IS OFFERED A RUDE STRAW MATTRESS ON THE FLOOR.

WHILE THE BENDER SON FEEDS AND TENDS HIS HORSE IN THE STABLE OUT BACK.

THE SURROUNDING COMMUNITY ACCEPTS THE STRANGE FAMILY AS A RATHER HARMLESS GROUP OF ECCENTRICS.

THE OLDER COUPLE KEEP LARGELY TO THEMSELVES. "PA" IS NOTED FOR HIS HULKING, "APELIKE" PRESENCE.

"MA," LIKE HER HUSBAND, HAS SCANT COMMAND OF ENGLISH. SILENT AND SULLEN, SHE ATTRACTS LITTLE NOTICE AT ALL.

JOHN JR., THOUGH FRIENDLY ENOUGH, IS JUDGED BY SOME TO BE FEEBLE-MINDED.

HIS EVERY UTTERANCE COMES WITH A DISTURBING GIGGLE.

BUT IT IS KATE WHO LEAVES THE DEEPEST IMPRESSION. THE MOST OUTGOING OF THE FAMILY, HER EXOTIC BEAUTY IS UNUSUAL FOR THIS RAW FRONTIER REGION.

SHE IS SAID TO MOVE WITH A "TIGERISH" GRACE.

THE TWO BENDER SIBLINGS PROVE THEMSELVES A MOST NEIGHBORLY PAIR.

THEY ATTEND LOCAL CHURCH SOCIALS, PRAYER MEETINGS AND THE WEEKEND DANCES IN PRIVATE HOMES.

THEY ARE REGULAR ATTENDEES OF THE SUNDAY SCHOOL AND CHOIR PRACTICE HELD AT THE HARMONY GROVE SCHOOLHOUSE AND CONDUCTED BY MR. LEROY DICK...

WHO HOLDS THE POSITION OF TOWNSHIP "OFFICER" OR "TRUSTEE," THE CLOSEST THING TO LAW ENFORCEMENT IN THIS PART OF THE COUNTY.

THE LOCAL MENFOLK ARE QUITE NATURALLY DRAWN TO KATE...

WHILE THE WOMEN REMAIN SUSPICIOUS AND STANDOFFISH.

FOR ABOUT SIX MONTHS IN 1871, KATE WORKS AS A WAITRESS IN THE DINING ROOM OF THE CHERRY VALE HOTEL.

ECCENTRIC AND INDEPENDENT, SHE WALKS THE COUNTRYSIDE, VISITING DIFFERENT HOMESTEADS TO OFFER HER SERVICES AS A HEALER AND SPIRIT-MEDIUM.

SHE PROVES HERSELF QUITE SEDUCTIVE TO THE BOYS OF THE SURROUNDING TOWNS AND FARMS, WHOM SHE KEEPS IN A CONSTANT STATE OF DESIRE AND EXPECTATION.

AMONG THEM IS THE SMITTEN NEIGHBOR RUDOLPH BROCKMAN.

THEY ARE CONTENT TO LOITER AT THE BENDER PLACE, PERFORM CHORES FOR THE FAMILY, TRAVEL TO OTHER TOWNS TO PURCHASE SUPPLIES FOR THE GROCERY.

ON OCCASION, THEY HELP THE FAMILY SELL THE HORSES, SADDLES, RIGS AND OTHER POSSESSIONS THAT ARE LEFT BEHIND BY GUESTS UNABLE TO PAY WITH CASH.

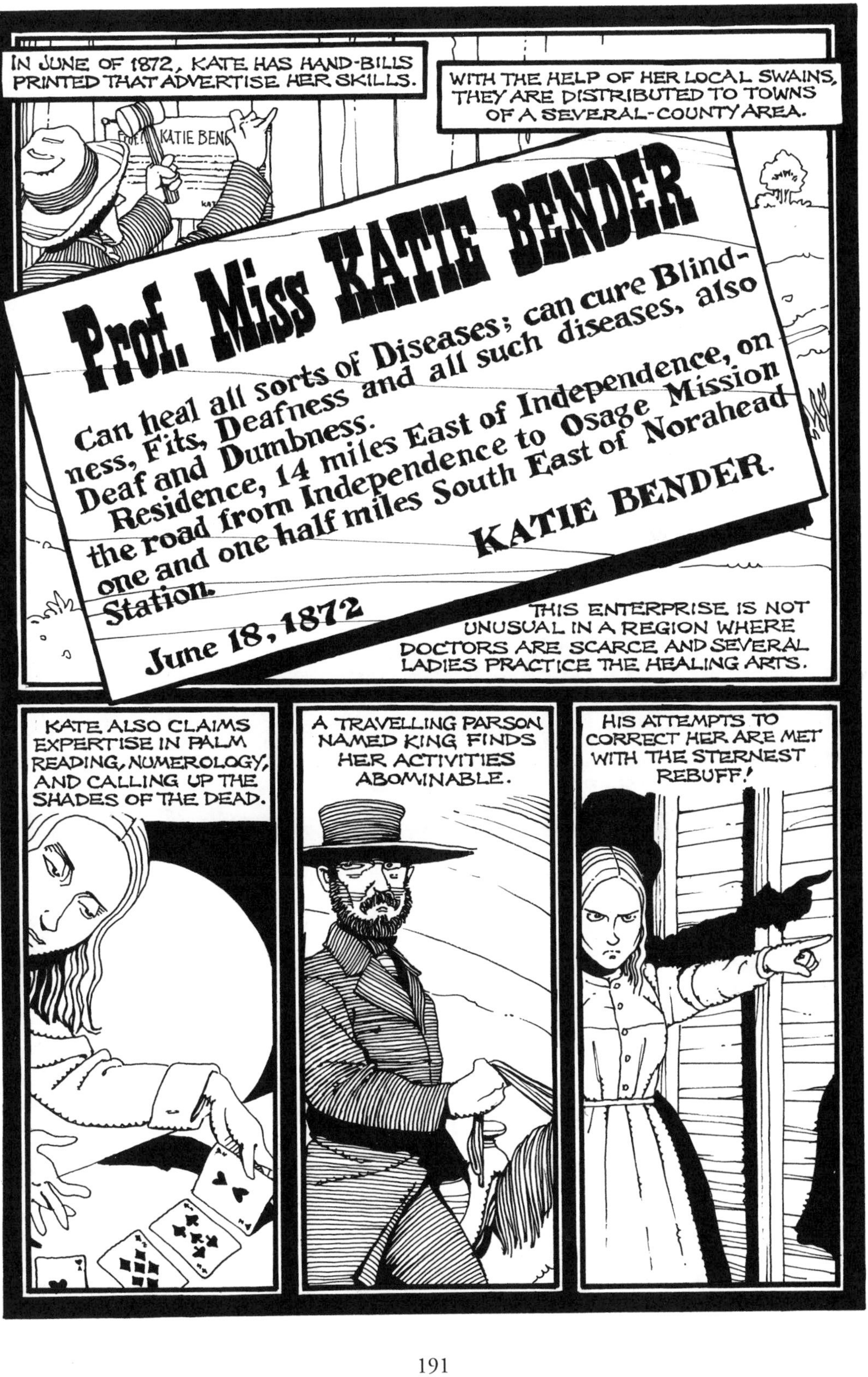
IN JUNE OF 1872, KATE HAS HAND-BILLS PRINTED THAT ADVERTISE HER SKILLS.
WITH THE HELP OF HER LOCAL SWAINS, THEY ARE DISTRIBUTED TO TOWNS OF A SEVERAL-COUNTY AREA.
Prof. Miss KATIE BENDER
Can heal all sorts of Diseases; can cure Blindness, Fits, Deafness and all such diseases, also Deaf and Dumbness.
Residence, 14 miles East of Independence, on the road from Independence to Osage Mission one and one half miles South East of Norahead Station.
KATIE BENDER.
June 18, 1872
THIS ENTERPRISE IS NOT UNUSUAL IN A REGION WHERE DOCTORS ARE SCARCE AND SEVERAL LADIES PRACTICE THE HEALING ARTS.
KATE ALSO CLAIMS EXPERTISE IN PALM READING, NUMEROLOGY, AND CALLING UP THE SHADES OF THE DEAD.
A TRAVELLING PARSON NAMED KING FINDS HER ACTIVITIES ABOMINABLE.
HIS ATTEMPTS TO CORRECT HER ARE MET WITH THE STERNEST REBUFF!

A LOCAL WOMAN VISITS KATE SEVERAL TIMES, IN HOPE OF BEING CURED OF A LINGERING MALADY.

BUT ONE DAY, FEELING THAT THE TREATMENT IS TAKING TOO LONG, SHE COMES TO DEMAND A REFUND.

KATE TRIES TO CONVINCE THE LADY TO STAY THE NIGHT...

AND, FAILING THAT, PERSUADES HER TO PARTICIPATE IN A SEANCE.

THE VISITOR BECOMES ALARMED WHEN THE FAMILY INTONE A FRIGHTENING GIBBERISH...

AND PASS AROUND A CLUB, A KNIFE AND A PISTOL.

SHE RUNS FROM THE HOUSE, HIDING IN THE TALL GRASS, AS THE BENDER MEN, ON HORSEBACK, SEARCH FOR HER.

SHE MANAGES TO ESCAPE UNHARMED AND CHOOSES — FOR NOW — TO TELL NO ONE ABOUT THE INCIDENT.

ANOTHER LOCAL LADY, INTERESTED IN SPIRITUALISM, COMES TO THE BENDERS FOR A SEANCE.

SHE IS SHOCKED WHEN KATE AND HER BROTHER DRAW HUMAN FIGURES ON THE WALL...

AND THEN PLUNGE KNIVES INTO THESE IMAGES.

KATE DECLARES THAT THE SPIRITS COMMAND HER TO KILL.

THE VISITOR FLEES IN HORROR.

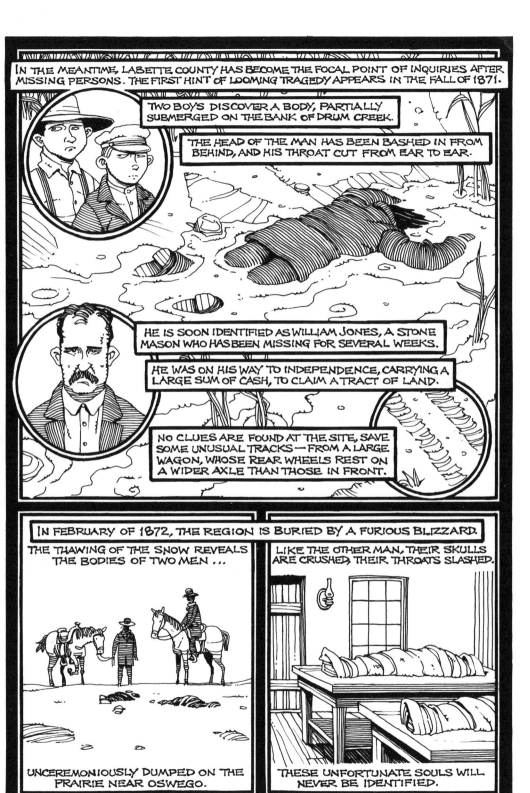

IN THE MEANTIME, LABETTE COUNTY HAS BECOME THE FOCAL POINT OF INQUIRIES AFTER MISSING PERSONS. THE FIRST HINT OF LOOMING TRAGEDY APPEARS IN THE FALL OF 1871.

TWO BOYS DISCOVER A BODY, PARTIALLY SUBMERGED ON THE BANK OF DRUM CREEK.

THE HEAD OF THE MAN HAS BEEN BASHED IN FROM BEHIND, AND HIS THROAT CUT FROM EAR TO EAR.

HE IS SOON IDENTIFIED AS WILLIAM JONES, A STONE MASON WHO HAS BEEN MISSING FOR SEVERAL WEEKS.

HE WAS ON HIS WAY TO INDEPENDENCE, CARRYING A LARGE SUM OF CASH, TO CLAIM A TRACT OF LAND.

NO CLUES ARE FOUND AT THE SITE, SAVE SOME UNUSUAL TRACKS — FROM A LARGE WAGON, WHOSE REAR WHEELS REST ON A WIDER AXLE THAN THOSE IN FRONT.

IN FEBRUARY OF 1872, THE REGION IS BURIED BY A FURIOUS BLIZZARD.

THE THAWING OF THE SNOW REVEALS THE BODIES OF TWO MEN ...

LIKE THE OTHER MAN, THEIR SKULLS ARE CRUSHED, THEIR THROATS SLASHED.

UNCEREMONIOUSLY DUMPED ON THE PRAIRIE NEAR OSWEGO.

THESE UNFORTUNATE SOULS WILL NEVER BE IDENTIFIED.

THROUGHOUT THE YEAR 1872, THE DISAPPEARANCES MOUNT, AND THE OSAGE TRAIL AREA DEVELOPS AN UNPLEASANT REPUTATION.

BEN BROWN, OF CEDAR VALE, VANISHES WHILE TRAVELLING ON BUSINESS...

WILLIAM F. McCROTTY, WHO LIVES NEAR THE OSAGE MISSION...

JOHNNY BOYLE, A YOUNG BACHELOR, TREKS SOUTHWARD FROM THE OSAGE MISSION, WITH ABOUT $1900 CASH MONEY.

ALONG WITH HIS NEW WAGON AND TEAM OF MATCHING SORRELS.

IS KNOWN TO HAVE BEEN CARRYING $2600 IN CASH.

HE IS NEVER SEEN AGAIN.

HENRY McKENZIE, AT AGE 29 A NOMADIC SORT, WITH A TASTE FOR EXPENSIVE-LOOKING OUTFITS.

HE IS LAST SEEN BY MR. AND MRS. DICK IN LATE NOVEMBER, ON HIS WAY TO VISIT RELATIONS NEAR INDEPENDENCE.

HE IS A COUSIN TO THE WIFE OF MR. LEROY DICK, THE TOWNSHIP OFFICER.

HE CARRIES WITH HIM A LARGE SUM OF MONEY, PERHAPS AS MUCH AS $2000.

BY THE DAWN OF 1873, LEROY DICK HAS RECEIVED HALF A DOZEN LETTERS FROM DISTRAUGHT RELATIVES SEEKING THEIR MISSING LOVED ONES.

ON MORE THAN ONE OCCASION, A PARTY OF SEARCHERS STOPS TO MAKE INQUIRIES.

IN MARCH, GEORGE LONCHER PREPARES TO LEAVE HIS FARM OUTSIDE INDEPENDENCE.

HIS WIFE HAVING RECENTLY DIED, HE SETS OUT TO TAKE HIS YOUNG DAUGHTER TO LIVE WITH HER GRANDPARENTS IN IOWA.

FOR THE JOURNEY, HE HAS PURCHASED A WAGON AND TEAM FROM A LOCAL DOCTOR, WILLIAM YORK.

LONCHER AND HIS DAUGHTER WILL NEVER REACH THEIR DESTINATION.

LATER IN THE MONTH, DR. YORK RIDES NORTHWARD FOR BUSINESS DEALINGS IN FT. SCOTT.

WHILE THERE, HE HEARS DISTURBING NEWS...

THE WAGON AND HORSES THAT HE SOLD TO GEORGE LONCHER HAVE BEEN FOUND ABANDONED IN THE WOODS OUTSIDE OF TOWN.

DETERMINED TO ORGANIZE A SEARCH, HE DEPARTS AT ONCE FOR INDEPENDENCE.

SOMEWHERE ALONG THE WAY, HE VANISHES.

AN EASTERNER NAMED PICKERING IS INVITED TO OCCUPY THE "GUEST SEAT."

BUT HE DECLINES, NOTING AN UNAPPEALING GREASE SPOT ON THE CANVAS CURTAIN BEHIND IT.

HE TAKES ANOTHER CHAIR, PROMPTING A FURIOUS SCOLDING FROM KATE.

WHEN SHE PULLS OUT A KNIFE, MR. PICKERING CHOOSES TO TAKE HIS LEAVE.

AT ANOTHER TIME, A MRS. FITTS, WHILE SITTING AT DINNER, SENSES A MOVEMENT BEHIND THE CANVAS.

KATE ISSUES AN IMPATIENT COMMAND...

NOW!

BUT BEFORE ANYTHING CAN HAPPEN, THE TERRIFIED LADY FLEES.

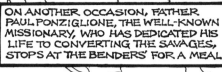
ON ANOTHER OCCASION, FATHER PAUL PONZIGLIONE, THE WELL-KNOWN MISSIONARY, WHO HAS DEDICATED HIS LIFE TO CONVERTING THE SAVAGES, STOPS AT THE BENDERS' FOR A MEAL.

THE ATMOSPHERE WITHIN THE HOUSE MAKES HIM FEEL DECIDEDLY UNSAFE.

AS HE SITS, KATE AND HER FATHER CONVERSE IN LOW TONES.

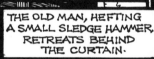
THE OLD MAN, HEFTING A SMALL SLEDGE HAMMER, RETREATS BEHIND THE CURTAIN.

FATHER PONZIGLIONE TAKES THE FIRST OPPORTUNITY TO VACATE THE PREMISES...

MAKING THE EXCUSE THAT HE NEEDS TO TEND HIS HORSE.

HE THEN RIDES AWAY.

UNFORTUNATELY, NONE OF THESE WORTHY CITIZENS REPORT THEIR EXPERIENCES UNTIL LONG AFTER THE FACT— WHEN IT IS TOO LATE.

AS A RESULT, THE BENDERS—SUSPECTED BY SOME AND KNOWN AS STRANGE BY ALL—ATTRACT NO LEGAL SCRUTINY.

PART III

THE BENDERS
DEPART

THE SAD ANSWER TO THE "OSAGE HILLS MYSTERY" HAS ITS BEGINNING ON APRIL 8, 1873 ...

DURING THE ANNUAL SCHOOL BOARD MEETING AT THE HARMONY GROVE SCHOOLHOUSE.

75 TO 100 CITIZENS ARE PRESENT...

INCLUDING THE MALE BENDERS, SENIOR AND JUNIOR.

SCHOOL BUSINESS IS QUICKLY FINISHED, SO THAT THOSE PRESENT CAN GET DOWN TO THE REAL REASON FOR THE MEETING ...

WHAT TO DO ABOUT THE DISAPPEARANCES THAT HAVE PUT A BLOT UPON THE COMMUNITY.

A LIVELY AND OPEN DISCUSSION ENSUES, WITH MANY PEOPLE IN A HIGH STATE OF INDIGNATION.

SOME FEAR THAT A "SECRET DEN OF HUMAN BUTCHERY" OPERATES IN THEIR MIDST.

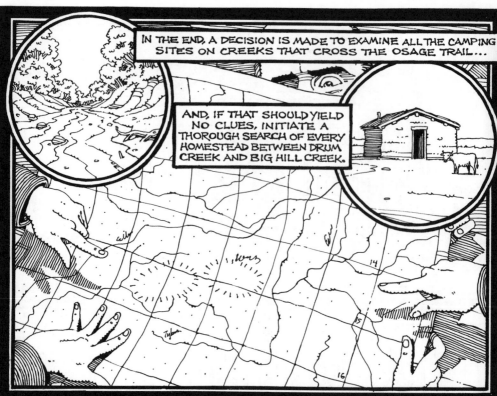

IN THE END, A DECISION IS MADE TO EXAMINE ALL THE CAMPING SITES ON CREEKS THAT CROSS THE OSAGE TRAIL...

AND, IF THAT SHOULD YIELD NO CLUES, INITIATE A THOROUGH SEARCH OF EVERY HOMESTEAD BETWEEN DRUM CREEK AND BIG HILL CREEK.

THE MEETING ADJOURNS AMIDST A GENERAL FEELING OF ACCOMPLISHMENT.

THE BENDERS CLIMB INTO THEIR WAGON AND HEAD HOME.

DESPITE THE ENTHUSIASTIC RESOLUTIONS OF THE MEETING, LITTLE IS DONE OVER THE FOLLOWING WEEKS.

IN MID-APRIL, A SEARCH IS UNDERTAKEN FOR THE MISSING DOCTOR WILLIAM YORK OF INDEPENDENCE...

ORGANIZED AND LED BY THE DOCTOR'S BROTHER, COL. ALEXANDER YORK.

THOUGH SMALL OF STATURE, THE COLONEL IS A HARD AND DETERMINED MAN, A FORMER COMMANDER IN THE UNION ARMY AND KANSAS STATE SENATOR.

THE PARTY OF FIFTY OR SIXTY MEN ALSO INCLUDES A THIRD BROTHER, EDWARD YORK.

THEY COMB THE AREA ALONG THE OSAGE TRAIL.

THE GROUP SPLITS INTO SMALLER UNITS TO MAKE INQUIRIES AT DIFFERENT TOWNS.

DR. YORK, THEY LEARN, WAS LAST SEEN ON MARCH 10, IN PARSONS.

WHILE THERE, HE PURCHASED CIGARS AND WAS ADVISED BY THE STOREKEEPER TO SPEND THE NIGHT AT THE BENDER INN.

ON APRIL 14, A SMALL GROUP LED BY EDWARD YORK ARRIVES AT THE ESTABLISHMENT IN QUESTION.

PARSONS

CHERRY VALE

INDEPENDENCE

FOR A TRAVELLER GOING WEST FROM PARSONS, THE BENDERS' WOULD BE THE LOGICAL STOPPING-PLACE.

THE FAMILY CONFIRMS THAT DR. YORK DID INDEED STOP THERE.

HE STAYED THE NIGHT AND DEPARTED IN THE MORNING.

KATE OFFERS TO GO INTO A TRANCE AND CONSULT HER "SPIRIT GUIDE"— AN OLD INDIAN CHIEF—TO DISCOVER THE FATE OF THE MISSING MAN.

BUT SHE CAUTIONS THEM THAT THIS MIGHT TAKE SOME TIME — SINCE SHE HAS NOT YET REACHED HER "MAJORITY" AS A MEDIUM.

BESIDES, SHE SENSES THAT THERE ARE SEVERAL UNBELIEVERS PRESENT.

PLEASE, WOULD THEY RETURN TOMORROW?

ALTHOUGH SEVERAL OF THE PARTY ARE SKEPTICAL, EDWARD YORK AGREES TO RETURN.

GROCERIES

205

THE NEXT DAY, EDWARD YORK, WITH HIS BROTHER THE COLONEL AND ABOUT FIFTY MEN, ARRIVES AT THE BENDER HOUSE.

REGRETTABLY, KATE HAS GATHERED NO NEW INFORMATION FROM HER TRANCE.

COL. YORK THEN INTERROGATES THE FAMILY AS TO THE 1871 MURDER OF WILLIAM JONES, WHOSE BODY WAS FOUND NEARBY ON DRUM CREEK.

JOHN BENDER JR. TELLS A STORY ABOUT BEING AMBUSHED HIMSELF, LAST YEAR, AT THAT VERY CROSSING. HE CLAIMS TO HAVE BARELY ESCAPED WITH HIS LIFE.

THE POSSE ACCOMPANIES HIM TO THE LOCATION, WHERE HE RE-ENACTS THE EPISODE. FEW, IF ANY, BELIEVE HIS TALE.

THE PARTY AT LAST DEPARTS FOR INDEPENDENCE. SOME HOT-HEADS IN THE GROUP BELIEVE THAT THE FAMILY SHOULD BE ARRESTED ON THE SPOT.

COL. YORK, HOWEVER, SEES THEM AS "SIMPLE, CREDULOUS FOLK," WITH NOTHING TO INDICATE THAT THEY ARE KILLERS.

OVER THE NEXT SEVERAL WEEKS, THE COMMUNITY GOES ABOUT ITS BUSINESS IN A STATE OF MUTED AGITATION.

AN ARTICLE IN THE APRIL 29TH EDITION OF THE THAYER 'HEADLIGHT,' NOTICED BY FEW, TELLS OF A DISQUIETING DISCOVERY.

A WAGON AND HORSES WERE RECENTLY FOUND ABANDONED ON A RIVER BANK OUTSIDE OF TOWN.

THEY HAD APPARENTLY LANGUISHED THERE FOR SEVERAL DAYS ...

SINCE THE HUNGRY HORSES HAD GNAWED ON THE WOODEN SIDES OF THE WAGON.

BULLET HOLES WERE FOUND IN THE SIDES, AND DROPS OF BLOOD ON THE DASH-BOARD.

IN THE BOTTOM OF THE WAGON BED, A WOODEN SIGN.

OCERIES

A SMALL TERRIER GUARDED THE FIND.

MOST INTERESTINGLY, THE WAGON'S REAR WHEELS WERE SET WIDER ON THEIR AXLE THAN THOSE IN FRONT.

207

ON SUNDAY, MAY 1, BILLY TOLE, A NEIGHBOR OF THE BENDERS, DRIVES HIS CATTLE PAST THEIR PLACE.

HE NOTICES SEVERAL ANIMALS WANDERING ABOUT THE PROPERTY.

UPON CLOSER INVESTIGATION, HE FINDS A DEAD CALF IN THE STABLE YARD, A STARVING HOG, NEGLECTED CHICKENS DUCKS AND PEAFOWL.

THE FAMILY'S WAGON AND TEAM ARE MISSING.

THE HOUSE APPEARS TO BE VACANT.

THERE IS NO MISTAKE ABOUT IT. THE PROPERTY IS DESERTED.

THE BENDERS ARE GONE.

PART I V

TRAGIC DISCOVERIES

WORD SPREADS QUICKLY ABOUT THE DEPARTURE OF THE BENDERS.

ON MONDAY MORNING, A PARTY OF ABOUT FORTY MEN, ORGANIZED BY LEROY DICK VENTURE OUT TO THE SITE.

AND THROUGHOUT THE DAY, A STEADY STREAM OF CURIOUS HUMANITY ARRIVES FROM AROUND THE AREA.

A SEARCH OF THE HOUSE INTERIOR UNCOVERS SEVERAL ITEMS LEFT BEHIND BY THE FLEEING FAMILY.

THE ELEGANT AND ARTISTIC EIGHT-DAY CLOCK...

THE OLD MAN'S GERMAN BIBLE.

EDWARD YORK FINDS THE SPECTACLES OF HIS LOST BROTHER.

BENEATH THE STOVE ARE FOUND THESE HAMMERS ~
- A HANDMADE 6 LB. SLEDGE
- AN ALSATIAN SHOE HAMMER
- A COMMON 3-INCH CLAW HAMMER.

THE SEARCHERS ARE PUZZLED BY STRANGE DESIGNS AND FIGURES SCRAWLED ON THE FLOOR.

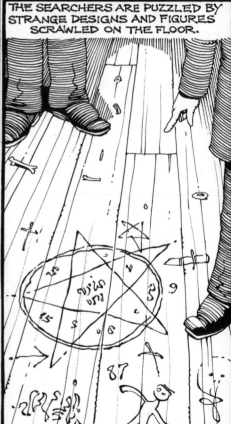

IN THE FLOOR BENEATH THE DINING TABLE IS FOUND A DOOR, WHICH OPENS WITH A LEATHER STRAP.

A HORRIBLE STENCH DRIFTS UPWARD. THOSE WHO SERVED IN THE LATE WAR RECOGNIZE THE SMELL OF ROTTING BLOOD.

WHAT CAN BE IN THE CELLAR?

TO GET TO IT, THE ENTIRE HOUSE IS PRIED OFF ITS FOUNDATION AND MOVED SEVERAL FEET.

THE STONE SLAB OF THE CELLAR FLOOR IS AWASH IN DRIED BLOOD...

AND BLOOD HAS SOAKED INTO THE DIRT AROUND IT.

WHEN THE SLAB IS BROKEN AND REMOVED, IT IS SEEN TO HAVE BEEN ELEVATED BY FIVE-INCH STONE COLUMNS ABOVE THE GORE-SUFFUSED EARTH BELOW.

A PASSAGE-WAY LEADS OUT TO THE REAR OF THE HOUSE.

TOWARD THE LATE AFTERNOON, THE SEARCHERS FEEL THAT THEY HAVE SEEN ALL THERE IS TO SEE AND PREPARE TO DEPART THE PROPERTY.

BUT SEVERAL PEOPLE NOTICE THAT THE RAYS OF THE SETTING SUN OUTLINE A DEPRESSED AREA OF GROUND IN THE NEGLECTED ORCHARD BEHIND THE HOUSE.

IT TAKES BUT LITTLE DIGGING TO OPEN THE SHALLOW GRAVE OF DR. WILLIAM YORK.

HIS BROTHER EDWARD SADLY IDENTIFIES THE CORPSE — ITS SKULL SMASHED, ITS THROAT CUT.

JUST TO MAKE SURE, A GRISLY PROCEDURE IS ENACTED.

LEROY DICK AND TWO OTHERS SEVER THE HEAD, CLEAN IT, AND MOUNT IT ON THE EDGE OF THE GRAVE, FOR A POSITIVE IDENTIFICATION.

ALL PRESENT ARE DISTURBED AND ANGRY... SURELY THERE ARE MORE GRAVES HERE!

AS DARKNESS FALLS, THEY VOW TO RETURN TOMORROW.

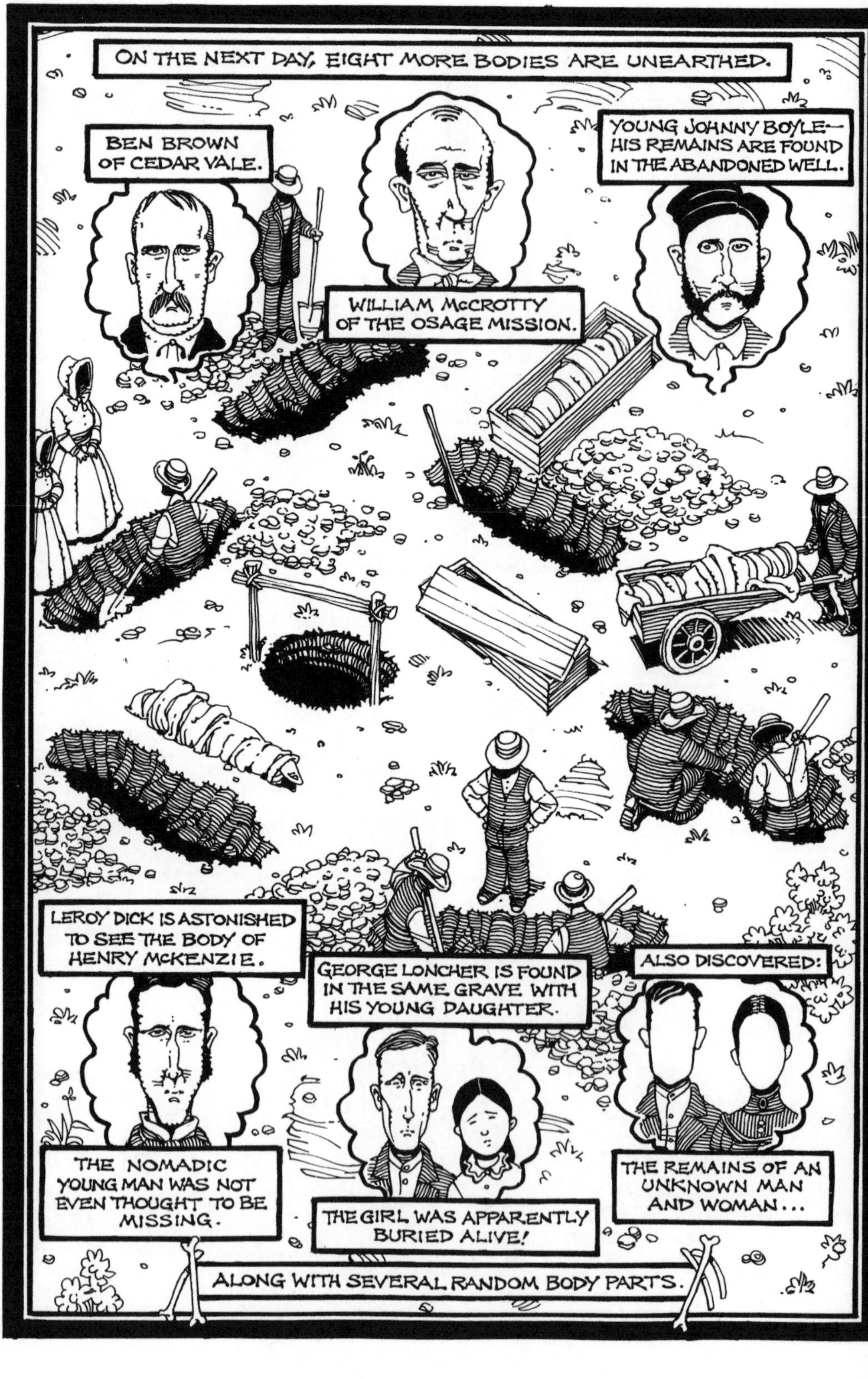
ON THE NEXT DAY, EIGHT MORE BODIES ARE UNEARTHED.
BEN BROWN OF CEDAR VALE.
WILLIAM McCROTTY OF THE OSAGE MISSION.
YOUNG JOHNNY BOYLE— HIS REMAINS ARE FOUND IN THE ABANDONED WELL.
LEROY DICK IS ASTONISHED TO SEE THE BODY OF HENRY McKENZIE.
THE NOMADIC YOUNG MAN WAS NOT EVEN THOUGHT TO BE MISSING.
GEORGE LONCHER IS FOUND IN THE SAME GRAVE WITH HIS YOUNG DAUGHTER.
THE GIRL WAS APPARENTLY BURIED ALIVE!
ALSO DISCOVERED:
THE REMAINS OF AN UNKNOWN MAN AND WOMAN...
ALONG WITH SEVERAL RANDOM BODY PARTS.

A THRONG OF ABOUT ONE THOUSAND HAS MADE ITS WAY TO THE PROPERTY TODAY.

THOSE SOUVENIR-HUNTERS AMONG THEM DISMANTLE THE BENDER HOUSE PIECE-BY-PIECE.

AN ANGRY MOB ATTEMPTS TO TERRIFY THE GERMAN NEIGHBOR RUDOLPH BROCKMAN INTO CONFESSING HIS COMPLICITY IN THE FAMILY'S CRIMES.

FOUR ATTEMPTS ARE MADE TO LYNCH HIM BEFORE CALMER MINDS PREVAIL, AND HE IS RELEASED.

HARPER'S WEEKLY PUBLISHES ILLUSTRATIONS THAT ARE DISTRIBUTED TO THE WORLD.

SEVERAL LOCAL PEOPLE ARE ARRESTED AS BEING IN LEAGUE WITH THE FUGITIVES, ALTHOUGH ALL WILL BE EVENTUALLY RELEASED.

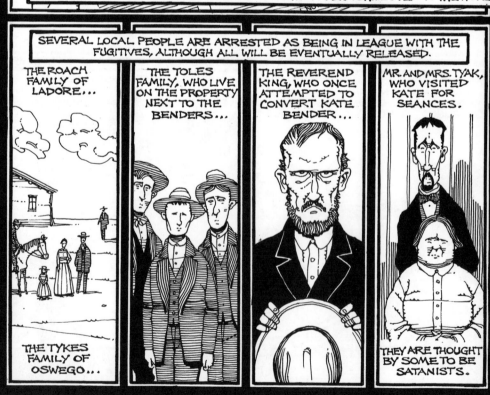

THE ROACH FAMILY OF LADORE...

THE TYKES FAMILY OF OSWEGO...

THE TOLES FAMILY, WHO LIVE ON THE PROPERTY NEXT TO THE BENDERS...

THE REVEREND KING, WHO ONCE ATTEMPTED TO CONVERT KATE BENDER...

MR. AND MRS. TYAK, WHO VISITED KATE FOR SEANCES.

THEY ARE THOUGHT BY SOME TO BE SATANISTS.

218

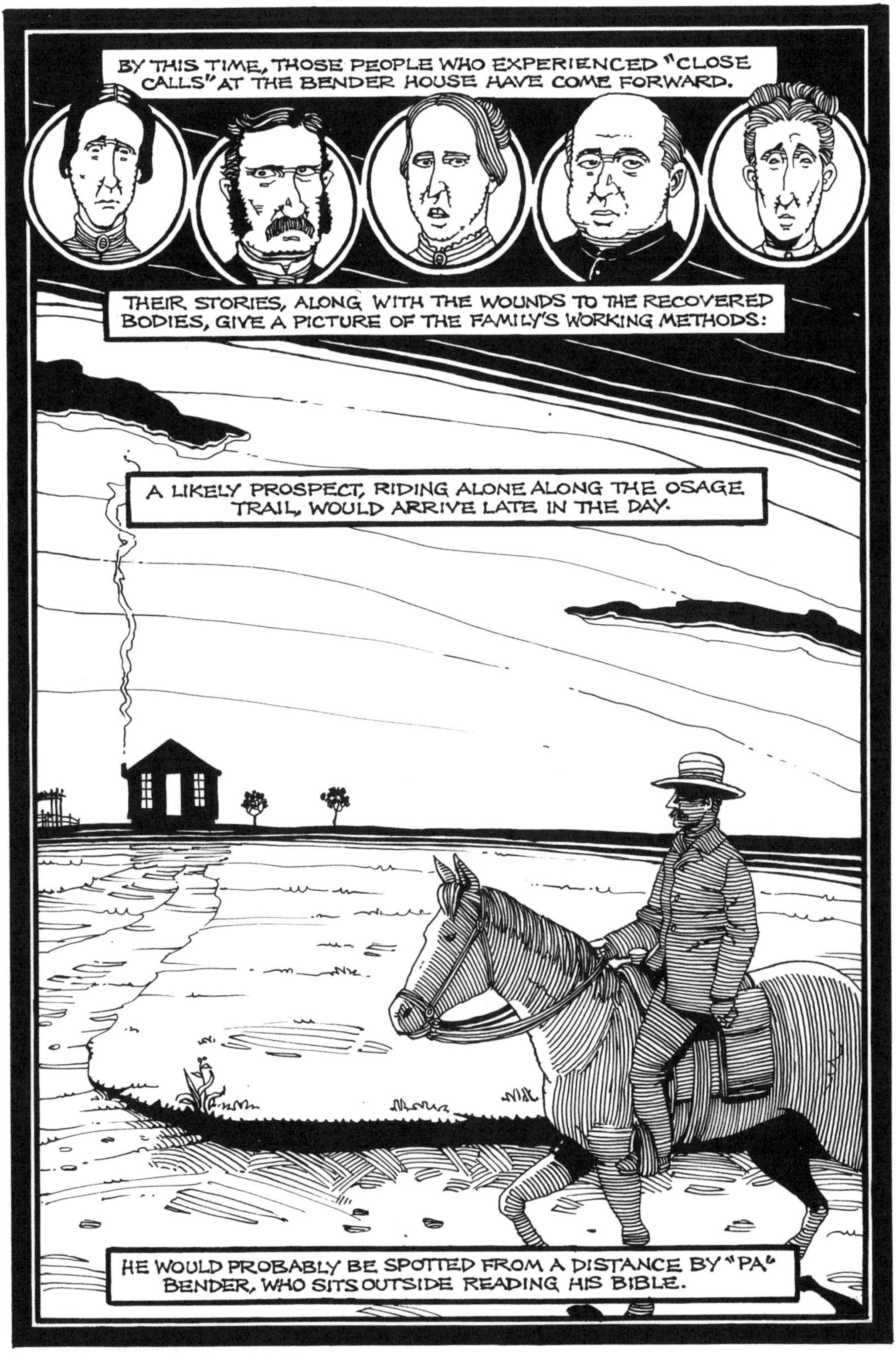
BY THIS TIME, THOSE PEOPLE WHO EXPERIENCED "CLOSE CALLS" AT THE BENDER HOUSE HAVE COME FORWARD.
THEIR STORIES, ALONG WITH THE WOUNDS TO THE RECOVERED BODIES, GIVE A PICTURE OF THE FAMILY'S WORKING METHODS:
A LIKELY PROSPECT, RIDING ALONE ALONG THE OSAGE TRAIL, WOULD ARRIVE LATE IN THE DAY.
HE WOULD PROBABLY BE SPOTTED FROM A DISTANCE BY "PA" BENDER, WHO SITS OUTSIDE READING HIS BIBLE.

THE TRAVELLER IS BROUGHT INSIDE AND OFFERED A MEAL, COOKED BY "MA" AND SERVED BY KATE.

VOLUBLE AND SEDUCTIVE, KATE INVITES HIM TO OCCUPY THE SPECIAL VISITOR'S PLACE IN FRONT OF THE CANVAS PARTITION.

SHE THEN CASUALLY PUMPS HIM FOR INFORMATION: WHERE IS HE FROM? WHAT IS HIS BUSINESS?

DOES KATE ALSO OFFER SEXUAL FAVORS AS PART OF THE PACKAGE? NO CERTAIN ANSWER WILL EVER BE KNOWN.

AS THE GUEST EATS HIS DINNER, PLEASANTLY DISTRACTED BY KATE, HE IS STRUCK FROM BEHIND THE CANVAS.

THE ACT IS PERFORMED BY EITHER "PA" OR JOHN JR., NO DOUBT WIELDING THE SIX-POUND SLEDGE.

THE DOOR BENEATH THE TABLE IS THEN OPENED...

AND THE VICTIM LOWERED INTO THE CELLAR.

HERE, THE DEED IS COMPLETED, MOST LIKELY BY KATE, WHO CUTS THE MAN'S THROAT WITH HER CARVING KNIFE.

BY ALL THAT CAN BE ASCERTAINED, THE DAUGHTER IS THE LEADER AND INSTIGATOR OF THE FAMILY'S HORRIFIC CAREER.

AFTER DARK, THE BODY IS REMOVED FROM THE CELLAR.

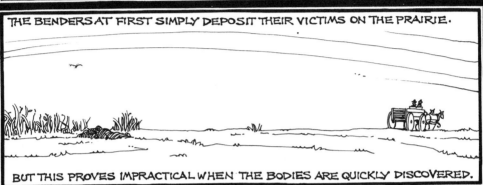

THE BENDERS AT FIRST SIMPLY DEPOSIT THEIR VICTIMS ON THE PRAIRIE.

BUT THIS PROVES IMPRACTICAL WHEN THE BODIES ARE QUICKLY DISCOVERED.

MOST LIKELY, THE NEXT VICTIM—JOHNNY BOYLE—IS PUT INTO THE WELL ON THEIR PROPERTY...

COMPELLING THEM TO DIG A NEW ONE FOR THEIR OWN USE.

THEREAFTER, THEY EXCAVATE THE UNPRODUCTIVE ORCHARD BEHIND THE HOUSE.

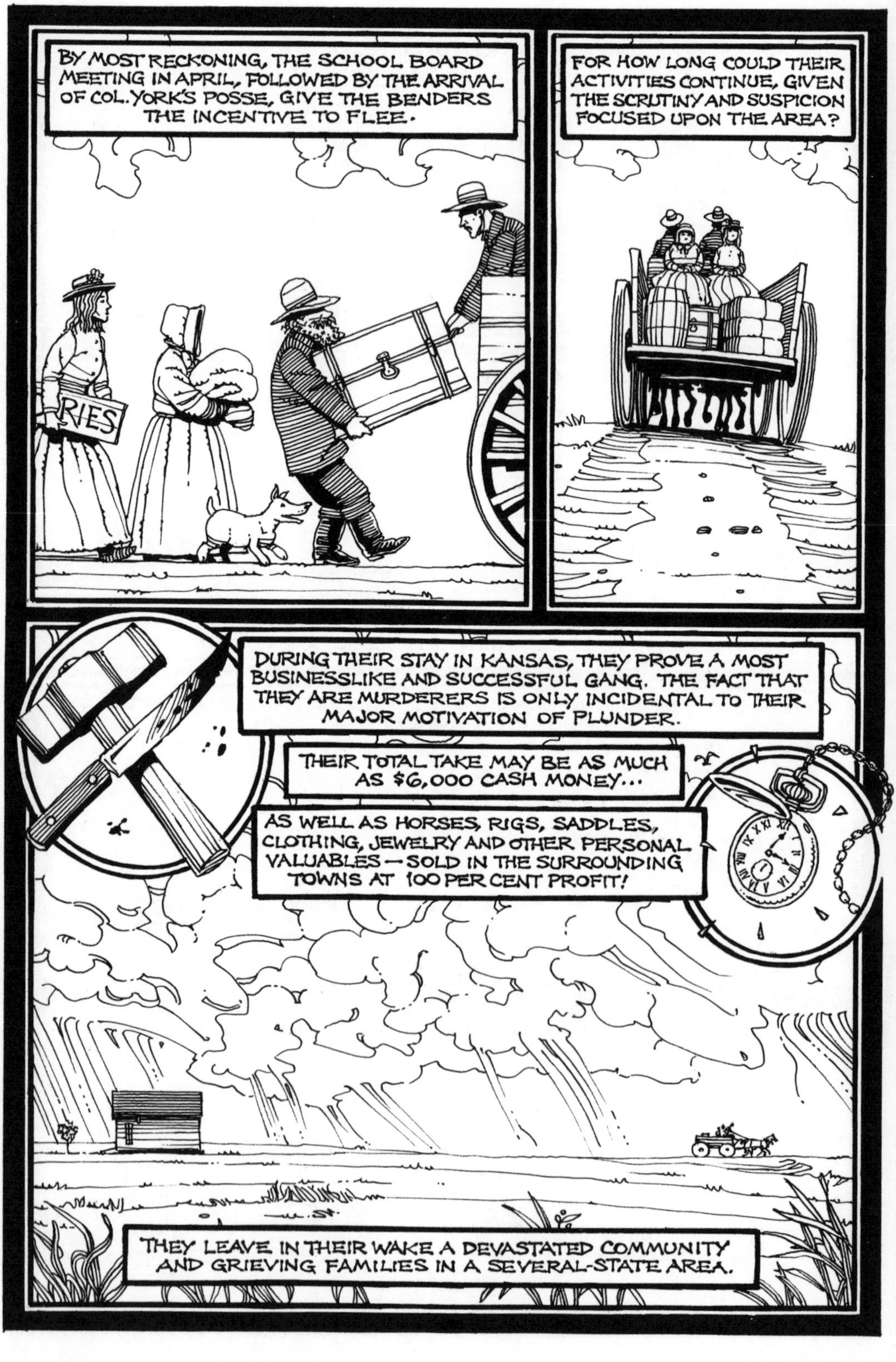
BY MOST RECKONING, THE SCHOOL BOARD MEETING IN APRIL, FOLLOWED BY THE ARRIVAL OF COL. YORK'S POSSE, GIVE THE BENDERS THE INCENTIVE TO FLEE.
RIES
FOR HOW LONG COULD THEIR ACTIVITIES CONTINUE, GIVEN THE SCRUTINY AND SUSPICION FOCUSED UPON THE AREA?
DURING THEIR STAY IN KANSAS, THEY PROVE A MOST BUSINESSLIKE AND SUCCESSFUL GANG. THE FACT THAT THEY ARE MURDERERS IS ONLY INCIDENTAL TO THEIR MAJOR MOTIVATION OF PLUNDER.
THEIR TOTAL TAKE MAY BE AS MUCH AS $6,000 CASH MONEY...
AS WELL AS HORSES, RIGS, SADDLES, CLOTHING, JEWELRY AND OTHER PERSONAL VALUABLES — SOLD IN THE SURROUNDING TOWNS AT 100 PER CENT PROFIT!
THEY LEAVE IN THEIR WAKE A DEVASTATED COMMUNITY AND GRIEVING FAMILIES IN A SEVERAL-STATE AREA.

PART V

WHAT BECAME
OF THEM?

BEFORE THE MONTH OF MAY IS OUT, AN OFFICIAL REWARD IS OFFERED BY THOMAS OSBORN, THE GOVERNOR OF KANSAS.

COL. ALEXANDER YORK ALSO OFFERS $1000 FOR THE APPREHENSION OF THE "BLOODY BENDERS."

GOVERNOR'S PROCLAMATION.
$2,000 REWARD
State of Kansas, Executive Department.

WHEREAS several atrocious murders have been committed in Labette County, Kansas, under which fasten, beyond doubt, the commi... upon a family known as the "B... JOHN BENDER about... inches in he...

A STATION AGENT AT THAYER RECALLS THAT, ON AN AFTERNOON IN MID-APRIL, A GERMAN FAMILY OF FOUR CAUGHT A NORTH-BOUND TRAIN.

THAYER.

LEAVENWORTH, LAWRENCE & GALVESTON R.R.

CHERRY VALE

HE REMEMBERS THEM BECAUSE THEY HAD ARTICLES WRAPPED IN A WHITE BED-SPREAD AND CARRIED A "DOG-HIDE" TRUNK.

AN AGENT IN KANSAS CITY ALSO REMEMBERS THE DISTINCTIVE TRUNK.

ILLINOIS

MISSOURI

ST. LOUIS

KANSAS CITY

NSAS

A STORY LATER DEVELOPS THAT THE FOUR MADE THEIR WAY TO ST. LOUIS, WHERE THEY STAYED A WEEK WITH "PA" BENDER'S SISTER BEFORE MOVING ON.

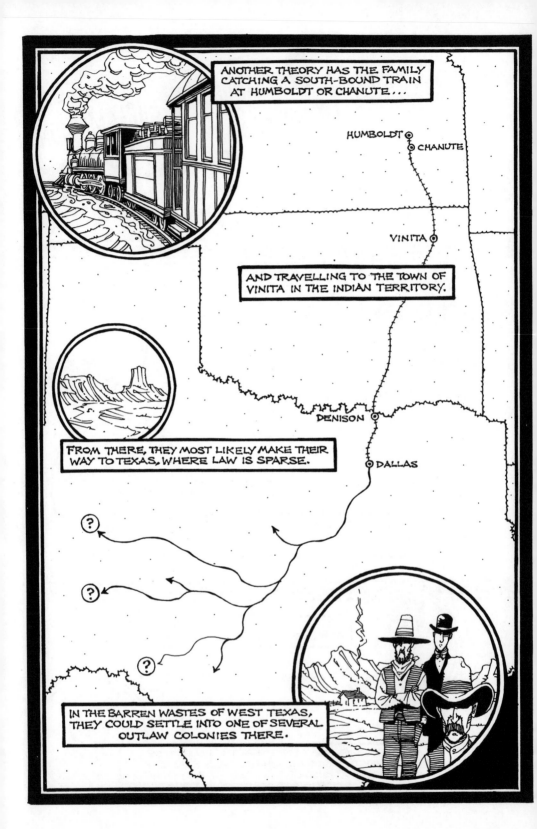

ANOTHER THEORY HAS THE FAMILY CATCHING A SOUTH-BOUND TRAIN AT HUMBOLDT OR CHANUTE...

HUMBOLDT
CHANUTE

VINITA

AND TRAVELLING TO THE TOWN OF VINITA IN THE INDIAN TERRITORY.

DENISON

DALLAS

FROM THERE, THEY MOST LIKELY MAKE THEIR WAY TO TEXAS, WHERE LAW IS SPARSE.

IN THE BARREN WASTES OF WEST TEXAS, THEY COULD SETTLE INTO ONE OF SEVERAL OUTLAW COLONIES THERE.

228

SEVERAL PRIVATELY-ORGANIZED SEARCH PARTIES COMB THE VAST AREA INTO WHICH THE FUGITIVES ARE THOUGHT TO HAVE VANISHED.

MARSHALL JAMES SNODDY, OF FT. SCOTT, WITH COL. C.J. PECKHAM AND HENRY BEERS, DOGGEDLY FOLLOW REPORTS OF THE BENDERS DEEP INTO TEXAS...

UNTIL THE TRAIL GOES COLD.

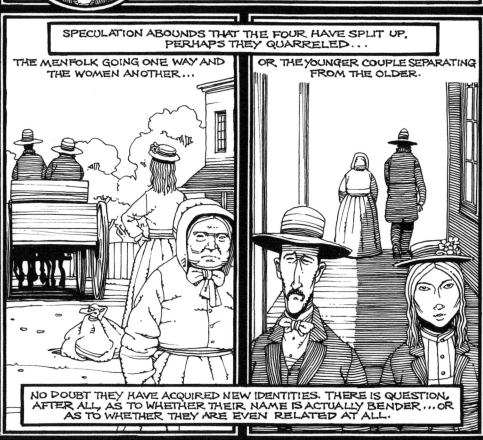

SPECULATION ABOUNDS THAT THE FOUR HAVE SPLIT UP. PERHAPS THEY QUARRELED...

THE MENFOLK GOING ONE WAY AND THE WOMEN ANOTHER...

OR THE YOUNGER COUPLE SEPARATING FROM THE OLDER.

NO DOUBT THEY HAVE ACQUIRED NEW IDENTITIES. THERE IS QUESTION, AFTER ALL, AS TO WHETHER THEIR NAME IS ACTUALLY BENDER... OR AS TO WHETHER THEY ARE EVEN RELATED AT ALL.

THE MOST PERSISTENT RUMORS, HOWEVER, ASSERT THAT THE FAMILY NEVER LEFT LABETTE COUNTY.

A POSSE COMES UPON THEM AS THEY PREPARE TO CAMP FOR THE NIGHT.

FROM HERE, SEVERAL SCENARIOS PLAY OUT.

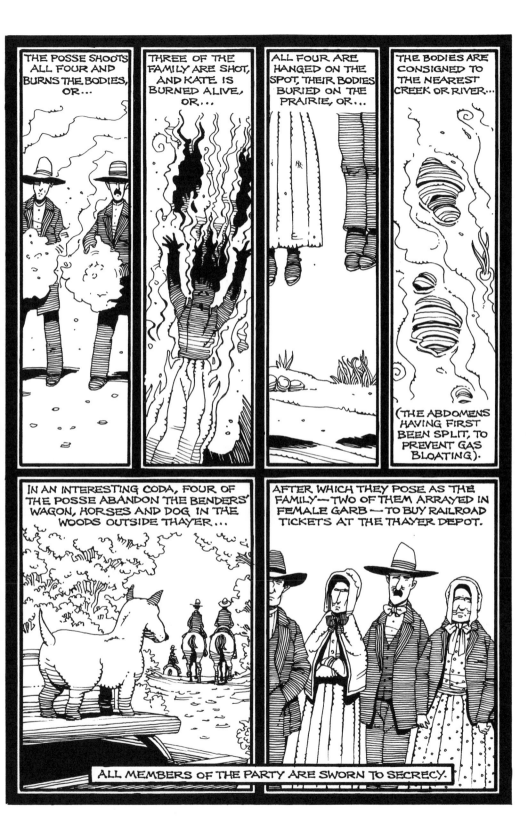

THE POSSE SHOOTS ALL FOUR AND BURNS THE BODIES, OR...

THREE OF THE FAMILY ARE SHOT, AND KATE IS BURNED ALIVE, OR...

ALL FOUR ARE HANGED ON THE SPOT, THEIR BODIES BURIED ON THE PRAIRIE, OR...

THE BODIES ARE CONSIGNED TO THE NEAREST CREEK OR RIVER...

(THE ABDOMENS HAVING FIRST BEEN SPLIT, TO PREVENT GAS BLOATING).

IN AN INTERESTING CODA, FOUR OF THE POSSE ABANDON THE BENDERS' WAGON, HORSES AND DOG IN THE WOODS OUTSIDE THAYER...

AFTER WHICH THEY POSE AS THE FAMILY—TWO OF THEM ARRAYED IN FEMALE GARB—TO BUY RAILROAD TICKETS AT THE THAYER DEPOT.

ALL MEMBERS OF THE PARTY ARE SWORN TO SECRECY.

231

IN ANY CASE, THE BENDER FAMILY IS NEVER OFFICIALLY SEEN AGAIN, EITHER AS A GROUP OR INDIVIDUALLY.

RUMORS OF SIGHTINGS, HOWEVER, CONTINUE THROUGH THE FOLLOWING DECADE.

KATE IS A SOCIETY MATRON IN SAN FRANCISCO...

OR A WHORE IN MONTANA...

OR A PRACTICING OUTLAW IN SEVERAL CITIES.

JOHN, JR. IS SEEN AS A SECTION HAND IN TEXAS...

OR AS THE ROBBER "DUTCH FRANK," DISPATCHED BY THE LAW...

WHILE THE OLD MAN IS A SUICIDE IN MICHIGAN.

NONE OF THESE REPORTS WILL EVER BE VERIFIED.

THE MOST FANCIFUL TALE COMES FROM A MEXICAN CAPTAIN NAMED DON PIEPPO.

IN HIS ACCOUNT, THE BENDERS MAKE IT AS FAR AS THE CALIFORNIA COAST.

HERE, THEY ACQUIRE A HOT-AIR BALLOON, IN WHICH THEY ATTEMPT AN ESCAPE INTO MEXICO.

BUT HIGH WINDS CARRY THEM OUT TO SEA, WHERE ALL PERISH SAVE ONE.

THAT ONE IS DON PIEPPO HIMSELF, WHO ADMITS THAT HE IS ACTUALLY JOHN BENDER, JR.

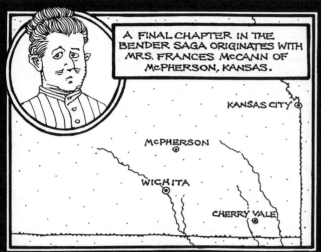

A FINAL CHAPTER IN THE BENDER SAGA ORIGINATES WITH MRS. FRANCES McCANN OF McPHERSON, KANSAS.

KANSAS CITY

McPHERSON

WICHITA

CHERRY VALE

IN 1888, SHE BECOMES FRIENDLY WITH A YOUNG WOMAN, LIVING NEARBY, WHO HAS BEEN ABANDONED BY HER HUSBAND.

WHILE ILL WITH FEVER, THE YOUNG WOMAN CONFESSES TO MRS. McCANN THAT SHE IS NONE OTHER THAN KATE BENDER!

AND THAT HER MOTHER, THE NOTORIOUS "MA" BENDER, STOLE MONEY FROM HER AND ESCAPED TO MICHIGAN.

ONCE RECOVERED, "KATE" REPAYS HER FRIEND BY CONDUCTING SPIRIT READINGS FOR HER.

SHE REVEALS TO MRS. McCANN — WHO GREW UP AN ORPHAN — THAT HER PARENTS WERE MURDERED BY THIS SAME MRS. BENDER.

NOT LONG THEREAFTER, "KATE" LEAVES McPHERSON, ON HER WAY TO MICHIGAN, SHE SAYS, TO SEARCH FOR HER MOTHER.

MRS. McCANN SOON FOLLOWS, DETERMINED TO UNCOVER THE SECRET OF HER OWN FAMILY HISTORY.

IN MICHIGAN, MRS. McCANN INITIATES INQUIRIES AMONG THE LUMBER TOWNS AND LOGGING CAMPS INTO WHICH HER FRIEND HAS VANISHED.

SHE HEARS STORIES ABOUT A CERTAIN ALMIRA GRIFFITH, A WICKED OLD LADY WHO, THROUGH SEVERAL HUSBANDS, GAVE BIRTH TO AS MANY AS EIGHT CHILDREN— MOST OF WHOM JOINED HER IN VARIOUS CRIMINAL PURSUITS.

SHE CATCHES UP WITH HER QUARRY IN THE TOWN OF NILES, WHERE MRS. GRIFFITH IS IN JAIL WITH HER DAUGHTER ELIZA.

IT SEEMS THAT MOTHER AND DAUGHTER HAVE MADE ACCUSATIONS OF THEFT AGAINST EACH OTHER.

CONVINCED THAT THE TWO WOMEN ARE "MA" AND KATE BENDER, MRS. McCANN RETURNS TO REPORT HER FINDINGS TO AUTHORITIES IN LABETTE COUNTY.

SHE TRAVELS BACK TO MICHIGAN IN THE COMPANY OF MR. LEROY DICK.

THOUGH INITIALLY SKEPTICAL, MR. DICK IS ASTOUNDED TO FIND THAT, AFTER SIXTEEN YEARS, HE CAN POSITIVELY IDENTIFY BOTH WOMEN.

IN NOVEMBER OF 1889, THEY ARE BROUGHT TO KANSAS IN HOPES OF A TRIAL, THE YOUNGER ONE NOW WITH A BABY.

A GROUP OF SIXTEEN CITIZENS WHO HAD DEALINGS WITH THE BENDERS ARE BROUGHT TO THE JAIL IN PARSONS TO SCRUTINIZE THE PRISONERS.

SEVEN OF THEM SAY THAT THEY ARE DEFINITELY THE SAME LADIES... SIX SAY THAT THEY DEFINITELY ARE NOT... THREE ARE UNDECIDED.

A TRIAL IS SET FOR MAY OF 1890... BUT IT IS NEVER TO TAKE PLACE.

A DEFENSE ATTORNEY NAMED JOHN T. JAMES APPEARS.

HE PAINTS A PATHETIC PICTURE OF HIS CLIENTS...

HOMELESS, FRIENDLESS, UNJUSTLY ACCUSED.

MRS. GRIFFITH, HE POINTS OUT, CAN BE SHOWN TO HAVE BEEN SERVING A JAIL SENTENCE IN MICHIGAN AT THE TIME OF THE BENDER ATROCITIES.

IN ADDITION, MANY PEOPLE WONDER WHY THIS LADY SPEAKS WITH NO ACCENT, WHILE "MA" BENDER COULD BARELY GRUNT A WORD OR TWO OF ENGLISH.

IN FEBRUARY OF 1890, TO THE SURPRISE OF ALL, THE WOMEN ARE RELEASED AND THEIR CASE DISMISSED.

THE REASON FOR THIS REMAINS UNCLEAR. THE COUNTY CLAIMS THAT SUCH A LARGE-SCALE TRIAL WOULD BE TOO EXPENSIVE, ESPECIALLY SINCE THE VERDICT IS IN DOUBT.

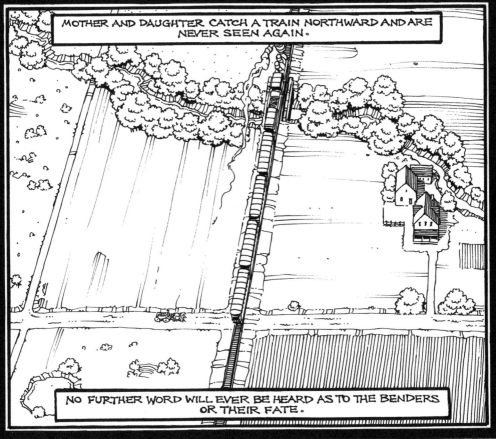

MOTHER AND DAUGHTER CATCH A TRAIN NORTHWARD AND ARE NEVER SEEN AGAIN.

NO FURTHER WORD WILL EVER BE HEARD AS TO THE BENDERS OR THEIR FATE.

BY THIS TIME, THE FORMER BENDER PROPERTY CONSISTS OF A MERE HOLE IN THE GROUND ~ THE NOXIOUS CELLAR!

IN TIME, THE HOLE IS FILLED IN AND THE PROPERTY, LIKE THE OSAGE TRAIL THAT RAN THROUGH IT, IS RECLAIMED BY THE PRAIRIE.

THE CORN THAT GROWS THERE IS SAID TO COME UP BLOOD-RED.

CHERRY VALE BOASTS A BENDER MUSEUM, WHICH OPERATES FROM 1961 TO 1978.

AMONG THE ARTIFACTS ON EXHIBIT ARE THE FAMILY'S THREE DEADLY HAMMERS...

AND A WREATH, SUPPOSEDLY WOVEN FROM THE HAIR OF THE MURDERED LONCHER GIRL.

FOR MANY YEARS, THE TOWN SPONSORS AN ANNUAL "BENDER DAYS" CELEBRATION.

THE HILLS TO THE EAST ARE OFFICIALLY RENAMED THE "BENDER MOUNDS."

A STATE HISTORICAL MARKER ON HIGHWAY 160 COMMEMORATES THE BRUTAL EPISODE.

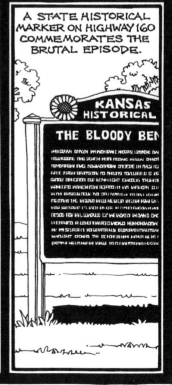

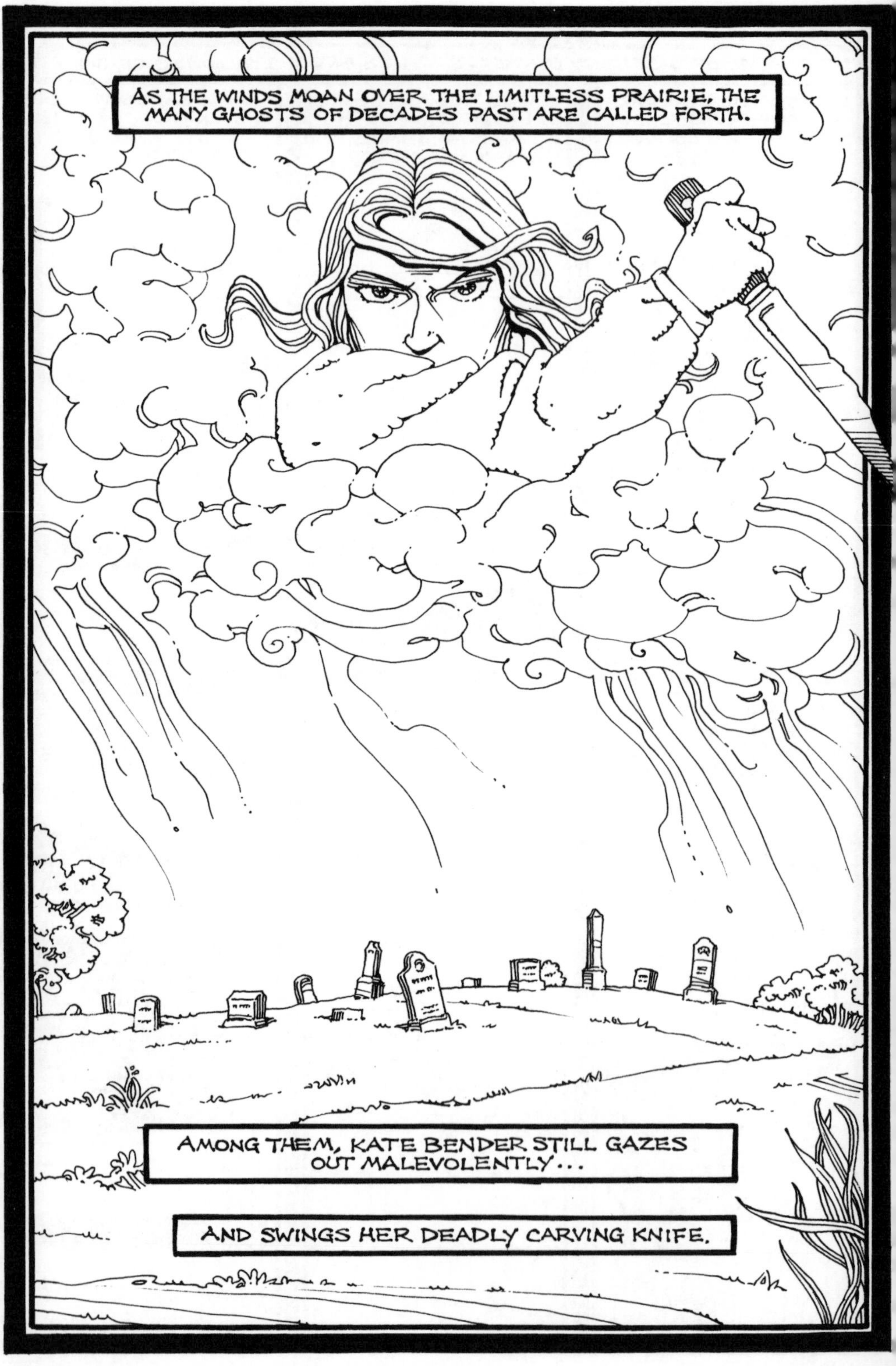
AS THE WINDS MOAN OVER THE LIMITLESS PRAIRIE, THE MANY GHOSTS OF DECADES PAST ARE CALLED FORTH.
AMONG THEM, KATE BENDER STILL GAZES OUT MALEVOLENTLY...
AND SWINGS HER DEADLY CARVING KNIFE.

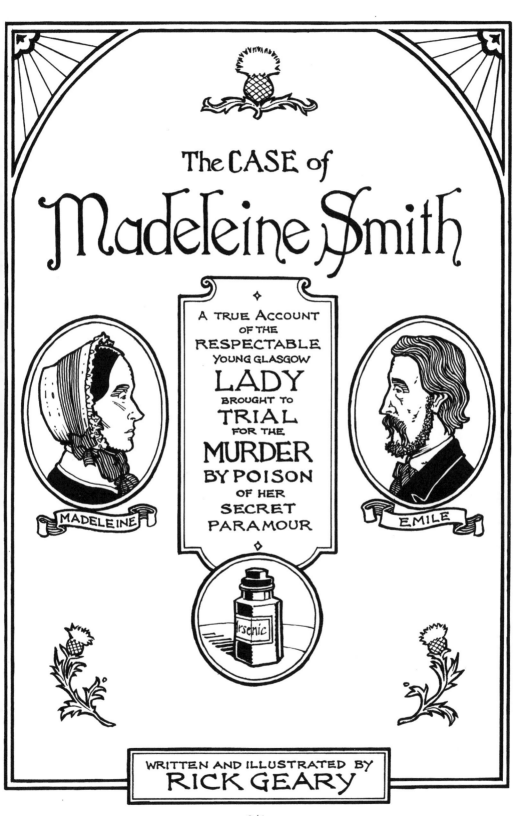

The CASE of

Madeleine Smith

A TRUE ACCOUNT OF THE RESPECTABLE YOUNG GLASGOW **LADY** BROUGHT TO **TRIAL** FOR THE **MURDER** BY POISON OF HER SECRET PARAMOUR

MADELEINE

EMILE

WRITTEN AND ILLUSTRATED BY
RICK GEARY

BIBLIOGRAPHY

Crimes of Passion. (London, Verdict Press, 1975)

Hartman, Mary S., *Victorian Murderesses: A True History of Thirteen Respectable French and English Women Accused of Unspeakable Crimes.* (New York, Schoken Books, 1977)

House, Jack, *Square Mile of Murder.* (London, Magnum Books, 1980)

MacGowan, Douglas, *Murder in Victorian Scotland: The Trial of Madeleine Smith.* (Westport, CT, Praeger Publishers, 1999)

Roughead, William, *Classic Crimes.* (New York, Vintage Books, 1977)

Thompson, C. J. S., *Poison Mysteries in History, Romance and Crime.* (Philadelphia and London, J.B. Lippincott Co., no date)

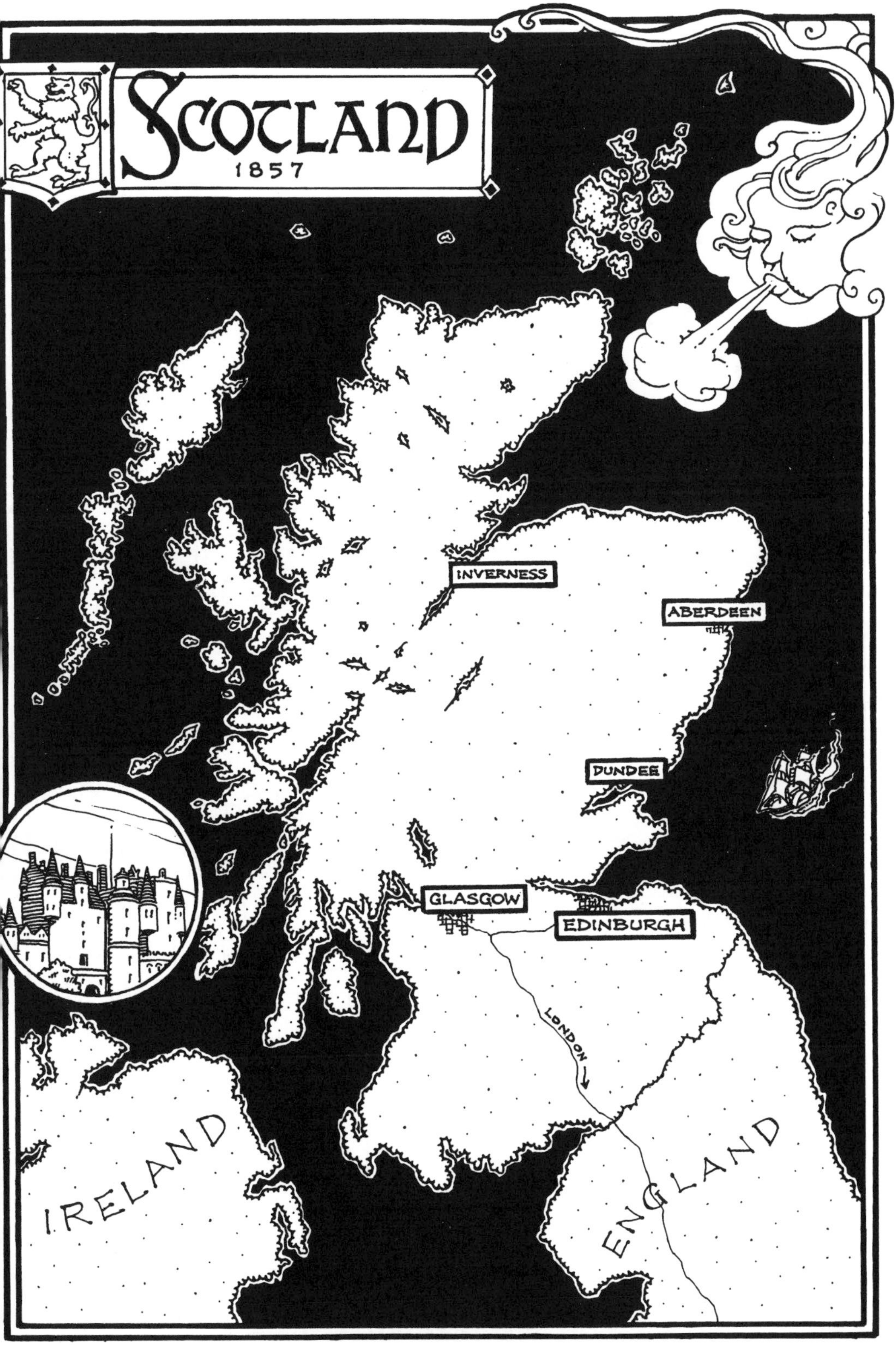
SCOTLAND
1857
INVERNESS
ABERDEEN
DUNDEE
GLASGOW
EDINBURGH
LONDON
IRELAND
ENGLAND

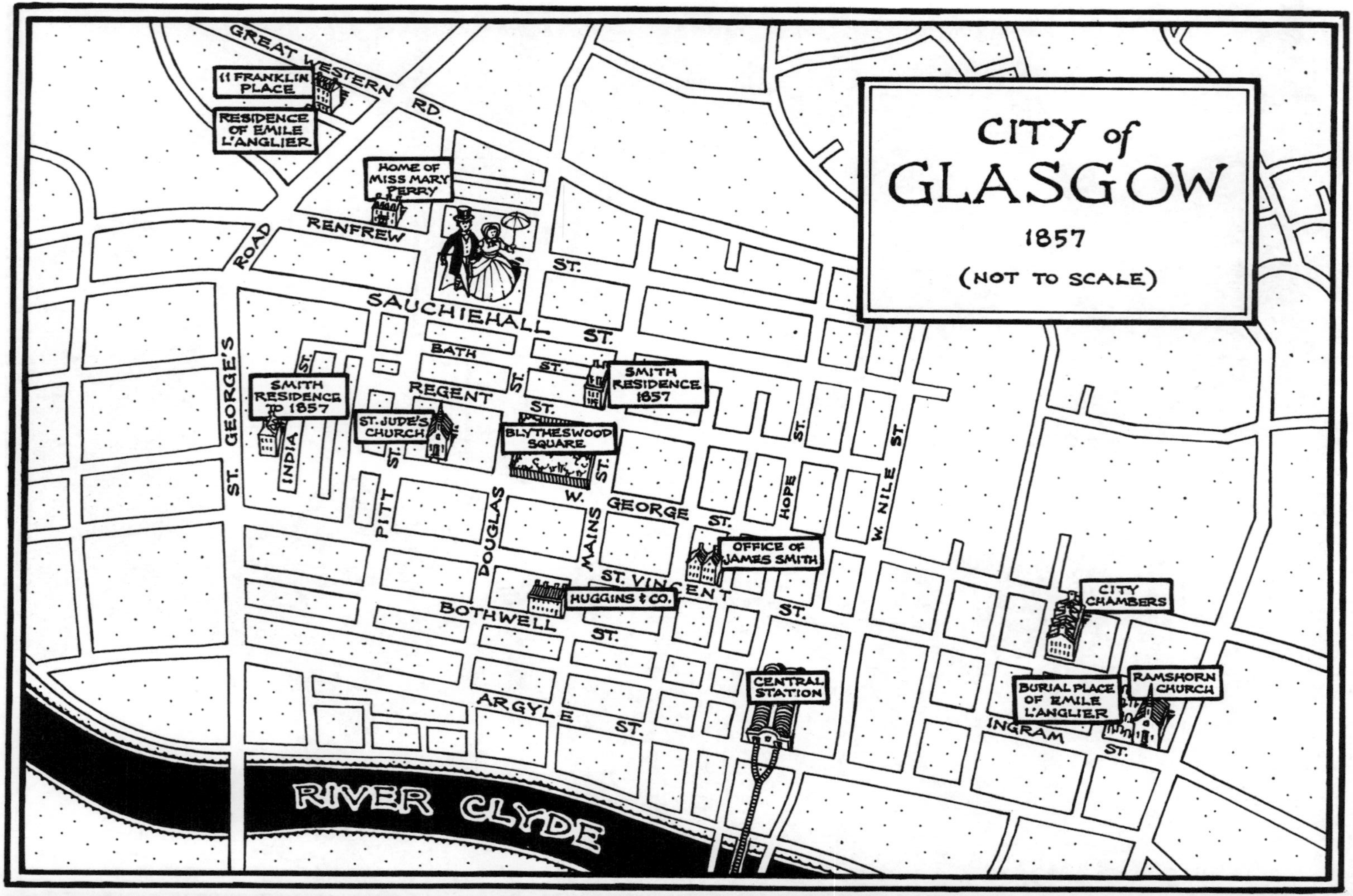
CITY of GLASGOW
1857
(NOT TO SCALE)
11 FRANKLIN PLACE
RESIDENCE OF EMILE L'ANGLIER
HOME OF MISS MARY PERRY
SMITH RESIDENCE TO 1857
ST. JUDE'S CHURCH
SMITH RESIDENCE 1857
BLYTHESWOOD SQUARE
OFFICE OF JAMES SMITH
HUGGINS & CO.
CENTRAL STATION
CITY CHAMBERS
BURIAL PLACE OF EMILE L'ANGLIER
RAMSHORN CHURCH
GREAT WESTERN RD.
RENFREW ST.
ROAD
SAUCHIEHALL ST.
BATH ST.
REGENT ST.
ST. GEORGE'S
INDIA ST.
PITT ST.
DOUGLAS
W. GEORGE ST.
MAINS ST.
HOPE ST.
W. NILE ST.
ST. VINCENT ST.
BOTHWELL ST.
ARGYLE ST.
INGRAM ST.
RIVER CLYDE

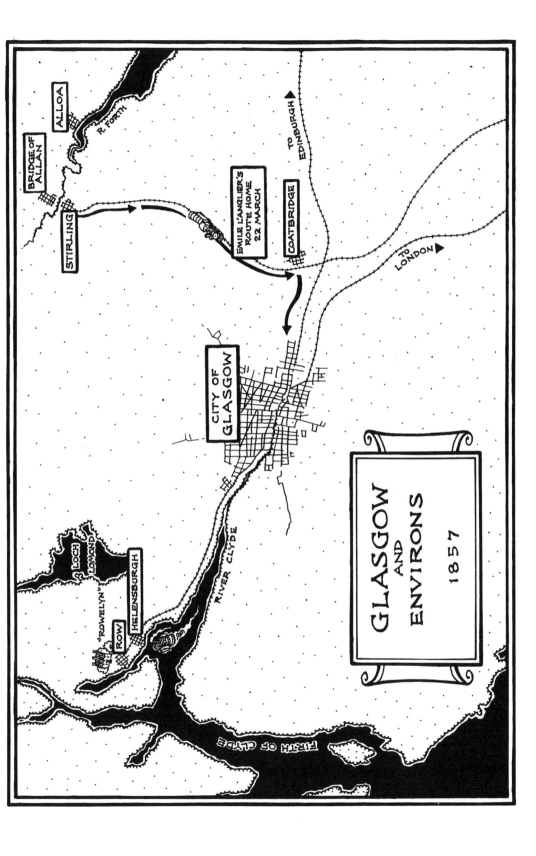

GLASGOW AND ENVIRONS 1857

ALLOA

R. FORTH

BRIDGE OF ALLAN

STIRLING

TO EDINBURGH

EMILE L'ANGLIER'S ROUTE HOME 22 MARCH

COATBRIDGE

TO LONDON

CITY OF GLASGOW

LOCH LOMOND

"ROWELYN"

ROW

HELENSBURGH

RIVER CLYDE

FIRTH OF CLYDE

PART I

DEATH BY POISON

"THE HANDFUL OF DUST
THAT LIES BENEATH THE
LEANING TOMBSTONE."

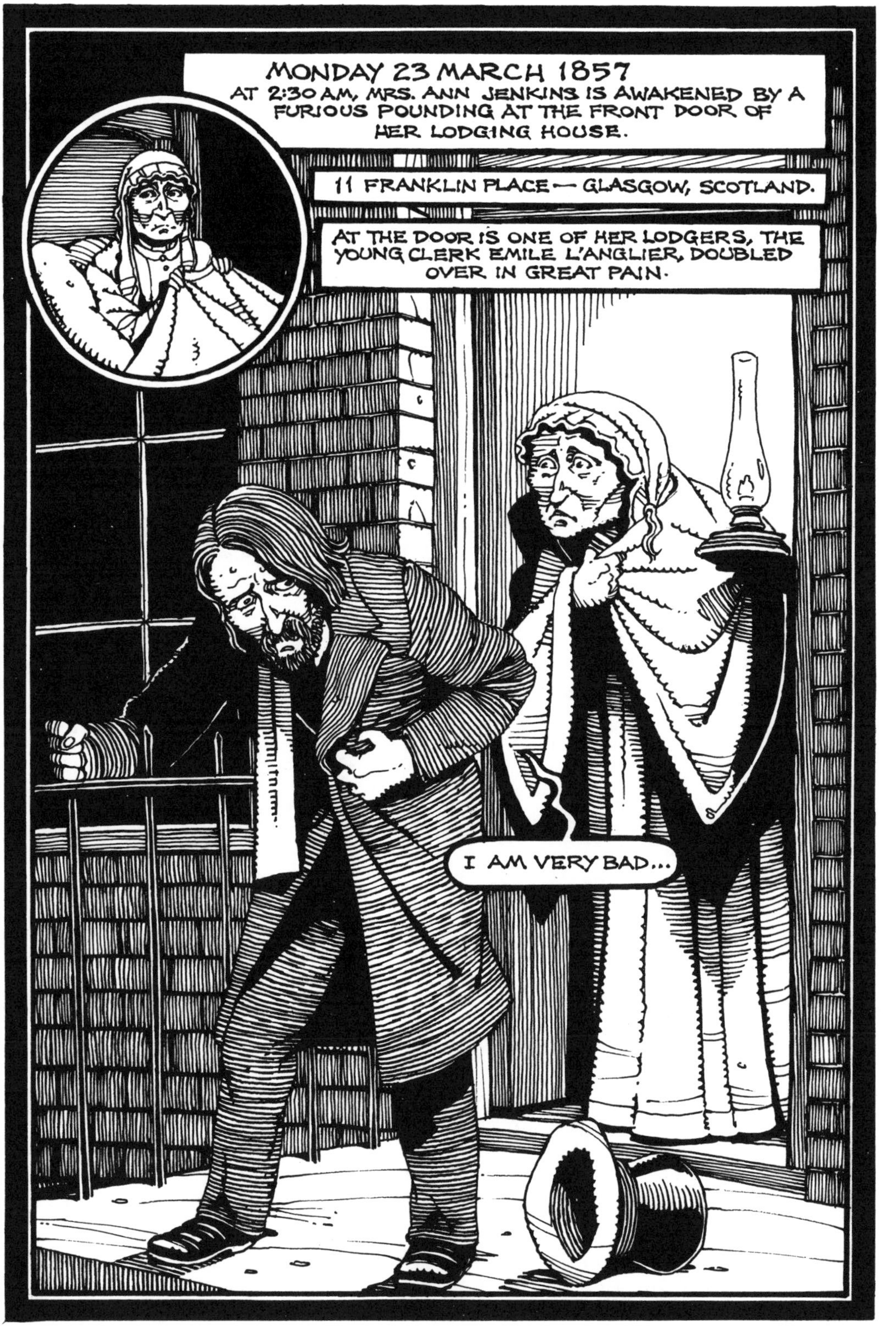
MONDAY 23 MARCH 1857
AT 2:30 AM, MRS. ANN JENKINS IS AWAKENED BY A FURIOUS POUNDING AT THE FRONT DOOR OF HER LODGING HOUSE.
11 FRANKLIN PLACE — GLASGOW, SCOTLAND.
AT THE DOOR IS ONE OF HER LODGERS, THE YOUNG CLERK EMILE L'ANGLIER, DOUBLED OVER IN GREAT PAIN.
I AM VERY BAD...

THE LANDLADY HELPS HIM TO HIS ROOM.

I AM GOING TO HAVE ANOTHER VOMITING OF THAT BILE.

THIS IS THE FOURTH SUCH ATTACK THE MAN HAS EXPERIENCED IN RECENT WEEKS.

HE SIPS A TUMBLER OF HOT WATER AND VOMITS FOUL LIQUID INTO HIS CHAMBER POT. THEN, COMPLAINING OF COLD, HE CLIMBS INTO BED.

MRS. JENKINS COVERS HIM WITH SEVERAL BLANKETS.

AT 7:00 AM, AS HIS CONDITION APPEARS TO WORSEN, SHE GOES OUT TO FETCH A NEARBY PHYSICIAN.

DR. JAMES STEVEN OF STAFFORD PLACE.

THE DOCTOR APPLIES A MUSTARD POULTICE, ADVISES REST AND QUIET. HE PROMISES TO RETURN LATER IN THE MORNING.

OH MRS. JENKINS, THIS IS THE WORST ATTACK I EVER HAD.

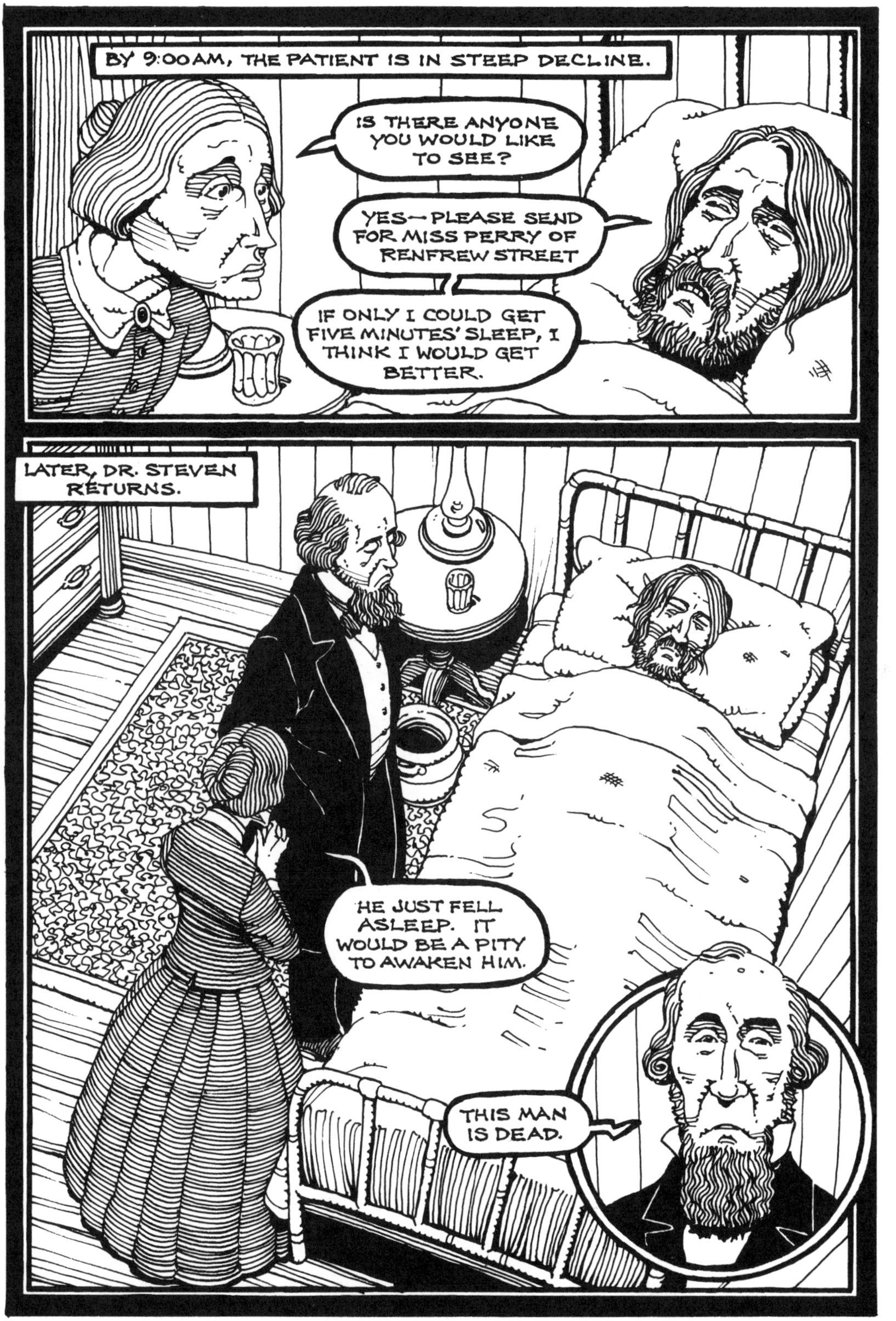
BY 9:00AM, THE PATIENT IS IN STEEP DECLINE.
IS THERE ANYONE YOU WOULD LIKE TO SEE?
YES—PLEASE SEND FOR MISS PERRY OF RENFREW STREET
IF ONLY I COULD GET FIVE MINUTES' SLEEP, I THINK I WOULD GET BETTER.
LATER, DR. STEVEN RETURNS.
HE JUST FELL ASLEEP. IT WOULD BE A PITY TO AWAKEN HIM.
THIS MAN IS DEAD.

MISS MARY PERRY ARRIVES TOO LATE.

ARE YOU THE INTENDED, MA'AM?

NO, I AM ONLY A FRIEND.

I HEARD HE WAS GOING TO BE MARRIED. HOW SORRY THE YOUNG LADY WILL BE.

MISS PERRY, CHOKING WITH GRIEF, KISSES THE POOR MAN'S FOREHEAD...

AND THEN DEPARTS.

SHORTLY THEREAFTER, THE MAN'S REGULAR PHYSICIAN, DR. THOMSON, ARRIVES.

ALSO PRESENT ARE: WILLIAM STEVENSON, HIS SUPERVISOR AT HUGGINS SEED WAREHOUSE; AND AMADEE THUAU, HIS FRIEND AND FELLOW LODGER.

MRS. JENKINS EXPLAINS TO THEM THAT MR. L'ANGLIER HAS BEEN AWAY FROM TOWN FOR SEVERAL DAYS — BUT RETURNED UNEXPECTEDLY LAST NIGHT.

MR. STEVENSON TAKES CHARGE OF THE DEAD MAN'S POSSESSIONS. IN THE POCKET OF HIS COAT IS FOUND THIS LETTER:

WHY, MY BELOVED, DID YOU NOT COME TO ME? OH, BELOVED, ARE YOU ILL? COME TO ME, SWEET ONE. I WAITED AND WAITED FOR YOU, BUT YOU CAME NOT. I SHALL WAIT AGAIN TOMORROW NIGHT — SAME HOUR AND ARRANGEMENT. DO COME, SWEET LOVE, MY OWN DEAR LOVE OF A SWEETHEART. COME, BELOVED, AND CLASP ME TO YOUR HEART. COME AND WE SHALL BE HAPPY. A KISS, FOND LOVE. ADIEU, WITH TENDER EMBRACES, EVER BELIEVE ME TO BE YOUR OWN DEAR FOND

"MIMI"

THIS EXPLAINS ALL.

252

AMONG THE MAN'S BELONGINGS ARE FOUND:

VARIOUS KEYS...

SEVERAL PACKAGES OF LETTERS...

A NOTEBOOK, APPARENTLY KEPT AS A JOURNAL.

IN HIS DESK AT THE SEED WAREHOUSE ARE FOUND MANY MORE LETTERS, — WRAPPED IN BUNDLES — ALL SIGNED BY THE SAME "MIMI"...

A CORRESPONDENCE EXTENDING BACK TWO YEARS!

MISS PERRY KNOWS WHO SENT THESE LETTERS.

SHE GOES AT ONCE TO THE HOME OF THE ARCHITECT JAMES SMITH ON BLYTHESWOOD SQUARE,

HER SPECIAL INTEREST IS THE SMITHS' ELDEST DAUGHTER MADELEINE, AGE 20...

WHO EVINCES SCANT EMOTION UPON HEARING THE GRIM NEWS.

TUESDAY 24 MARCH
A POST-MORTEM IS CONDUCTED UPON THE REMAINS OF EMILE L'ANGLIER, BY THE DOCTORS THOMSON AND STEVEN.

HIS ORGANS SHOW SIGNS OF POISON. THE DOCTORS REMOVE THE STOMACH AND ITS CONTENTS AND PRESERVE THEM FOR FURTHER ANALYSIS.

THURSDAY 26 MARCH
THE POOR MAN IS BURIED. HAVING NO RELATIONS IN GLASGOW, HE IS PLACED IN THE STEVENSON FAMILY VAULT AT THE RAMSHORN CHURCHYARD ON INGRAM STREET.

WEDNESDAY 25 MARCH ON THIS DAY, THE PROCURATOR-FISCAL, JAMES HART, HAS IN HIS POSSESSION SEVERAL PIECES OF THE NOTORIOUS CORRESPONDENCE.

THE CONTENTS OF THESE LETTERS ARE PROFOUNDLY DISTURBING TO ALL WHO HAVE SO FAR READ THEM.

MADELEINE SMITH IS INTERVIEWED AT HER HOME BY AUGUSTE DE MEAN, THE FRENCH CONSULATE (AND FRIEND TO THE DECEASED).

TO HIM SHE STATES THAT, YES, SHE CARRIED ON A ROMANTIC CORRESPONDENCE WITH MR. L'ANGLIER — BUT SHE HAS NOT SEEN HIM FOR SEVERAL WEEKS.

IN ANY CASE, SHE IS NOW ENGAGED TO MARRY ANOTHER MAN.

HER POSITION IS NOT HELPED, HOWEVER, BY THE DISCOVERY THAT SHE MADE THREE PURCHASES OF ARSENIC IN RECENT WEEKS.

FRIDAY 27 MARCH DR. FREDERICK PENNY, PROFESSOR OF CHEMISTRY AT THE ANDERSONIAN UNIVERSITY, MAKES HIS ANALYSIS OF THE DEAD MAN'S STOMACH CONTENTS.

HIS CONCLUSION: DEATH FROM ARSENIC POISONING. EIGHTY-FIVE GRAINS — SUFFICIENT TO DISPATCH FORTY MEN.

TUESDAY 31 MARCH 1857 ON THIS DAY, THE PROCURATOR-FISCAL ISSUES A WARRANT FOR THE ARREST OF MADELEINE SMITH.

SHE IS PROMPTLY TAKEN INTO CUSTODY.

PART II

MADELEINE AND EMILE

"IN CHILD-HOOD AND
YOUTH ARE SOWN THE SEEDS."

How does a well-born and respectable young lady find herself under arrest for the ultimate crime?

Let us examine the life of Miss Madeleine Hamilton Smith, heretofore unremarkable for a girl of her station.

She was born in Glasgow in 1836, the eldest of five children born to the architect James Smith and his wife, the former Elizabeth Hamilton.

HER YOUNGER SIBLINGS:

JOHN (JACK)

JANET

ELIZABETH (BESSIE)

JAMES

THE FAMILY OCCUPIED A FINE HOUSE ON FASHIONABLE INDIA STREET.

THE FATHER'S OFFICE WAS NEARBY, AT 124 ST. VINCENT STREET.

257

MADELEINE'S CHILDHOOD WAS OF THE ORDINARY KIND FOR A FAMILY OF WEALTH AND POSITION.

HER FATHER WAS A DOMINANT PRESENCE: FOND YET STERN.

HER MOTHER WAS OF DELICATE HEALTH, OFTEN TAKING TO HER BED.

IN CONSEQUENCE, MANY OF THE DUTIES OF CHILD-RAISING FELL TO MADELEINE, AS ELDEST DAUGHTER.

AT AGE FOURTEEN, AS WAS CUSTOMARY, SHE WAS SENT AWAY TO A PROPER FINISHING SCHOOL.

GLASGOW

LONDON

GORTON'S ACADEMY FOR YOUNG LADIES, IN LONDON.

(MR. SMITH BELIEVED THAT ONLY IN ENGLAND COULD SHE RECEIVE THE CORRECT EDUCATION.)

MADELEINE BECAME ONE OF SEVENTEEN GIRLS UNDER THE TUTELAGE OF MRS. ALICE GORTON.

THE CURRICULUM CONSISTED OF COPIOUS PRAYER, ALONG WITH LESSONS IN MUSIC, NEEDLE-WORK AND GOOD MANNERS.

WHEN APPROPRIATE, A DISCUSSION OF CURRENT EVENTS, OR VARIOUS SUBJECTS OF HISTORY AND CLASSICAL CULTURE.

MADELEINE LEARNED THE PROPER COMPOSITION OF LETTERS OF ALL KINDS. SHE PROVED A LOYAL CORRESPONDENT, WITH TWICE-WEEKLY MESSAGES HOME.

MRS. GORTON KEPT A STRICT EYE UPON HER GIRLS, ENSURING THEM VERY LITTLE PRIVACY.

THUS A STUDENT BECAME SKILLED IN THE ARTS OF INTRIGUE AND SECRECY.

MADELEINE IMPRESSED HER INSTRUCTORS AS DILIGENT, ATTENTIVE AND BRIGHT...

ALTHOUGH SOMETIMES PRONE TO "STUBBORN SULKS."

IN 1853, MADELEINE GRADUATED AND RETURNED HOME, TO INDIA STREET.

LIKE ALL SUCH "FINISHED" YOUNG LADIES, SHE NOW MERELY WAITED FOR A SUITABLE OFFER OF MARRIAGE.

BUT PERHAPS SHE HAD OTHER IDEAS.

IDLE AND RESTLESS, SHE DEVOURED THE POPULAR MAGAZINES OF SENSATIONAL FICTION...

LADIES CONFIDANTE MONTHLY

BLACKWELL'S GAZETTE

STORIES OF ROMANTIC HEROINES — YOUNG LADIES OF PASSION AND SUFFERING — WOMEN WHO STRUGGLED AND REBELLED.

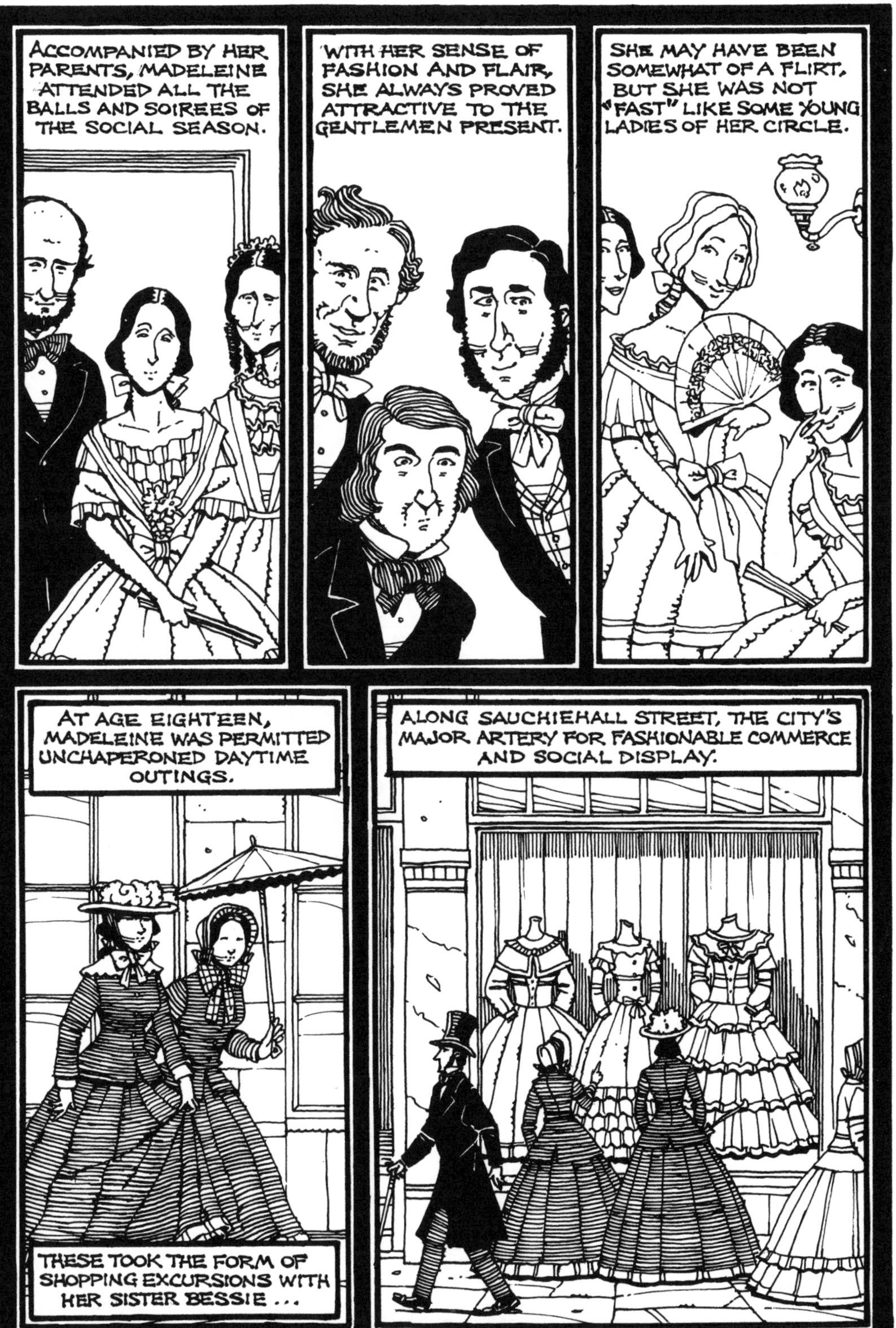
ACCOMPANIED BY HER PARENTS, MADELEINE ATTENDED ALL THE BALLS AND SOIREES OF THE SOCIAL SEASON.
WITH HER SENSE OF FASHION AND FLAIR, SHE ALWAYS PROVED ATTRACTIVE TO THE GENTLEMEN PRESENT.
SHE MAY HAVE BEEN SOMEWHAT OF A FLIRT, BUT SHE WAS NOT "FAST" LIKE SOME YOUNG LADIES OF HER CIRCLE.
AT AGE EIGHTEEN, MADELEINE WAS PERMITTED UNCHAPERONED DAYTIME OUTINGS.
THESE TOOK THE FORM OF SHOPPING EXCURSIONS WITH HER SISTER BESSIE ...
ALONG SAUCHIEHALL STREET, THE CITY'S MAJOR ARTERY FOR FASHIONABLE COMMERCE AND SOCIAL DISPLAY.

IT IS UNDOUBTEDLY DURING ONE OF THESE OUTINGS, SOMETIME EARLY IN 1855, THAT MADELEINE'S EYE IS ATTRACTED BY A CERTAIN HANDSOME AND WELL-DRESSED GENTLEMAN.

THE EYE OF EMILE L'ANGLIER IS LIKEWISE DRAWN TO HER.

THEREAFTER, WHEN THEY PASS ON THE SIDEWALK, A GLANCE OF ADMIRATION IS EXCHANGED.

HOW ARE THEY TO MEET?

EMILE L'ANGLIER KNOWS THAT A GENTLEMAN CANNOT SIMPLY INTRODUCE HIMSELF TO A STRANGE LADY ON THE STREET.

AND EMILE IS, FIRST AND ALWAYS, A GENTLEMAN.

HE WAS BORN, IN 1822, ON THE ISLE OF JERSEY, AT THAT TIME HOME TO EXPATRIATES OF NATIONS.

ENGI

ENGLISH CHA

FRA

LIKE MADELEINE, HE WAS ELDEST OF FIVE CHILDREN — BORN TO A FRENCH COUPLE: PIERRE L'ANGLIER AND HIS WIFE VICTOIRE.

ANASTASIE

ELMIRE

ACHILLE

ZEPHRINE

THE FATHER WAS A SUCCESSFUL SEED MERCHANT AND NURSERYMAN.

YOUNG EMILE ATTENDED THE LOCAL SCHOOLS AND GREW UP FLUENT IN BOTH FRENCH AND ENGLISH.

AT AGE FOURTEEN, HE BEGAN AN APPRENTICESHIP IN THE NURSERY BUSINESS.

HE WORKED HARD AND LEARNED ALL ASPECTS OF THE TRADE.

UPON HIS FATHER'S DEATH IN 1840, EMILE, WITH HIS MOTHER AND SIBLINGS, RAN THE FAMILY BUSINESS AS BEST THEY COULD.

IN 1842, THE YOUNG MAN TOOK ADVANTAGE OF AN OPPORTUNITY OFFERED BY A VISITING ARISTOCRAT TO CONTINUE HIS APPRENTICESHIP IN SCOTLAND.

AT AGE NINETEEN, HE LEFT HOME FOR THE FIRST TIME.

EDINBURGH

LONDON

HE SETTLED FIRST IN EDINBURGH AND WORKED AT THE LARGE NURSERY OF DICKSONS AND CO.

BEFORE LONG, HE ENTERED INTO HIS FIRST SERIOUS LOVE AFFAIR.

HER NAME IS LOST TO HISTORY, BUT EMILE PROVED THE MOST ARDENT OF SUITORS TO THIS "LADY OF FIFE" (AS SHE IS LATER CALLED).

AT SOME POINT, THEY MAY HAVE BECOME ENGAGED, BUT OVER TIME, THE ROMANCE COOLED.

THIS WAS PERHAPS THE REASON FOR EMILE'S DECISION, IN 1846, TO LEAVE EDINBURGH.

HE RETURNED AT FIRST TO HIS HOME ON JERSEY, AND THEN MOVED TO PARIS, WHERE HE LIVED WITH RELATIONS OF HIS MOTHER.

HERE HE REMAINED FOR FIVE YEARS, WHERE HE . . .

WORKED AS A CLERK IN A MERCANTILE ESTABLISHMENT...

DRANK DEEPLY OF THE CITY'S NIGHT LIFE. . .

PURSUED INTENSE AND DOOMED ROMANCES . . .

AND SERVED, FOR A TIME, IN THE ARMY.

IN 1851, FOR REASONS UNKNOWN, EMILE DECIDED TO RETURN TO SCOTLAND. HE RESETTLED IN EDINBURGH.

HAVING FOUND HIS FORMER LOVE ENGAGED TO ANOTHER, HE PURSUED ROMANTIC ATTACHMENTS WITH SEVERAL LADIES.

HIS PARISIAN SOPHISTICATION MADE HIM QUITE ATTRACTIVE, AT FIRST.

BUT HIS EFFORTS NEARLY ALWAYS LED TO DISAPPOINTMENT AND REJECTION...

RESULTING IN DEPRESSION AND EVEN CONTEMPLATION OF SUICIDE.

IN ADDITION, HE COULD NOT FIND SUITABLE EMPLOYMENT IN EDINBURGH.

HE MOVED NORTHWARD, TO DUNDEE, WHERE HE LABORED FOR SIX MONTHS AT A NURSERY.

DUNDEE

GLASGOW

EDINBURGH

AND THEN, IN THE SUMMER OF 1852, HE DECIDED TO SETTLE IN GLASGOW.

EMILE FOUND LODGING AT KINGSTON PLACE, SOUTH OF THE RIVER CLYDE.

HE SECURED EMPLOYMENT AT THE SEED WAREHOUSE OF HUGGINS AND CO., LOCATED AT 10 BOTHWELL STREET.

HE POSITIONED HIMSELF TO RISE IN SOCIETY. DRESSING TO THE LATEST TASTE, HE CRUISED THE BOULEVARDS WITH AN EYE OUT FOR BEAUTIFUL LADIES.

ALTHOUGH A ROMAN CATHOLIC, HE ATTENDED SERVICES AT ST. JUDE'S EPISCOPAL CHURCH ON JANE STREET.

HE FOUND A WILLING CONFIDANTE IN THE PERSON OF AN OLDER MAIDEN LADY NAMED MARY PERRY.

FROM HER HOME ON RENFREW STREET, MISS PERRY INVOLVED HERSELF, AS FRIEND AND ADVISOR, IN THE LIVES OF A LARGE CIRCLE OF PEOPLE.

IN 1854, SHE ADVISED EMILE TO MOVE HIS RESIDENCE TO A MORE SOCIALLY ACCEPTABLE LOCATION: ALONG GREAT WESTERN ROAD, NEAR THE BOTANICAL GARDENS.

SOMETIME EARLY IN 1855, DURING ONE OF HIS PERAMBULATIONS ALONG SAUCHIEHALL STREET, EMILE'S EYE IS CAUGHT BY A GRAVELY BEAUTIFUL YOUNG LADY.

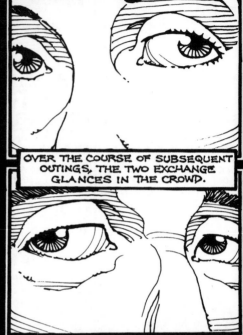

OVER THE COURSE OF SUBSEQUENT OUTINGS, THE TWO EXCHANGE GLANCES IN THE CROWD.

IN TIME, THEY FIND THEMSELVES UNCONSCIOUSLY SEARCHING OUT THE OTHER.

HOW ARE THEY TO MEET?

PART III

A FORBIDDEN ROMANCE

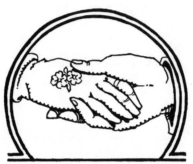

" PLEASANT ACQUAINTANCE
MADE, RESULTING IN
LASTING FRIENDSHIP. "

EMILE WORKS TO SOLVE THE PROBLEM OF HOW TO MEET THIS
BEAUTIFUL LADY.   THE GOAL BECOMES HIS OBSESSION.

AS A FIRST STEP, HE BECOMES FRIENDLY WITH THE BROTHERS CHARLES AND ROBERT BAIRD, NEPHEWS OF A CO-WORKER AT HUGGINS, WHO ARE ACQUAINTANCES OF THE SMITH FAMILY.

ONE DAY IN LATE FEBRUARY OR EARLY MARCH, 1855, HE AND ROBERT BAIRD STROLL DOWN SAUCHIEHALL STREET.

HE SPIES THE OBJECT OF HIS DESIRE (WITH HER SISTER) ENTERING A FASHIONABLE SHOP.

HE ASKS ROBERT TO GO INSIDE AND BRING THEM OUT.

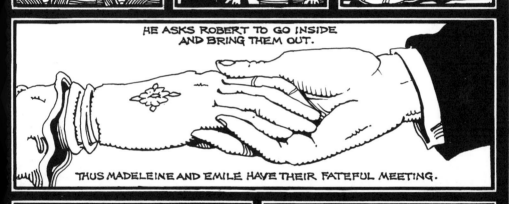

THUS MADELEINE AND EMILE HAVE THEIR FATEFUL MEETING.

OVER THE ENSUING WEEKS, THEY MEET BY PRE-ARRANGEMENT IN SHOPS OR ALONG THE STREET.

THE THREE STROLL TOGETHER, EXCHANGING PLEASANTRIES IN A MANNER CONSISTENT WITH PROPRIETY.

IN APRIL, THE SMITH FAMILY LEAVES FOR ITS COUNTRY RESIDENCE: A LARGE HOUSE CALLED "ROWELYN," NEAR THE TOWN OF ROW, TWENTY MILES UP THE RIVER CLYDE FROM GLASGOW.

ROW

HELENSBURG

RIVER CLYDE

GLASGOW

THE FAMILY SPENDS LEISURELY DAYS. MADELEINE TENDS THE GARDEN AND EVEN SUPERVISES THE LIVESTOCK.

IT IS HERE, ONE DAY IN APRIL, THAT MADELEINE PENS HER FIRST LETTER TO EMILE: RESTRAINED AND POLITE, GIVING LITTLE HINT OF WHAT IS TO COME. ✳

"THOUGH OUR INTERCOURSE HAS BEEN VERY SHORT, YET WE HAVE BECOME AS FAMILIAR FRIENDS. MAY WE LONG CONTINUE SO...

I AM TRYING TO BREAK MYSELF OF ALL MY VERY BAD HABITS. IT IS YOU I HAVE TO THANK FOR THIS...

YOUR FLOWER IS FADING...

WITH KIND LOVE, BELIEVE ME, YOURS VERY SINCERELY, MADELEINE."

✳ A TOTAL OF 198 LETTERS FROM MADELEINE WILL EVENTUALLY BE FOUND AMONG EMILE'S POSSESSIONS—BUT NONE FROM HIM AMONG HERS. PERHAPS THE TWO HAVE MADE A PACT TO DESTROY EACH OTHER'S CORRESPONDENCE—A PACT THAT ONLY THE YOUNG LADY KEEPS.

BY THE TIME OF MADELEINE'S SECOND LETTER, AN OBSTACLE HAS EMERGED.

"WELL, SOME FRIEND WAS KIND ENOUGH TO TELL PAPA THAT YOU WERE IN THE HABIT OF WALKING WITH US...

PAPA WAS VERY ANGRY WITH ME FOR WALKING WITH A GENTLEMAN UNKNOWN TO HIM."

THROUGH THIS SAME "FRIEND," MR. SMITH LEARNS THAT THE GENTLEMAN IS NOT ONLY A FOREIGNER BUT A MERE CLERK.

THE BEARER OF THIS NEWS IS UNDOUBTEDLY MADELEINE'S SISTER BESSIE.

DID BESSIE ACT OUT OF JEALOUSY...

OR THE DESIRE TO PROTECT HER SISTER'S GOOD NAME?

"FOR THE PRESENT, OUR CORRESPONDENCE MUST STOP...

BY CONTINUING TO CORRESPOND, HARM MAY ARISE."

THE ATTRACTION BETWEEN THEM IS TOO STRONG, HOWEVER, AND WITHIN DAYS, THEIR EXCHANGE OF LETTERS BEGINS ANEW.

273

AS THE YEAR PASSES, A SECRET ROMANCE GROWS.

MADELEINE RETRIEVES EMILE'S LETTERS AT THE POST OFFICE, UNDER THE NAME "MISS RICHARD."

WHEN THE FAMILY IS AT ROWELYN, EMILE JOURNEYS THERE AT EVERY SAFE OPPORTUNITY.

SHE CAUTIONS HIM TO GET OFF THE FERRY AT HELENSBURGH, THE PRECEDING STOP, AND WALK THE REMAINING DISTANCE.

THEY ARE ABLE TO MEET BRIEFLY, AFTER DARK, IN THE ESTATE'S WALLED GARDEN.

WHEN THE FAMILY IS IN GLASGOW, EMILE HAUNTS THEIR INDIA STREET NEIGHBORHOOD.

ON CERTAIN EVENINGS, WHEN HER PARENTS ARE OUT, MADELEINE ALLOWS HIM INTO THE HOUSE— THOUGH ONLY AS FAR AS THE LAUNDRY ROOM.

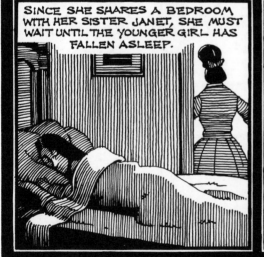

SINCE SHE SHARES A BEDROOM WITH HER SISTER JANET, SHE MUST WAIT UNTIL THE YOUNGER GIRL HAS FALLEN ASLEEP.

OF GREAT ASSISTANCE TO MADELEINE'S SUBTERFUGE IS A CO-OPERATIVE HOUSEMAID, CHRISTINA HAGGART.

SINCE MISS HAGGART IS IN A LOVE AFFAIR HERSELF, SHE CANNOT BUT SYMPATHIZE.

THE HOUSEMAID OFTEN SERVES AS LETTER-CARRIER FOR HER MISTRESS...

WHILE EMILE'S FRIEND, THE SYMPATHETIC MISS MARY PERRY, SOMETIMES LENDS HER PARLOR AS MEETING PLACE FOR THE LOVERS.

TO MISS PERRY HE CONFIDES HIS DETERMINATION TO MEET AND WIN OVER MADELEINE'S FATHER AND MARRY HIS BELOVED.

IN JULY OF 1855, HOWEVER, MADELEINE AGAIN ATTEMPTS TO BREAK OFF THEIR CORRESPONDENCE. HER FATHER HAS LAID DOWN THE LAW.

"FATHER HATES YOU WITH ALL HIS HEART. HE DESPISES YOU... HE CARES NOT FOR WHAT I SAY."

EMILE IS DEVASTATED AND CONSIDERS TAKING A NURSERY POSITION IN LIMA, PERU.

BUT MADELEINE IS TOO MUCH IN LOVE. SHE DEFIES HER FATHER AND RE-INITIATES THE CORRESPONDENCE.

"FOR THE LOVE OF HEAVEN, WRITE TO ME, IF IT SHOULD ONLY BE A LINE. I KNOW YOU MUST HATE ME, BUT, OH, FORGIVE ME."

SHE NOW SIGNS HER LETTERS "MIMI."

BY THE END OF 1855, MADELEINE AND EMILE ARE WORKING AT CROSS-PURPOSES. HE PRESSES FOR EVER MORE PUBLIC DECLARATION OF THEIR LOVE — WHILE HER OVERWHELMING NEED IS TO KEEP IT A SECRET.

NEVERTHELESS, THEY NOW CONSIDER THEMSELVES "ENGAGED" AND SET THEIR WEDDING DATE FOR SEPTEMBER OF THE COMING YEAR.

"MY OWN DARLING HUSBAND — I DID NOT EXPECT THE PLEASURE OF SEEING YOU LAST EVENING — OF BEING FONDLED BY YOU...

SWEET ONE OF MY SOUL. MY ALL, MY OWN BEST BELOVED."

THE ROMANCE CONTINUES IN THIS VEIN INTO THE YEAR 1856 — AND AND CULMINATES ONE SUMMER EVENING IN THE GARDEN AT ROWELYN.

HERE THEY AT LAST GIVE THEIR LOVE ITS FULLEST EXPRESSION!

AFTERWARD, MADELEINE FINDS THAT SHE FEELS LITTLE REGRET.

"IF WE DID WRONG LAST NIGHT, IT WAS IN THE EXCITEMENT OF OUR LOVE. YES, BELOVED, I DID TRULY LOVE YOU WITH MY SOUL...

I MUST HAVE BEEN VERY STUPID TO YOU LAST NIGHT, BUT EVERYTHING GOES OUT OF MY HEAD WHEN I SEE YOU...

AM I NOT YOUR WIFE? YES, I AM!...

I DID NOT BLEED LAST NIGHT BUT I HAD A GREAT DEAL OF PAIN IN THE NIGHT...

TELL ME, PET, WERE YOU ANGRY AT ME FOR ALLOWING YOU TO DO WHAT YOU DID? WAS IT VERY BAD OF ME?"

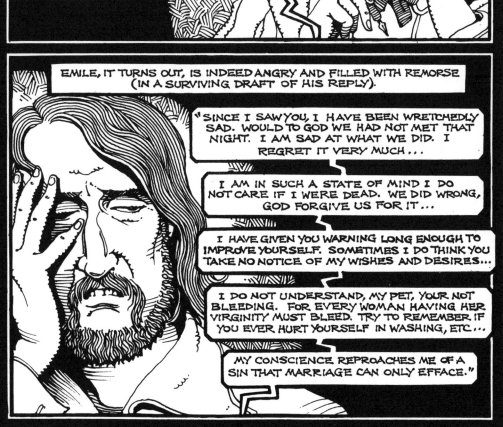

EMILE, IT TURNS OUT, IS INDEED ANGRY AND FILLED WITH REMORSE (IN A SURVIVING DRAFT OF HIS REPLY).

"SINCE I SAW YOU, I HAVE BEEN WRETCHEDLY SAD. WOULD TO GOD WE HAD NOT MET THAT NIGHT. I AM SAD AT WHAT WE DID. I REGRET IT VERY MUCH...

I AM IN SUCH A STATE OF MIND I DO NOT CARE IF I WERE DEAD. WE DID WRONG, GOD FORGIVE US FOR IT...

I HAVE GIVEN YOU WARNING LONG ENOUGH TO IMPROVE YOURSELF. SOMETIMES I DO THINK YOU TAKE NO NOTICE OF MY WISHES AND DESIRES...

I DO NOT UNDERSTAND, MY PET, YOUR NOT BLEEDING. FOR EVERY WOMAN HAVING HER VIRGINITY MUST BLEED. TRY TO REMEMBER IF YOU EVER HURT YOURSELF IN WASHING, ETC...

MY CONSCIENCE REPROACHES ME OF A SIN THAT MARRIAGE CAN ONLY EFFACE."

NOW FULLY INTO HER DOUBLE LIFE, MADELEINE, LIKE A DUTIFUL "FIANCEE," TRIES TO LIMIT HER SOCIAL OBLIGATIONS, THE PARTIES AND BALLS THAT HER PARENTS EXPECT HER TO ATTEND.

HOWEVER, AN OBSTACLE EMERGES IN THE PERSON OF WILLIAM "BILLY" MINNOCH, A WELL-TO-DO MERCHANT IN HIS THIRTIES, SOCIALLY CONNECTED AND MUCH ATTRACTED TO THE (SUPPOSEDLY AVAILABLE) YOUNG LADY.

MORE IMPORTANT, HE HAS THE APPROVAL OF MR. SMITH.

THEY ARE SEEN IN EACH OTHER'S COMPANY OFTEN ENOUGH THAT MADELEINE ATTEMPTS TO ALLAY EMILE'S FEARS ...

"DON'T GIVE AN EAR TO ANY REPORTS YOU MAY HEAR. THERE ARE SEVERAL I HEAR GOING ABOUT THAT I AM TO BE MARRIED. REGARD THEM NOT! ...

TRUE AND CONSTANT I WILL PROVE. DON'T FEAR ME. I SHALL BE THINE ...

WERE IT NOT FOR THESE THOUGHTS, I WOULD BE WEARY OF THIS COLD, UNFEELING, THOUGHTLESS WORLD."

NEVERTHELESS, THEIR PLANNED SEPTEMBER WEDDING IS INDEFINITELY POSTPONED.

FROM ROWELYN, SHE WRITES ...

"MR. MINNOCH HAS BEEN HERE SINCE FRIDAY. HE IS MOST AGREEABLE, I THINK. WE SHALL SEE HIM VERY OFTEN THIS SUMMER."

SOMETIME IN THE FALL, EMILE MOVES HIS RESIDENCE, TO A ROOMING HOUSE AT 11 FRANKLIN PLACE.

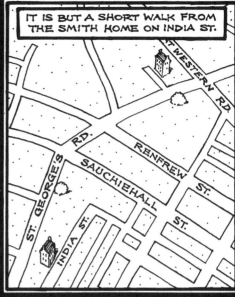

IT IS BUT A SHORT WALK FROM THE SMITH HOME ON INDIA ST.

HE OCCUPIES A SMALL SINGLE ROOM.

THE LANDLADY, MRS. ANN JENKINS, IS CORDIAL AND SYMPATHETIC.

AS HER NEW BOARDER MOVES IN, SHE NOTICES A PHOTOGRAPH ON HIS BUREAU.

IS THAT YOUR INTENDED?

PERHAPS, SOMEDAY...

LATER IN THE FALL, AFTER THE SMITH FAMILY RETURNS FROM ROWELYN, THEY MOVE INTO A NEW AND LARGER RESIDENCE ON EXCLUSIVE BLYTHESWOOD SQUARE.

THEY OCCUPY THE GROUND FLOOR AND BASEMENT. AS IT HAPPENS, THE UPPER FLAT IS OCCUPIED BY WILLIAM MINNOCH.

MADELEINE, AS PER HER REQUEST, TAKES A BASEMENT BEDROOM, WHICH SHE OCCUPIES, AGAIN, WITH HER SISTER JANET.

HER WINDOW, ON THE MAINS STREET SIDE OF THE HOUSE, IS LEVEL WITH THE SIDEWALK — AND SEEMINGLY IDEAL FOR THE PASSING OF MESSAGES.

SHE CAUTIONS EMILE TO USE BROWN ENVELOPES, SO HIS LETTERS WILL NOT BE NOTICED IN THE WINDOW-WELL.

HE DROPS THEM THERE, AND RETRIEVES THOSE FROM HER, WHEN STOOPING DOWN AS IF TO TIE HIS SHOE.

AS THE AUTUMN PASSES, HER LETTERS BECOME BRIEFER AND COOLER...

AS SHE SPENDS MORE TIME AT PUBLIC EVENTS IN THE COMPANY OF WILLIAM MINNOCH. THIS SENDS POOR EMILE INTO PAROXISMS OF AGONY.

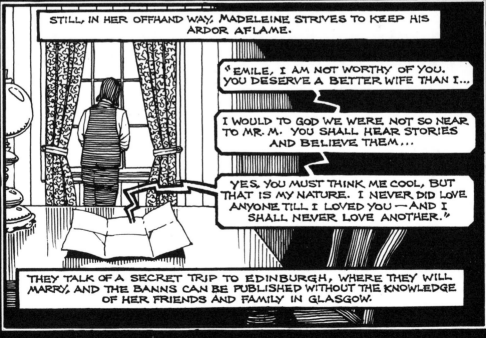

STILL, IN HER OFFHAND WAY, MADELEINE STRIVES TO KEEP HIS ARDOR AFLAME.

"EMILE, I AM NOT WORTHY OF YOU. YOU DESERVE A BETTER WIFE THAN I...

I WOULD TO GOD WE WERE NOT SO NEAR TO MR. M. YOU SHALL HEAR STORIES AND BELIEVE THEM...

YES, YOU MUST THINK ME COOL, BUT THAT IS MY NATURE. I NEVER DID LOVE ANYONE TILL I LOVED YOU — AND I SHALL NEVER LOVE ANOTHER."

THEY TALK OF A SECRET TRIP TO EDINBURGH, WHERE THEY WILL MARRY, AND THE BANNS CAN BE PUBLISHED WITHOUT THE KNOWLEDGE OF HER FRIENDS AND FAMILY IN GLASGOW.

281

SHE ASSURES HIM THAT SHE TRIES TO LIMIT HER "BAD HABITS"— HER FLIRTING, HER ATTENDANCE AT SOCIAL GATHERINGS, HER EXTRAVAGANT SHOPPING EXCURSIONS ALONG SAUCHIEHALL STREET.

AT THE SAME TIME, SHE WRITES FREELY OF WILLIAM MINNOCH'S ATTENTIONS TO HER, AND OF HIS SEEMINGLY CONSTANT PRESENCE IN HER FAMILY'S LIFE.

"YOU ALWAYS LISTEN TO REPORTS ABOUT ME IF THEY ARE BAD. I COULD NOT SIT THERE A WHOLE EVENING WITHOUT TALKING—BUT I DID NOT FLIRT. THERE IS A DIFFERENCE BETWEEN TALKING AND FLIRTING...

DOES MADELEINE ENJOY MAKING EMILE JEALOUS? OR DOES SHE MERELY SEEK TO SOFTEN MALICIOUS GOSSIP?

DARLING, DO NOT THINK OF DARK CLOUDS—THEY MAY PASS AWAY AND ALL WILL BE SUNSHINE."

IT CUTS EMILE DEEPLY TO ENCOUNTER HIS LOVE ON THE BUSY SIDEWALK...

AND WATCH HER WALK SERENELY PAST, STUDIOUSLY IGNORING HIM.

282

BUT EMILE CONTINUES TO VISIT MADELEINE'S WINDOW BY NIGHT.

HE CARRIES CIGARS TO OFFER ANY PATROLMAN WHO MIGHT QUESTION HIS PRESENCE.

HE POSES AS THE FIANCE OF A SERVANT WHO OCCUPIES A BASEMENT ROOM.

ON CERTAIN NIGHTS, WHEN HER PARENTS ARE AWAY, AND WITH THE COMPLIANCE OF CHRISTINA HAGGART, EMILE MIGHT BE ALLOWED INTO THE PARLOR FOR A BRIEF MEETING.

ON OTHER NIGHTS, AS THE WEATHER TURNS COLDER, MADELEINE MIGHT BRING A CUP OF HOT COCOA OUT TO HER LOVER THROUGH THE BASEMENT'S REAR DOOR.

SINCE HER BEDROOM IS NEAR THE KITCHEN, IT IS EASY FOR HER TO MIX THE CONCOCTION HERSELF.

AS 1856 DRAWS TO A CLOSE, MADELEINE FINDS HER LIFE OF DECEPTION EVER MORE DIFFICULT TO SUSTAIN.

WILLIAM MINNOCH IS A CONSTANT VISITOR IN THE SMITH HOME OVER THE CHRISTMAS HOLIDAYS.

MR. AND MRS. SMITH ASSUME THAT AN OFFER OF MARRIAGE WILL BE SOON FORTHCOMING.

YET MADELEINE CONTINUES TO WRITE EMILE IN THE MOST PASSIONATE OF TERMS...

"EMILE, I FEEL SAD TONIGHT, AND WHY I CANNOT TELL. IF I WERE WITH YOU, I WOULD BE ALL RIGHT. BUT I FEEL READY TO WEEP AND SIGH ..."

AND REMAINS SENSITIVE TO HIS SCOLDINGS.

"SWEET PEA, I KNOW YOUR LOVE FOR ME IS GREAT WHEN I AM GOOD — BUT YOU ARE COOL WHEN I AM BAD, AND THEN I TRY TO DROWN MY BAD THOUGHTS IN BEING CARELESS."

SHE STILL CLOSES HER LETTERS:

"ADIEU, MY DEAR EMILE. BELIEVE ME, THINE EVER TRUE, DEVOTED, AFFECTIONATE WIFE, MIMI L'ANGLIER."

HOW THE WEARY SWAIN MUST READ AND RE-READ THESE MISSIVES IN THE ISOLATION OF HIS TINY ROOM, SQUEEZING THE LAST DROP OF MEANING FROM EVERY WORD.

PART IV

AN ATTACHMENT
SEVERED

"IF A MISUNDERSTANDING
HAPPENS, IT SHOULD BE
REMOVED BY THE LADY."

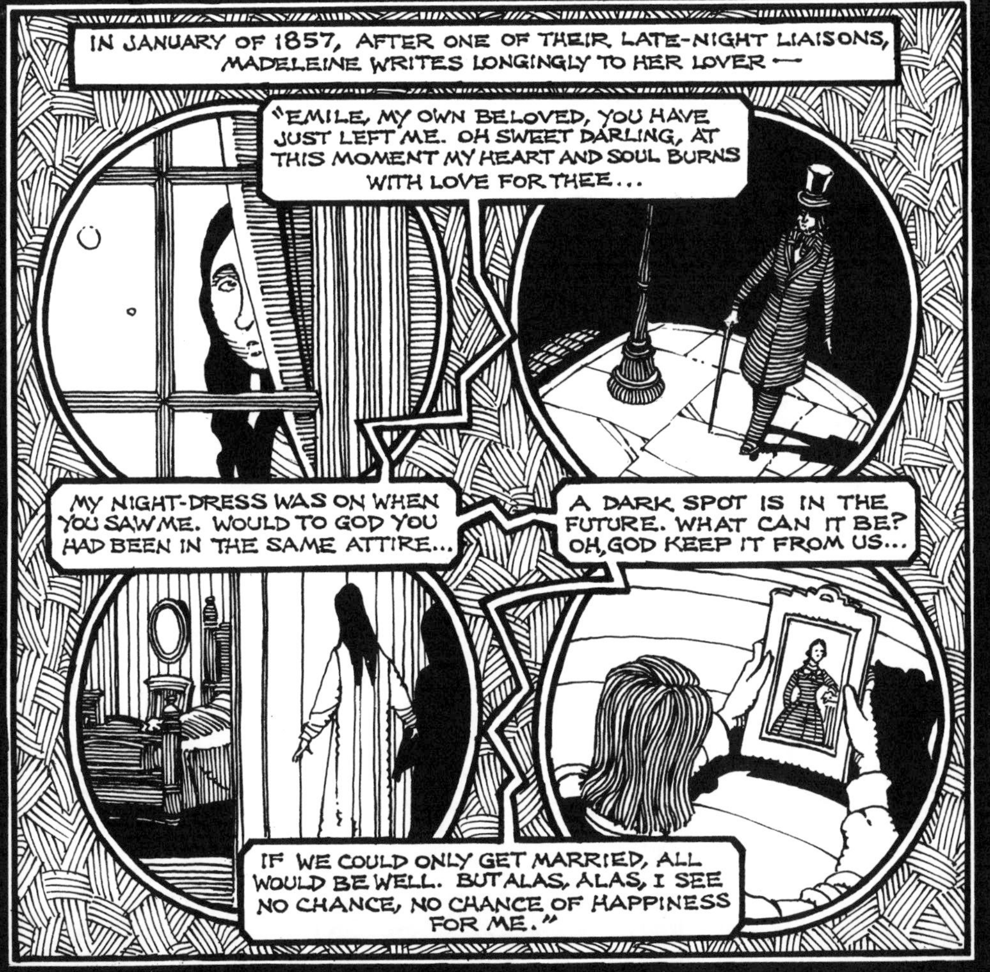
IN JANUARY OF 1857, AFTER ONE OF THEIR LATE-NIGHT LIAISONS, MADELEINE WRITES LONGINGLY TO HER LOVER —
"EMILE, MY OWN BELOVED, YOU HAVE JUST LEFT ME. OH SWEET DARLING, AT THIS MOMENT MY HEART AND SOUL BURNS WITH LOVE FOR THEE...
MY NIGHT-DRESS WAS ON WHEN YOU SAW ME. WOULD TO GOD YOU HAD BEEN IN THE SAME ATTIRE...
A DARK SPOT IS IN THE FUTURE. WHAT CAN IT BE? OH, GOD KEEP IT FROM US...
IF WE COULD ONLY GET MARRIED, ALL WOULD BE WELL. BUT ALAS, ALAS, I SEE NO CHANCE, NO CHANCE OF HAPPINESS FOR ME."

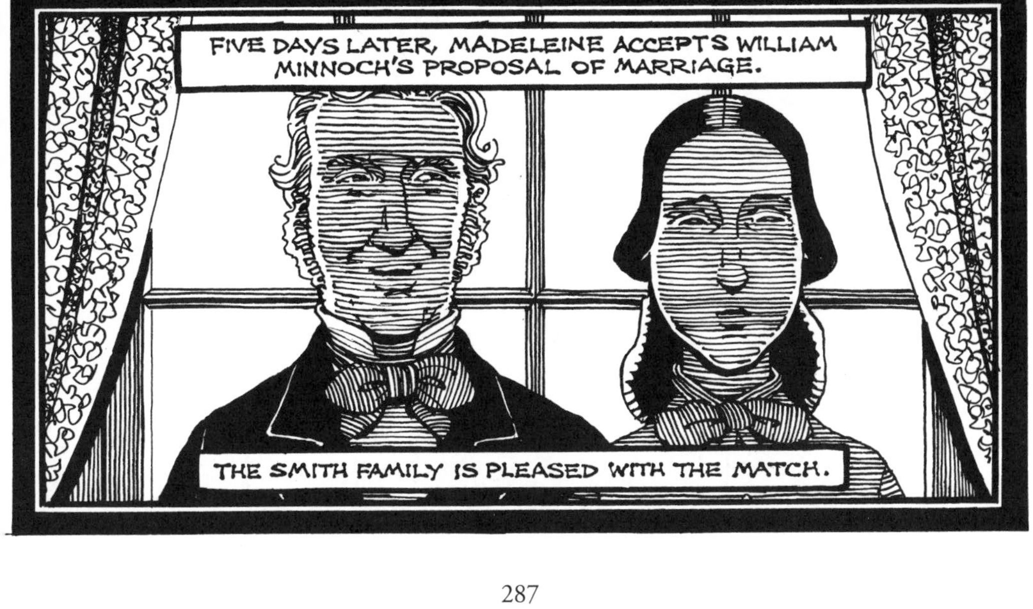
FIVE DAYS LATER, MADELEINE ACCEPTS WILLIAM MINNOCH'S PROPOSAL OF MARRIAGE.
THE SMITH FAMILY IS PLEASED WITH THE MATCH.

IN FEBRUARY, AS SHE FEELS HER SITUATION CLOSING IN UPON HER, MADELEINE ATTEMPTS TO TAKE ACTION. THE OPPORTUNITY ARRIVES WHEN EMILE, IN A PIQUE, RETURNS ONE OF HER LETTERS, AND SHE WRITES:

"WHEN YOU ARE NOT PLEASED WITH THE LETTERS I SEND YOU, THEN OUR CORRESPONDENCE SHALL BE AT AN END, AND AS THERE IS A COOLNESS ON BOTH SIDES, OUR ENGAGEMENT HAD BETTER BE BROKEN...

MY LOVE FOR YOU HAS CEASED...

I TRUST TO YOUR HONOR AS A GENTLEMAN THAT YOU WILL NOT REVEAL ANYTHING THAT MAY HAVE PASSED BETWEEN US. I SHALL FEEL OBLIGED BY YOUR BRINGING ME MY LETTERS AND LIKENESS ON THURSDAY EVENING AT 7...

I KNOW YOU WILL NEVER INJURE THE CHARACTER OF ONE YOU SO FONDLY LOVED."

BUT EMILE HAS NO INTENTION OF RETURNING HER CORRESPONDENCE.

HE STILL REGARDS MADELEINE AS HIS WIFE.

IN FACT, HIS HONOR AS A GENTLEMAN DICTATES THAT HE SHOW THE LETTERS TO HER FATHER AS PROOF OF THEIR UNION.

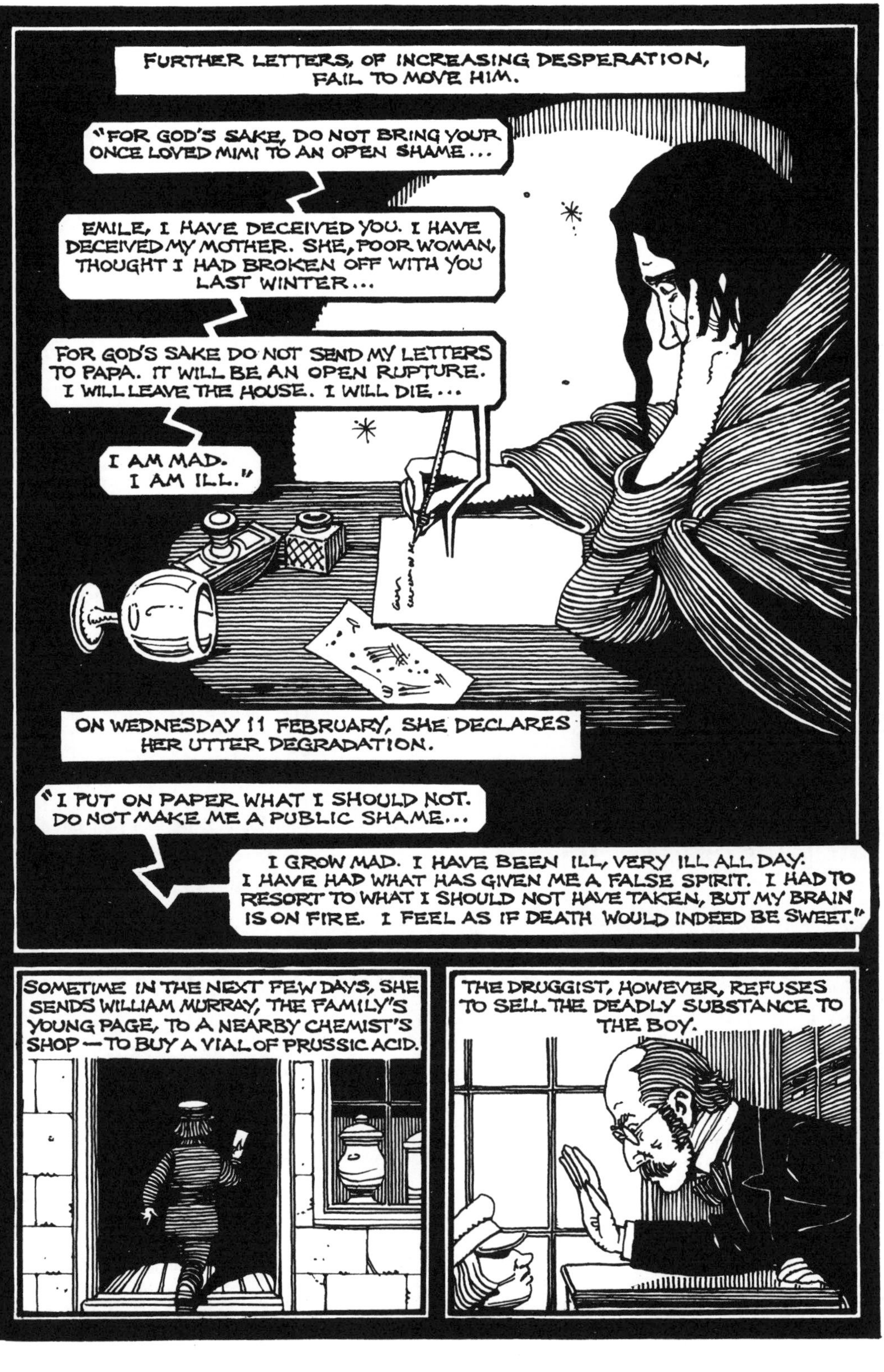
FURTHER LETTERS, OF INCREASING DESPERATION, FAIL TO MOVE HIM.
"FOR GOD'S SAKE, DO NOT BRING YOUR ONCE LOVED MIMI TO AN OPEN SHAME...
EMILE, I HAVE DECEIVED YOU. I HAVE DECEIVED MY MOTHER. SHE, POOR WOMAN, THOUGHT I HAD BROKEN OFF WITH YOU LAST WINTER...
FOR GOD'S SAKE DO NOT SEND MY LETTERS TO PAPA. IT WILL BE AN OPEN RUPTURE. I WILL LEAVE THE HOUSE. I WILL DIE...
I AM MAD. I AM ILL."
ON WEDNESDAY 11 FEBRUARY, SHE DECLARES HER UTTER DEGRADATION.
"I PUT ON PAPER WHAT I SHOULD NOT. DO NOT MAKE ME A PUBLIC SHAME...
I GROW MAD. I HAVE BEEN ILL, VERY ILL ALL DAY. I HAVE HAD WHAT HAS GIVEN ME A FALSE SPIRIT. I HAD TO RESORT TO WHAT I SHOULD NOT HAVE TAKEN, BUT MY BRAIN IS ON FIRE. I FEEL AS IF DEATH WOULD INDEED BE SWEET."
SOMETIME IN THE NEXT FEW DAYS, SHE SENDS WILLIAM MURRAY, THE FAMILY'S YOUNG PAGE, TO A NEARBY CHEMIST'S SHOP—TO BUY A VIAL OF PRUSSIC ACID.
THE DRUGGIST, HOWEVER, REFUSES TO SELL THE DEADLY SUBSTANCE TO THE BOY.

ALSO ON 11 FEBRUARY, FOR REASONS UNKNOWN, EMILE L'ANGLIER BEGINS TO KEEP A JOURNAL.

HE RECORDS THAT HE AND "MIMI" MEET ON THE 11TH, AND AGAIN ON 13 FEBRUARY.

APPARENTLY SOME KIND OF RECONCILIATION IS EFFECTED BETWEEN THEM...

OR HAS MADELEINE MERELY DECIDED TO TAKE A DIFFERENT APPROACH TO HER PROBLEM?

IT IS SUBSEQUENT TO ONE OF THESE VISITS THAT EMILE REPORTS THE FIRST ATTACK OF A MYSTERIOUS STOMACH AILMENT.

MRS. JENKINS FINDS HIM IN AGONY, HAVING VOMITED A DARK BILE.

THURSDAY 19 FEBRUARY: AFTER SEEING MADELEINE FOR "A FEW MOMENTS" DURING THE DAY, EMILE AGAIN FALLS VIOLENTLY ILL IN THE NIGHT...

WHILE THE LADY AND HER NEW FIANCE ATTEND A PERFORMANCE OF THE OPERA "LUCREZIA BORGIA."

SATURDAY 21 FEBRUARY 1857
MADELEINE ENTERS THE MURDOCH BROS. APOTHECARY ON SAUCHIEHALL STREET TO PURCHASE A SIXPENCE WORTH OF ARSENIC POWDER.

SHE REQUIRES IT, SHE SAYS, FOR RIDDING THE GARDEN AT HER COUNTRY HOME OF PESTS AND VERMIN.

SHE DULY SIGNS HER NAME TO THE "POISON BOOK," AS REQUIRED BY LAW.

ALSO REQUIRED BY LAW: ARSENIC IS NOT TO BE SOLD IN ITS PURE WHITE FORM. IT MUST BE MIXED WITH A COLORING AGENT LIKE SOOT OR INDIGO — TO PREVENT ITS BEING MISTAKEN FOR COMMON SALT OR SUGAR.

SUNDAY 22 FEBRUARY
EMILE RECORDS IN HIS JOURNAL A MEETING WITH HIS LOVE IN THE DRAWING ROOM AT BLYTHESWOOD SQUARE.

AT NIGHT HE IS AGAIN STRICKEN BY THE MYSTERIOUS STOMACH ILLNESS...
CHILLS! FEVER! VOMITING!

HIS FRIEND AND FELLOW LODGER AMADEE THAU SENDS FOR DOCTOR THOMSON, WHO PRESCRIBES SOME SOOTHING STOMACH POWDERS.

MONDAY 2 MARCH
AFTER A WEEK IN BED, EMILE FEELS RECOVERED ENOUGH TO TAKE TEA AT THE HOME OF MISS MARY PERRY.

SHE REMARKS UPON HOW SICK HE STILL LOOKS.

I NEVER EXPECTED TO SEE YOU AGAIN, I WAS SO ILL.

I BELIEVE IT WAS FROM A CUP OF CHOCOLATE I TOOK FROM MISS SMITH.

MONDAY 9 MARCH
ONE WEEK LATER, HE OFFERS MISS PERRY FURTHER CONFIDENCES.

IT IS A PERFECT FASCINATION, MY ATTRACTION TO THAT GIRL. IF SHE WERE TO POISON ME, I WOULD FORGIVE HER.

BUT WHAT MOTIVE WOULD SHE HAVE FOR GIVING YOU ANYTHING TO HURT YOU?

PERHAPS SHE MIGHT NOT BE SORRY TO BE RID OF ME.

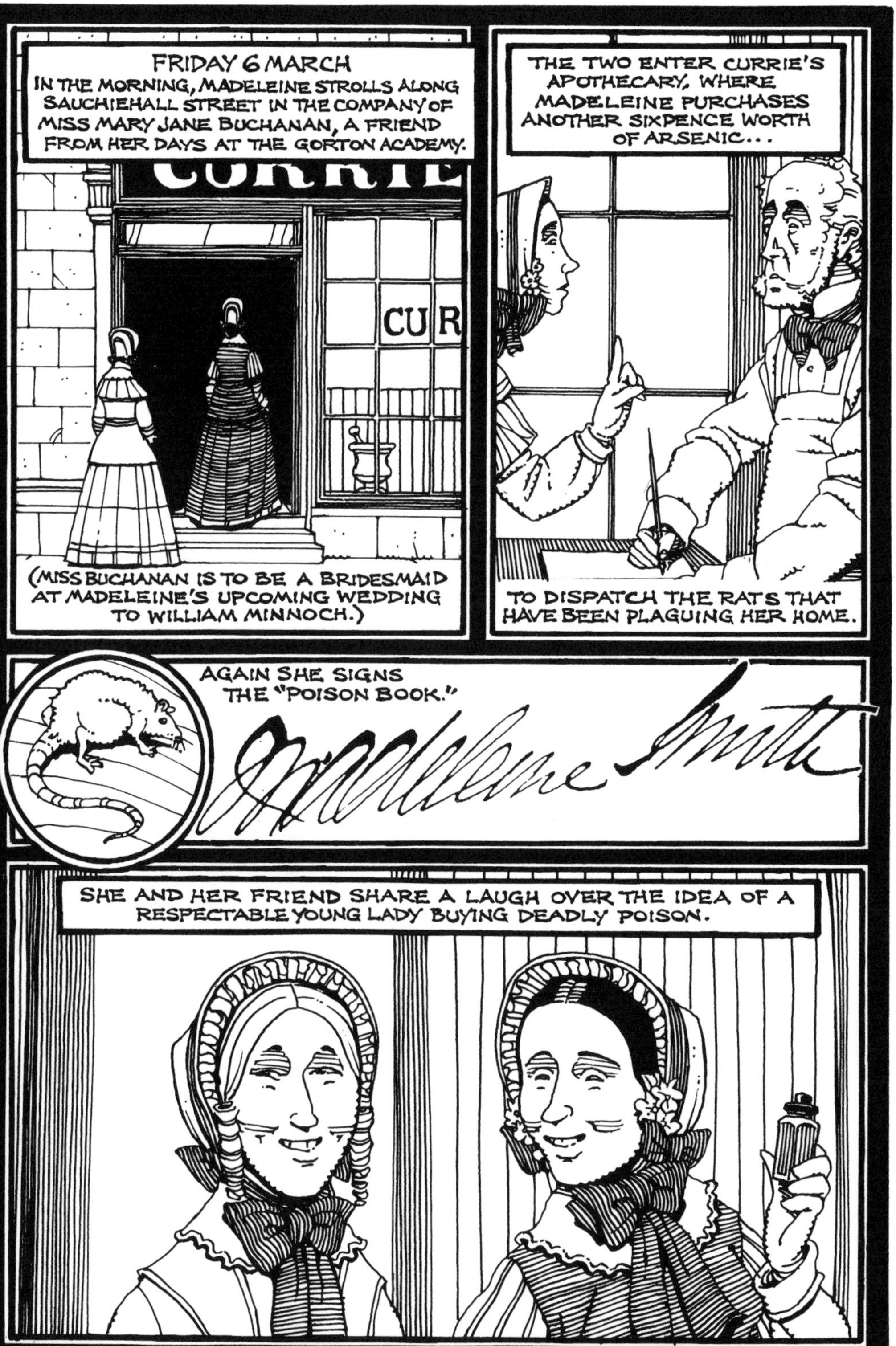
FRIDAY 6 MARCH
IN THE MORNING, MADELEINE STROLLS ALONG SAUCHIEHALL STREET IN THE COMPANY OF MISS MARY JANE BUCHANAN, A FRIEND FROM HER DAYS AT THE GORTON ACADEMY.
CURRIE
CUR
(MISS BUCHANAN IS TO BE A BRIDESMAID AT MADELEINE'S UPCOMING WEDDING TO WILLIAM MINNOCH.)
THE TWO ENTER CURRIE'S APOTHECARY, WHERE MADELEINE PURCHASES ANOTHER SIXPENCE WORTH OF ARSENIC...
TO DISPATCH THE RATS THAT HAVE BEEN PLAGUING HER HOME.
AGAIN SHE SIGNS THE "POISON BOOK."
Madeleine Smith
SHE AND HER FRIEND SHARE A LAUGH OVER THE IDEA OF A RESPECTABLE YOUNG LADY BUYING DEADLY POISON.

IN THE AFTERNOON, MADELEINE DEPARTS, WITH HER MOTHER AND SISTERS FOR A HOLIDAY IN THE SPA TOWN OF BRIDGE OF ALLAN.

BRIDGE OF ALLAN

R. FORTH

SHE HAS WARNED EMILE NOT TO FOLLOW HER THERE, FOR THEY WOULD HAVE NO OPPORTUNITY TO MEET (WHILE NEGLECTING TO MENTION THAT WILLIAM MINNOCH WILL BE IN ATTENDANCE).

GLASGOW

AT BRIDGE OF ALLAN, THE COUPLE SETS THEIR WEDDING FOR 18 JUNE.

TUESDAY 10 MARCH
ON THIS DAY, EMILE LEAVES FOR A WEEK'S STAY IN EDINBURGH.

HE TAKES DINNER ONE EVENING IN THE HOME OF MRS. TOWERS, THE MARRIED SISTER OF MISS PERRY.

MR. AND MRS. TOWERS MARK THE WEAKNESS OF HIS DEMEANOR.

HE TALKS ABOUT HIS RECENT BOUTS OF ILL HEALTH.

TUESDAY, 17 MARCH
ON THE SAME DAY, MADELEINE AND EMILE RETURN TO GLASGOW.

WEDNESDAY 18 MARCH

MADELEINE ONCE AGAIN VISITS CURRIE'S APOTHECARY FOR A SIXPENCE WORTH OF ARSENIC POWDER.

SHE REPORTS THAT IT HAS BEEN MOST EFFECTIVE IN KILLING THE RATS THAT INVADE HER HOME.

SHE THEN WRITES EMILE TO ARRANGE A MEETING FOR THE FOLLOWING NIGHT.

POST

THURSDAY 19 MARCH

UNBEKNOWNST TO MADELEINE, EMILE DEPARTS FOR BRIDGE OF ALLAN...

NO DOUBT IN AN ATTEMPT TO ACHIEVE A COMPLETE RECOVERY FROM HIS LINGERING ILLNESS.

MADELEINE'S LETTER HAS BEEN FORWARDED TO HIS HOTEL — BUT IT ARRIVES TOO LATE FOR HIM TO ARRANGE A RETURN TRIP TO — GLASGOW.

FRIDAY 20 MARCH

EMILE WRITES TO MARY PERRY —

"I FEEL MUCH BETTER. AND I HOPE TO BE HOME THE MIDDLE OF NEXT WEEK...

I SHOULD HAVE COME TO SEE SOMEONE LAST NIGHT, BUT THE LETTER CAME TOO LATE, SO WE ARE BOTH DISAPPOINTED."

ON THE SAME DAY, MADELEINE, WHO BELIEVES EMILE TO BE IN GLASGOW, IS PUZZLED TO HAVE RECEIVED NO REPLY.

"I SHALL WAIT AGAIN TOMORROW NIGHT..."

SHE WRITES ANOTHER LETTER, THIS ONE MORE PLAINTIVE.

SATURDAY 21 MARCH
THE LETTER ARRIVES AT EMILE'S ROOMING HOUSE.

AMADEE THUAU SENDS IT AHEAD TO BRIDGE OF ALLAN.

SUNDAY 22 MARCH
THIS MORNING, EMILE RECEIVES THE SECOND LETTER.

(THIS IS THE FATAL MISSIVE FOUND IN HIS COAT POCKET AFTER HIS DEATH.)

THE URGENCY OF ITS TONE STIRS HIM TO IMMEDIATE ACTION.

IN THE AFTERNOON, HE WALKS TO THE TOWN OF STERLING AND CATCHES THE FIRST TRAIN BACK TO GLASGOW.

HE GETS OFF AT THE NEAREST STATION, IN THE TOWN OF COATBRIDGE.

COAT

HERE, HE CONSUMES A DINNER OF BEEF...

AND, IN THE COMPANY OF ANOTHER TRAVELLER, HE WALKS THE EIGHT MILES TO HIS HOME, COVERING THE DISTANCE IN ABOUT TWO HOURS.

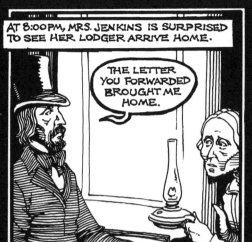

AT 8:00 PM, MRS. JENKINS IS SURPRISED TO SEE HER LODGER ARRIVE HOME.

THE LETTER YOU FORWARDED BROUGHT ME HOME.

AT ABOUT 9:00 PM, HE GOES OUT AGAIN, INFORMING THE LADY THAT HE MAY NOT RETURN UNTIL QUITE LATE.

AT THIS SAME HOUR, THE SMITH FAMILY AND THEIR SERVANTS GATHER IN THE DRAWING ROOM FOR THEIR REGULAR EVENING PRAYERS.

SHORTLY THEREAFTER, MADELEINE AND JANET RETIRE TO THEIR BASEMENT BEDROOM.

AT 9:20, EMILE ATTEMPTS TO CALL UPON A FRIEND AT A LODGING HOUSE OFF ST. VINCENT ST.

BUT HE IS INFORMED THAT THE MAN IS NOT AT HOME.

HE IS LATER SEEN BY AN ACQUAINTANCE WALKING ALONG SAUCHIEHALL STREET, IN THE DIRECTION OF BLYTHESWOOD SQUARE.

THE MOVEMENTS OF EMILE L'ANGLIER ARE UNACCOUNTED FOR DURING THE NEXT SEVERAL HOURS.

AT 2:30 AM, AS WE HAVE SEEN, HE RETURNS TO HIS LODGINGS IN A STATE OF AGONY.

PART V

THE TRIAL OF MADELEINE SMITH

"AN UNTRAINED NATURE,
FOSTERED BY OVER-INDULGENCE
AT HOME, WILL RIPEN INTO A
DANGEROUS ADULTHOOD."

TUESDAY 31 MARCH 1857

ON THE DAY OF HER ARREST, MADELEINE SMITH GIVES A STATEMENT TO POLICE. IT WILL BE ALL THE WORDS SHE EVER HAS TO SAY ABOUT HER CASE.

SHE CONFIRMS THAT SHE CARRIED ON A ROMANCE WITH EMILE L'ANGLIER. INDEED, THEY ONCE PLANNED TO BE MARRIED. HOWEVER, BECAUSE OF HIS CONTINUING ILL-HEALTH, SHE DID NOT SEE HIM FOR AT LEAST THREE WEEKS BEFORE HIS DEATH.

SHE AND THE DECEASED WERE IN THE HABIT OF EXCHANGING "NOTES."

SHE URGED A MEETING ON THAT FINAL WEEKEND IN ORDER TO INFORM HIM OF HER ENGAGEMENT TO WILLIAM MINNOCH.

BUT SHE EXPECTED HIM ON SATURDAY NIGHT, NOT AWARE THAT HE WAS AT BRIDGE OF ALLAN. HER LETTER'S DELAY IN REACHING HIM BROUGHT HIM BACK ON SUNDAY INSTEAD.

IN ANY CASE, SHE DID NOT SEE HIM ON EITHER EVENING.

YES, SHE PURCHASED ARSENIC ON THREE RECENT OCCASIONS. SHE USES IT AS A COSMETIC, IN DILUTED FORM, ON HER FACE, NECK AND ARMS...

(A PROCEDURE SHE LEARNED FROM A FELLOW STUDENT AT MRS. GORTON'S ACADEMY).

SHE ONCE OR TWICE GAVE EMILE A CUP OF COCOA THROUGH THE BARS OF HER BASEMENT WINDOW.

BUT OF COURSE SHE NEVER SERVED HIM POISON!

MADELEINE IS CHARGED WITH ONE COUNT OF MURDER AND TWO OF ATTEMPTED MURDER.

MADELEINE RESIDES IN A CELL IN GLASGOW'S NORTH PRISON FOR THE MONTHS PRECEEDING HER TRIAL...

WHILE THE CITY'S NEWSPAPERS STIR THE PUBLIC INTO A STATE OF EXCITEMENT.

AS A CONSEQUENCE, THE TRIAL'S LOCATION IS SHIFTED TO EDINBURGH.

GLASGOW

EDINBURGH

THURSDAY 30 JUNE 1857
THE TRIAL OPENS AT THE HIGH COURT OF THE JUSTICIARY.

THE STREETS ARE THRONGED WITH CURIOUS CITIZENS...

THE COURTROOM IS FILLED BEYOND CAPACITY.

AND AN ARMY OF THE INTERNATIONAL PRESS.

PRESIDING IS A THREE-JUDGE PANEL:

LORD IVORY

LORD HOPE
(THE LORD JUSTICE CLERK)

LORD HANDYSIDE.

PRESENTING THE CASE FOR THE CROWN IS THE LORD ADVOCATE JAMES MONCRIEFF.

THE DEFENSE (HIRED BY JAMES SMITH) CONSISTS OF THE DEAN OF FACULTY, JOHN INGLIS, AND TWO ADVOCATES.

CONSPICUOUSLY ABSENT FROM THE COURTROOM ARE MADELEINE'S PARENTS, WHO REMAIN IN SECLUSION IN GLASGOW.

ON HAND, HOWEVER, IS HER EVER-SUPPORTIVE YOUNGER BROTHER JACK.

ALL EYES ARE UPON THE DEFENDANT AS SHE ASCENDS INTO THE CHAMBER.

MANY REMARK UPON MADELEINE'S UTTER COMPOSURE AND CALM DURING THE ENTIRE PROCEEDING.

TO SOME, IT IS INDICATIVE OF HER INNER DIGNITY, REFINEMENT AND RESIGNATION.

TO OTHERS, IT IS EVIDENCE OF A "FOXLIKE," CUNNING AND DECEITFUL NATURE.

THE ENTIRE PUBLIC, IN FACT, IS DIVIDED ABOUT MADELEINE SMITH:

TO THE UPPER CLASSES, SHE IS THE TRUE VICTIM: OF L'ANGLIER, THE VILE SEDUCER, BLACKMAILER, MANIPULATOR AND SOCIAL PRETENDER — NOT TO MENTION A "FRENCHMAN."

IF SHE POISONED HIM, IT WAS NO MORE THAN HE DESERVED.

OTHERS BELIEVE THAT HE MOST LIKELY DID AWAY WITH HIMSELF.

HADN'T HE A HISTORY OF FAILED LOVE AFFAIRS AND SUICIDAL EPISODES?

THE COMMON MASSES, HOWEVER, KNOW THAT NO YOUNG LADY OF WEALTH AND POSITION WOULD HESITATE TO RID HERSELF OF AN INCONVENIENT SUITOR....

AND THAT SHE WILL MOST LIKELY GET AWAY WITH IT.

NEVERTHELESS, AN UNBIASED JURY OF FIFTEEN GOOD CITIZENS IS IMPANELED WITH RELATIVE EASE.

THREE FARMERS, ONE MERCHANT, A BOOTMAKER, A CURRIER, A TEACHER, A CLERK, A CABINET-MAKER, A CATTLE-FEEDER, A SHOE-MAKER, AND FOUR GENTLEMEN.

• THE CASE FOR THE CROWN •
AMONG THOSE CALLED TO TESTIFY:

THE MAN WHO ACCOMPANIED EMILE ON HIS WALK FROM COATBRIDGE TO GLASGOW:

HE SWEARS THAT THE DECEASED HAD NO OPPORTUNITY TO PURCHASE ARSENIC DURING THAT TIME.

A CHEMIST TESTIFIES AS TO THE EXTREME DIFFICULTY OF ADMINISTERING SUCH A LARGE DOSE OF THE POISON ACCIDENTALLY...

ALSO AS TO THE DANGER AND FOLLY OF USING ARSENIC AS A COSMETIC.

THE HOUSEMAID CHRISTINA HAGGART TELLS OF THE MANY MEETINGS BETWEEN THE DEFENDANT AND THE DECEASED...

(ALTHOUGH SHE DID NOT SEE HIM ON THE FATAL SUNDAY NIGHT.)

LANDLADY MRS. JENKINS TESTIFIES AS TO THE NUMBER AND SEVERITY OF HER LODGER'S ILLNESSES.

SHE HAD BEEN BOTH ALARMED AND MYSTIFIED.

MISS MARY PERRY DELIVERS ESPECIALLY DAMAGING TESTIMONY:

MR. L'ANGLIER HAD CONFIDED TO HER HIS SUSPICION THAT MISS SMITH WAS TRYING TO POISON HIM.

THE DEFENDANT'S FIANCE, WILLIAM MINNOCH SAYS HE NEVER KNEW OF THE EXISTENCE OF THE MAN.

(AFTER HE LEAVES THE COURTROOM, HE AND MADELEINE WILL NEVER SEE EACH OTHER AGAIN.)

"I DID NOT EXPECT THE PLEASURE OF SEEING YOU LAST EVENING — OF BEING FONDLED BY YOU..."

THE HIGHLIGHT OF THE CROWN'S CASE COMES ON THE FIFTH DAY, WHEN THE DEFENDANT'S LETTERS ARE READ INTO THE RECORD.
(OF THE 198 LETTERS RECOVERED, PARTS OF JUST 60 ARE DEEMED RELEVANT.)

EVEN SO, THE COURTROOM IS AGHAST.

THE PRESS, IN ITS TURN, BROADCASTS THE EXCERPTS TO AN INSATIABLE PUBLIC.

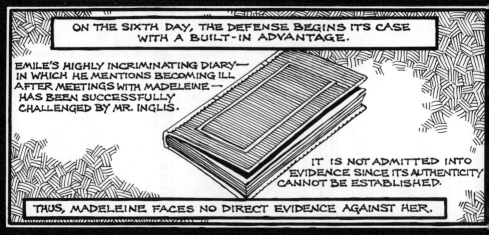

ON THE SIXTH DAY, THE DEFENSE BEGINS ITS CASE WITH A BUILT-IN ADVANTAGE.

EMILE'S HIGHLY INCRIMINATING DIARY— IN WHICH HE MENTIONS BECOMING ILL AFTER MEETINGS WITH MADELEINE— HAS BEEN SUCCESSFULLY CHALLENGED BY MR. INGLIS.

IT IS NOT ADMITTED INTO EVIDENCE SINCE ITS AUTHENTICITY CANNOT BE ESTABLISHED.

THUS, MADELEINE FACES NO DIRECT EVIDENCE AGAINST HER.

IN LIEU OF HER PERSONAL TESTIMONY, THE DEFENDANT'S STATEMENT OF 31 MARCH IS READ TO THE COURT.

SEVERAL ACQUAINTANCES OF EMILE'S TESTIFY AS TO HIS SENSITIVITY AND FRAGILITY WHERE LADIES ARE CONCERNED...

ALSO AS TO HIS THREATS OF SUICIDE OVER THE YEARS.

THREE DIFFERENT CHEMISTS, WITH SHOPS ALONG THE ROAD FROM COATBRIDGE TO GLASGOW...

DECLARE THAT THEY SOLD DRUGS ON 22 MARCH TO A MAN WHO LOOKED LIKE THE DECEASED.

ANOTHER SHOPKEEPER TESTIFIES THAT HE KEEPS HIS SUPPLY OF ARSENIC UNGUARDED AND IN PLAIN SIGHT DURING THE DAY...

THUS THE DECEASED COULD HAVE PILFERED A SMALL AMOUNT AT ANY TIME.

REPRESENTATIVES OF TWO PERIODICALS DESCRIBE CERTAIN SOCIETIES IN EASTERN EUROPE THAT USE ARSENIC...

TO MAINTAIN A "BLOOMING COMPLEXION AND THE APPEARANCE OF EXUBERANT HEALTH."

FINALLY, MADELEINE'S SISTER JANET GIVES TESTIMONY THAT MADELEINE FELL ASLEEP BESIDE HER ON SUNDAY, 22 MARCH...

AND AWOKE BESIDE HER THE NEXT MORNING.

DURING THE TIME OF HER TRIAL, MADELEINE REMAINS IMPRISONED IN EDINBURGH'S EAST JAIL.

LETTERS FROM PROSPECTIVE SUITORS AND EVEN PROPOSALS OF MARRIAGE ARRIVE DAILY.

NEWSPAPERS CHRONICLE SUCH DETAILS AS HER HEARTY BREAKFAST: COFFEE, ROLLS AND A MUTTON CHOP.

AT THE COURTHOUSE, PEOPLE PAY AS MUCH AS A GUINEA FOR A BRIEF GLIMPSE OF HER.

TUESDAY 7 JULY

MR. MONCRIEFF GIVES THE CROWN'S SUMMATION: TO HIS MIND, THE DEFENDANT'S LETTERS, ALONG WITH HER RECORDED PURCHASES OF ARSENIC, ARE ENOUGH TO OVERCOME ALL ARGUMENT.

I SEE NO OUTLET FOR THIS UNHAPPY PRISONER, AND IF YOU COME TO THE SAME RESULT AS I HAVE DONE, THERE IS BUT ONE COURSE OPEN TO YOU, AND THAT IS TO RETURN A VERDICT OF GUILTY.

WEDNESDAY 8 JULY

MR. INGLIS DELIVERS A RINGING DEFENSE SUMMATION THAT HOLDS THE COURTROOM RAPT. TO HIM, MADELEINE'S INNOCENCE HANGS UPON JUST THREE POINTS:

▶ FIRST: EMILE L'ANGLIER WAS AN UNBALANCED SEDUCER, WITH A HISTORY OF SUICIDAL EPISODES.
▶ SECOND: THERE IS NO EVIDENCE THAT MADELEINE SAW EMILE AFTER ANY OF HER THREE PURCHASES OF ARSENIC.
▶ THIRD: IF HER OBJECT WAS TO PREVENT HER LETTERS FROM BEING KNOWN TO HER FAMILY, KILLING HER LOVER WOULD GUARANTEE THAT THEY BE FOUND.

THE TIME MAY COME — IT CERTAINLY WILL COME — PERHAPS NOT BEFORE THE GREAT DAY IN WHICH THE SECRETS OF ALL HEARTS SHALL BE REVEALED — AND YET IT MAY BE THAT IN THIS WORLD, AND DURING OUR OWN LIFETIME, THE SECRET OF THIS EXTRAORDINARY STORY MAY BE BROUGHT TO LIGHT.

MAY THE SPIRIT OF TRUTH GUIDE YOU TO AN HONEST, A JUST AND A TRUE VERDICT.

WHEN HE FINISHES, THE SPECTATORS IN THE COURTROOM BURST INTO APPLAUSE.

307

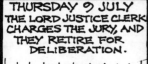

THURSDAY 9 JULY THE LORD JUSTICE CLERK CHARGES THE JURY, AND THEY RETIRE FOR DELIBERATION.

AFTER A MERE TWENTY-TWO MINUTES, ALL CONCERNED ARE SURPRISED WHEN IT IS ANNOUNCED THAT A VERDICT HAS BEEN REACHED.

ON THE FIRST COUNT OF ATTEMPTED MURDER: NOT GUILTY

ON THE SECOND COUNT OF ATTEMPTED MURDER AND THE CHARGE OF MURDER: THE PECULIARLY SCOTTISH VERDICT OF NOT PROVEN

THOUGH DOUBT MAY EXIST AS TO HER INNOCENCE, SHE IS FREE TO GO.

THE COURTROOM—AND THE STREET OUTSIDE—ERUPT IN WILD CHEERS AND HUZZAHS.

THE NOT-QUITE-EXONERATED LADY, IN THE COMPANY OF HER BROTHER, DEPARTS THE COURTHOUSE AND THE CITY OF EDINBURGH.

WHAT LIFE AWAITS HER?

PART VI

THE REST OF HER LIFE

"TO HAVE A BEAUTIFUL
HOME . . . IS A PLEASANT
DREAM AND A WORTHY
AMBITION."

IN THE WEEKS FOLLOWING HER TRIAL MADELEINE TRIES TO KEEP FROM THE PUBLIC'S EYE.

BUT IN GLASGOW, THIS IS DIFFICULT.

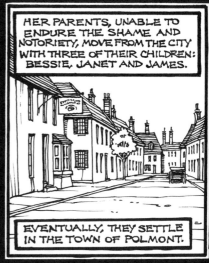

HER PARENTS, UNABLE TO ENDURE THE SHAME AND NOTORIETY, MOVE FROM THE CITY WITH THREE OF THEIR CHILDREN: BESSIE, JANET AND JAMES.

EVENTUALLY, THEY SETTLE IN THE TOWN OF POLMONT.

MR. SMITH CONTINUES IN HIS PRACTICE, WHILE MRS. SMITH REMAINS CONFINED TO HER BED.

THE DAUGHTERS BESSIE AND JANET WILL NEVER MARRY.

RUMOR HAS IT THAT MADELEINE HAS EMIGRATED TO CANADA OR AUSTRALIA.

IN FACT, SHE HAS MOVED TO LONDON WITH HER BROTHER JACK.

THEY RESIDE IN A FLAT ON SLOANE STREET.

MADELEINE NOW GOES BY HER CHILDHOOD NAME OF LENA.

SHE OCCUPIES HER TIME BY TAKING CLASSES IN WATERCOLOR.

HERE SHE ATTRACTS THE NOTICE OF HER TEACHER, GEORGE WARDLE...

WHO IS ALSO A DRAFTSMAN AND THE BUSINESS MANAGER FOR THE DESIGNER WILLIAM MORRIS,

WM. MORRIS

HE COURTS HER ARDENTLY, AND, IN TIME, SHE REVEALS TO HIM HER NOTORIOUS PAST.

BUT HE IS UNCONCERNED.

4 JULY 1861
THEY ARE UNITED IN WEDLOCK AT ST. PAUL'S CHURCH IN KNIGHTSBRIDGE.

THE BRIDE'S FATHER TRAVELS FROM SCOTLAND TO ATTEND THE CEREMONY.

THE WARDLES PRODUCE TWO OFFSPRING:

MARY ("KITTEN"), BORN IN 1863, THOMAS, BORN IN 1864.

FROM THEIR HOME IN THE PARRISH OF BLOOMSBURY, MR. AND MRS. WARDLE BECOME PART OF LONDON'S CULTURAL AND POLITICAL AVANT GARDE.

9 CHARLOTTE STREET.

LENA CONTINUES HER STUDY OF WATERCOLORS, AND ALSO PRODUCES FINE NEEDLEWORK.

THROUGH WILLIAM MORRIS, THEY COME IN CONTACT WITH THE ARTISTIC LUMINARIES OF THE DAY — INCLUDING THE PAINTERS OF THE PRE-RAPHAELITE BROTHERHOOD.

BURNE-JONES

HUNT

MILLAIS

ONE REPORT HAS HER POSING FOR DANTE GABRIEL ROSSETTI.

313

THE WARDLES ARE COMMITTED SOCIALISTS AND MEMBERS OF THE CENTRAL DEMOCRATIC CLUB.

LENA IS THE TREASURER OF A SPLINTER FACTION OF THE SOCIALIST LEAGUE, HEADED BY THE SON-IN-LAW OF KARL MARX.

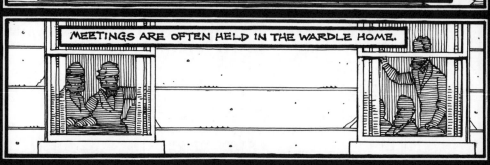

MEETINGS ARE OFTEN HELD IN THE WARDLE HOME.

THE INFAMOUS HISTORY OF THE HOSTESS IS APPARENTLY WELL KNOWN AMONG THE GROUP.

IN FACT, IT IS ALMOST A POINT OF PRIDE.

ONE OF THE MEMBERS, THE YOUNG WRITER GEORGE BERNARD SHAW, WILL LATER REMARK THAT MRS. WARDLE SEEMED "AN ORDINARY, GOOD-HUMOURED, CAPABLE WOMAN, WITH NOTHING SINISTER ABOUT HER."

HE TAKES COFFEE FROM HER, "TO NO ILL EFFECT."

314

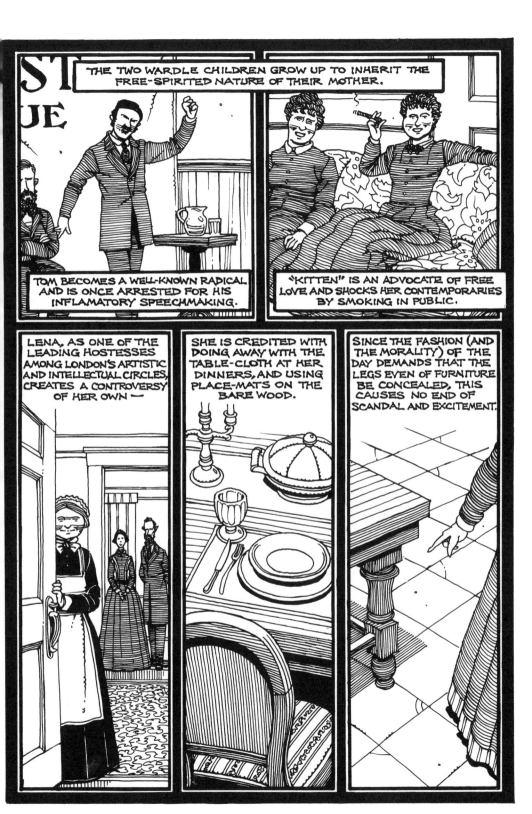

THE TWO WARDLE CHILDREN GROW UP TO INHERIT THE FREE-SPIRITED NATURE OF THEIR MOTHER.

TOM BECOMES A WELL-KNOWN RADICAL AND IS ONCE ARRESTED FOR HIS INFLAMATORY SPEECHMAKING.

"KITTEN" IS AN ADVOCATE OF FREE LOVE AND SHOCKS HER CONTEMPORARIES BY SMOKING IN PUBLIC.

LENA, AS ONE OF THE LEADING HOSTESSES AMONG LONDON'S ARTISTIC AND INTELLECTUAL CIRCLES, CREATES A CONTROVERSY OF HER OWN —

SHE IS CREDITED WITH DOING AWAY WITH THE TABLE-CLOTH AT HER DINNERS, AND USING PLACE-MATS ON THE BARE WOOD.

SINCE THE FASHION (AND THE MORALITY) OF THE DAY DEMANDS THAT THE LEGS EVEN OF FURNITURE BE CONCEALED, THIS CAUSES NO END OF SCANDAL AND EXCITEMENT.

-1889-
AFTER TWENTY-EIGHT YEARS OF MARRIAGE, GEORGE WARDLE RESIGNS FROM WILLIAM MORRIS AND LEAVES HIS WIFE.

NO REASON IS KNOWN FOR THIS, ALTHOUGH IT IS THOUGHT THAT THE MARRIAGE HAS NOT BEEN GOING WELL FOR QUITE SOME TIME.

(CAN HE BE AFRAID OF MEETING THE SAME FATE AS EMILE L'ANGLIER?)

HE SETTLES IN ITALY, AND THE TWO WILL NEVER SEE EACH OTHER AGAIN.

HE WILL DIE THERE IN 1910.

LENA WARDLE NOW LIVES ALONE FOR SEVERAL YEARS. SHE MOVES TO THE TOWN OF LEEK IN STAFFORDSHIRE.

HERE, SHE OCCUPIES A HOUSE LENT HER BY GEORGE'S BROTHER THOMAS.

SHE ACQUIRES A LOCAL REPUTATION AS AN ECCENTRIC RECLUSE, WEARING "AESTHETIC" CLOTHES AND A SHOCKING RED WIG.

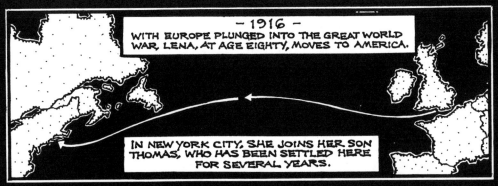

– 1916 –
WITH EUROPE PLUNGED INTO THE GREAT WORLD WAR, LENA, AT AGE EIGHTY, MOVES TO AMERICA.

IN NEW YORK CITY, SHE JOINS HER SON THOMAS, WHO HAS BEEN SETTLED HERE FOR SEVERAL YEARS.

LOOKING MUCH YOUNGER THAN HER YEARS, SHE ATTRACTS THE ATTENTION OF A MAN IN HIS SIXTIES: WILLIAM A. SHEEHY.

THEY MARRY AND SETTLE INTO A QUIET LIFE IN THEIR HOME ON EIGHTH AVENUE.

LENA FINDS, HOWEVER, THAT HER NOTORIOUS PAST IS NOT QUITE BEHIND HER.

ONE STORY HAS REPRESENTATIVES OF A MOVING PICTURE COMPANY ARRIVING AT HER DOOR, REQUESTING HER INVOLVEMENT IN A FILM PRODUCTION OF HER LIFE.

SHE REFUSES, OF COURSE.

AS A FORM OF PERSUASION, THE COMPANY THREATENS TO EXPOSE HER IDENTITY TO THE GOVERNMENT AND HAVE HER DEPORTED.

SHE SENDS THEM ON THEIR WAY, AND THE THREAT COMES TO NOTHING.

IN 1926, LENA'S HUSBAND DIES.

AS SHE LIVES ON ALONE, DOES SHE EVER THINK BACK TO THOSE DAYS OF PASSION AND TRAGEDY IN SCOTLAND.

IF SO, ARE THEY BUT A DREAM?

WHEN SHE DIES, FROM KIDNEY FAILURE, ON 12 APRIL 1928, HER RESIDENCE IS LISTED AS 4298 PARK AVE, NEW YORK CITY.

ALTHOUGH SHE HAS REACHED THE AGE OF NINETY-TWO, THE OFFICIAL DEATH CERTIFICATE GIVES HER AGE AS SIXTY-FOUR.

A FINAL MYSTERY IN THE LIFE OF THIS MOST MYSTERIOUS WOMAN.

TODAY, THE REMAINS OF EMILE L'ANGLIER CONTINUE TO RESIDE AT THE RAMSHORN CHURCHYARD IN GLASGOW.

LENA SHEEHY
DIED APRIL 12, 1928

LENA SHEEHY RESTS BENEATH A SIMPLE MARKER AT MOUNT HOPE CEMETERY, HASTINGS-ON-HUDSON, NEW YORK.

THE MURDER OF ABRAHAM LINCOLN

A CHRONICLE OF 62 DAYS IN THE LIFE OF THE AMERICAN REPUBLIC — MARCH 4 — MAY 4, 1865

WRITTEN AND ILLUSTRATED BY
RICK GEARY

BIBLIOGRAPHY

Bishop, Jim, *The Day Lincoln was Shot.* (New York, Gramercy Books, 1955)

Donald, David Herbert, *Lincoln.* (New York, Simon & Schuster, 1995)

Donovan, Robert J., *The Assasins.* (New York, Popular Library, 1962)

Hanchett, William, *The Lincoln Murder Conspiracies.* (Chicago & Urbana, University of Illinois Press, 1986)

Kunhardt, Dorothy Meserve and Philip B. Kunhardt, Jr., *Twenty Days.* (New York, Castle Books, 1965)

Lewis, Lloyd, *Myths After Lincoln.* (New York, Harcourt, Brace, 1929)

Reck, W. Emerson, A. *Lincoln, His Last 24 Hours.* (Jefferson NC and London, McFarland & Co., Inc, 1987)

Steers, Edward, Jr., *Blood on the Moon.* (Lexington KY, The University Press of Kentucky, 2001)

Stern, Philip Van Doren, *The Man Who Killed Lincoln.* (New York, The Literary Guild of America, Inc, 1939)

Winkler, H. Donald, Lincoln and Booth. (Nashville TN, Cumberland House, 2003)

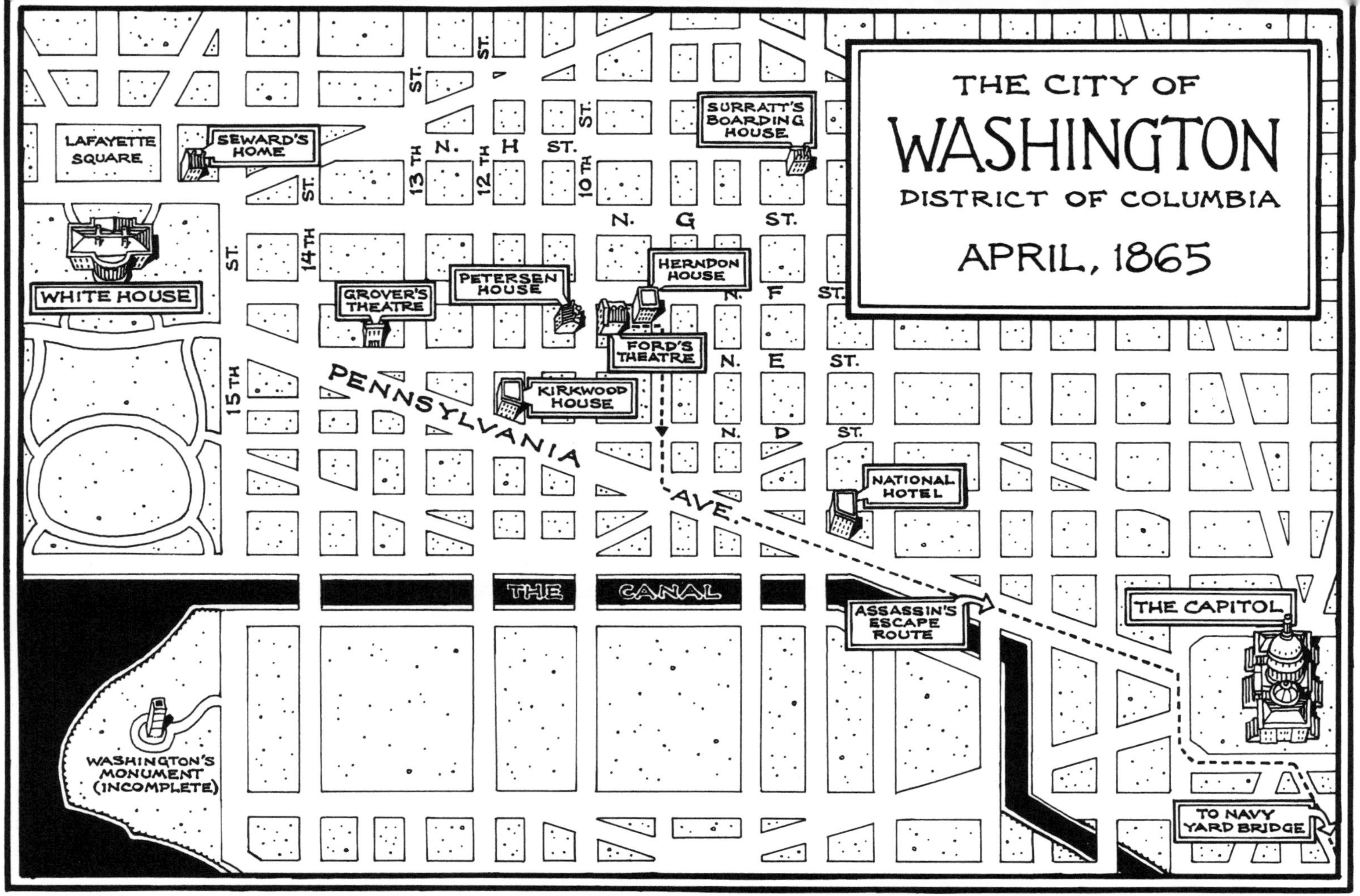
THE CITY OF
WASHINGTON
DISTRICT OF COLUMBIA
APRIL, 1865
LAFAYETTE SQUARE
SEWARD'S HOME
WHITE HOUSE
SURRATT'S BOARDING HOUSE
HERNDON HOUSE
PETERSEN HOUSE
GROVER'S THEATRE
FORD'S THEATRE
KIRKWOOD HOUSE
NATIONAL HOTEL
PENNSYLVANIA AVE.
THE CANAL
ASSASSIN'S ESCAPE ROUTE
THE CAPITOL
TO NAVY YARD BRIDGE
WASHINGTON'S MONUMENT (INCOMPLETE)
15TH ST.
14TH ST.
13TH ST.
12TH ST.
10TH ST.
H ST. N.
G ST. N.
F ST. N.
E ST. N.
D ST. N.

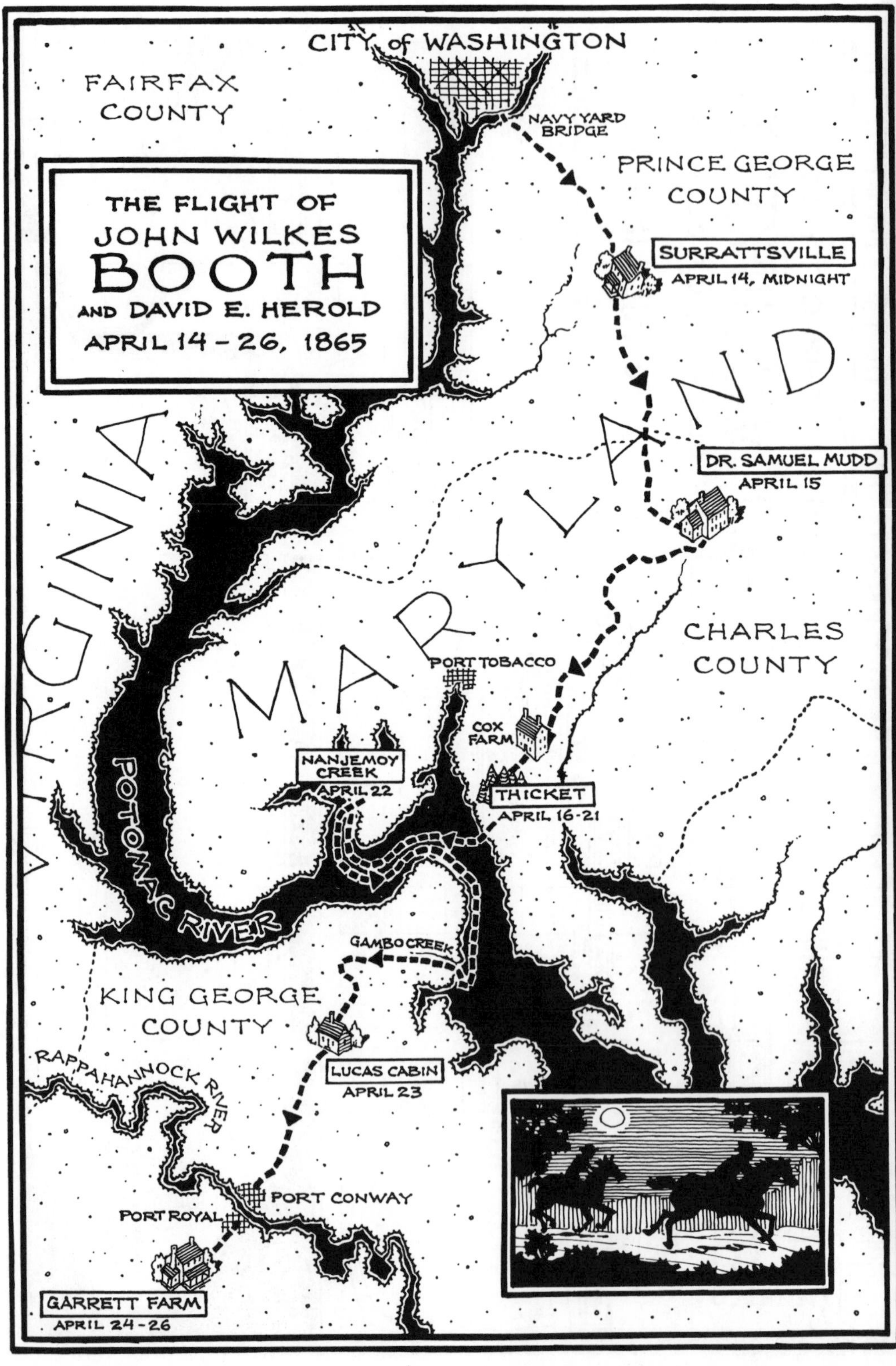

THE FLIGHT OF
JOHN WILKES
BOOTH
AND DAVID E. HEROLD
APRIL 14 – 26, 1865
CITY of WASHINGTON
FAIRFAX COUNTY
NAVY YARD BRIDGE
PRINCE GEORGE COUNTY
SURRATTSVILLE
APRIL 14, MIDNIGHT
MARYLAND
VIRGINIA
DR. SAMUEL MUDD
APRIL 15
CHARLES COUNTY
PORT TOBACCO
COX FARM
THICKET
APRIL 16-21
NANJEMOY CREEK
APRIL 22
POTOMAC RIVER
GAMBO CREEK
KING GEORGE COUNTY
LUCAS CABIN
APRIL 23
RAPPAHANNOCK RIVER
PORT CONWAY
PORT ROYAL
GARRETT FARM
APRIL 24-26

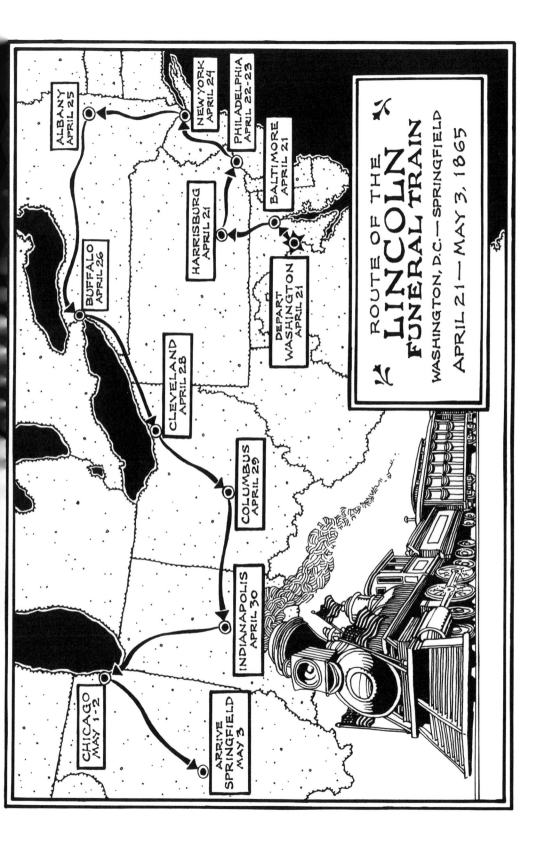

ROUTE OF THE
LINCOLN
FUNERAL TRAIN

WASHINGTON, D.C. — SPRINGFIELD

APRIL 21 — MAY 3, 1865

DEPART
WASHINGTON
APRIL 21

BALTIMORE
APRIL 21

HARRISBURG
APRIL 21

PHILADELPHIA
APRIL 22-23

NEW YORK
APRIL 24

ALBANY
APRIL 25

BUFFALO
APRIL 26

CLEVELAND
APRIL 28

COLUMBUS
APRIL 29

INDIANAPOLIS
APRIL 30

CHICAGO
MAY 1-2

ARRIVE
SPRINGFIELD
MAY 3

PART I
THE PRESIDENT

THE WHITE HOUSE

SATURDAY, MARCH 4, 1865
AT THE EAST FRONT OF THE CAPITOL, THE MAGNIFICENT, NEWLY-COMPLETED DOME OVERSEES THE SECOND INAUGURATION OF PRESIDENT ABRAHAM LINCOLN.

AT NOON PRECISELY, HE RECEIVES THE OATH FROM CHIEF JUSTICE SALMON P. CHASE...

AFTER WHICH HE GIVES AN ADDRESS SURPRISING IN ITS BREVITY—AND MOVING IN ITS POETRY.

AT THIS SECOND APPEARING TO TAKE THE OATH OF THE PRESIDENTIAL OFFICE, THERE IS LESS OCCASION FOR AN EXTENDED ADDRESS THAN THERE WAS AT THE FIRST.

ON THE OCCASION CORRESPONDING TO THIS FOUR YEARS AGO, ALL THOUGHTS WERE ANXIOUSLY DIRECTED TO AN IMPENDING CIVIL WAR. ALL DREADED IT — ALL SOUGHT TO AVERT IT.

THE COLD WINDS AND ANKLE-DEEP MUD OF THE CAPITAL DO LITTLE TO SUPPRESS THE ENTHUSIASM OF THE MULTITUDES IN ATTENDANCE.

BOTH PARTIES DEPRECATED WAR, BUT ONE OF THEM WOULD MAKE WAR RATHER THAN LET THE NATION SURVIVE, AND THE OTHER WOULD ACCEPT WAR RATHER THAN LET IT PERISH. AND THE WAR CAME.

EVERYONE CAN FEEL IT: AFTER FOUR BLOOD-SOAKED YEARS, THE TERRIBLE CONFLICT IS AT LAST COMING TO AN END.

ONE EIGHTH OF THE WHOLE POPULATION WERE COLORED SLAVES, NOT DISTRIBUTED GENERALLY OVER THE UNION, BUT LOCALIZED IN THE SOUTHERN PART OF IT. THESE SLAVES CONSTITUTED A PECULIAR AND POWERFUL INTEREST. ALL KNEW THAT THIS INTEREST WAS, SOMEHOW, THE CAUSE OF THE WAR.

NEWLY EMANCIPATED NEGROES AND OTHER RAGGED SURVIVORS HAVE SOUGHT REFUGE IN THE CAPITAL.

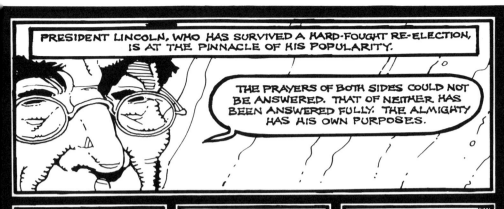

PRESIDENT LINCOLN, WHO HAS SURVIVED A HARD-FOUGHT RE-ELECTION, IS AT THE PINNACLE OF HIS POPULARITY.

THE PRAYERS OF BOTH SIDES COULD NOT BE ANSWERED. THAT OF NEITHER HAS BEEN ANSWERED FULLY. THE ALMIGHTY HAS HIS OWN PURPOSES.

AND YET, THERE ARE THOSE FOR WHOM HE REMAINS AN OBJECT OF SCORN AND DEEP LOATHING — A TYRANT!

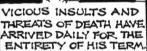

VICIOUS INSULTS AND THREATS OF DEATH HAVE ARRIVED DAILY FOR THE ENTIRETY OF HIS TERM.

HIS YOUNG SECRETARY, JOHN HAY, KEEPS THEM IN A BULGING FILE.

BUT THE PRESIDENT, NOTORIOUSLY CASUAL ABOUT HIS PERSONAL SECURITY, PREFERS TO TRUST IN PROVIDENCE.

IF I AM KILLED, I CAN DIE BUT ONCE, BUT TO LIVE IN CONSTANT DREAD OF IT IS TO DIE OVER AND OVER AGAIN.

(AFTER ALL, HE HAS OBSERVED, IF SOMEONE IS DETERMINED TO DO HIM HARM, AND CARES NOT ABOUT GIVING UP HIS OWN LIFE, THERE IS LITTLE THAT CAN BE DONE.)

FONDLY DO WE HOPE — FERVENTLY DO WE PRAY — THAT THIS MIGHTY SCOURGE OF WAR MAY SPEEDILY PASS AWAY.

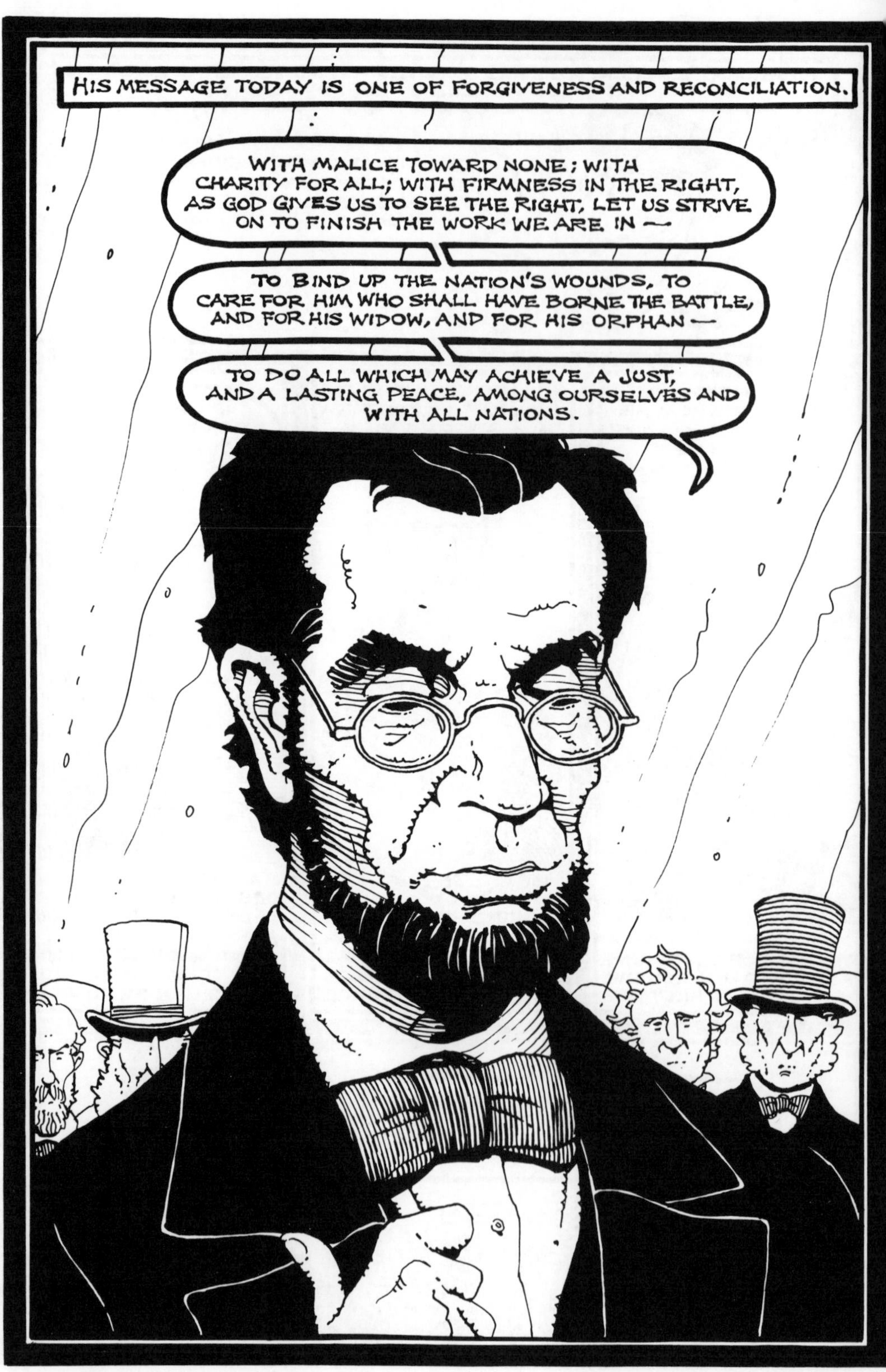
HIS MESSAGE TODAY IS ONE OF FORGIVENESS AND RECONCILIATION.
WITH MALICE TOWARD NONE; WITH CHARITY FOR ALL; WITH FIRMNESS IN THE RIGHT, AS GOD GIVES US TO SEE THE RIGHT, LET US STRIVE ON TO FINISH THE WORK WE ARE IN —
TO BIND UP THE NATION'S WOUNDS, TO CARE FOR HIM WHO SHALL HAVE BORNE THE BATTLE, AND FOR HIS WIDOW, AND FOR HIS ORPHAN —
TO DO ALL WHICH MAY ACHIEVE A JUST, AND A LASTING PEACE, AMONG OURSELVES AND WITH ALL NATIONS.

PART II.
THE CONSPIRATORS

SURRATT'S BOARDING HOUSE

SATURDAY, MARCH 4, 1865
WASHINGTON CITY IS, AT HEART, A SOUTHERN TOWN.

AND ON THIS INAUGURATION DAY, ITS STREETS TEEM WITH SECESSIONIST SPIES AND SYMPATHIZERS.

AMONG THE IMPORTANT GUESTS OBSERVING THE CEREMONY IS THE CELEBRATED YOUNG ACTOR JOHN WILKES BOOTH.

AT AGE 26, HE IS PREPARING FOR HIMSELF A ROLE THAT WILL ENSHRINE HIS NAME IN HISTORY...

FOR, UNKNOWN TO MANY, HE IS A FANATICAL PARTISAN OF THE CRUMBLING CONFEDERATE CAUSE—AND, WITHIN HIS HEART, CARRIES AN ABIDING HATRED OF THE NORTH, AND OF ITS PRESIDENT, ABRAHAM LINCOLN.

IT WILL BE INSTRUCTIVE, AT THIS POINT, TO REVIEW THE LIFE OF JOHN WILKES BOOTH...

A LIFE THAT BEGAN WITH BRIGHT PROMISE.

HIS FATHER WAS THE GREAT TRAGEDIAN JUNIUS BRUTUS BOOTH, AN ENGLISHMAN WHO SETTLED IN AMERICA.

HIS OLDER BROTHERS, JUNIUS, JR. AND EDWIN ALSO BECAME PROMINENT ACTORS.

JOHN WAS NEXT TO YOUNGEST OF HIS PARENTS' SIX SURVIVING OFFSPRING.

AND HIS WAS A RELATIVELY HAPPY CHILDHOOD, SPENT ON THE FAMILY FARM NEAR BEL AIR, MARYLAND.

DRAMATIC AND GREGARIOUS, HE WAS THE FAVORITE OF HIS MOTHER AND OF HIS DOTING OLDER SISTER, ASIA.

AS HE GREW, HE ACQUIRED A DEEP SYMPATHY AND SENTIMENT FOR THE SOUTHERN WAY OF LIFE.

AFTER AN INDIFFERENT EDUCATION, JOHN FOUND IT NATURAL TO ENTER THE FAMILY BUSINESS.

HE SET OUT TO BECOME A STAR OF THE FIRST MAGNITUDE.

HE TOURED THE SOUTH TO GREAT ACCLAIM AND WAS WELL-KNOWN FOR HIS FLAMBOYANT STYLE.

HIS DARK AND HANDSOME VISAGE MADE HIM A FAVORITE OF THE LADIES.

ONCE THE WAR BROKE OUT, HE SERVED THE REBEL CAUSE AS A COURIER, WHO COULD PASS UNCHALLENGED ACROSS STATE BORDERS.

HIS APPEARANCES ONSTAGE BECAME FEWER. SOME SPECULATED THAT HIS UNTRAINED VOICE HAD BEGUN TO DETERIORATE.

ACTUALLY, HE WAS SPENDING MORE AND MORE OF HIS TIME IN COLLUSION WITH THE CONFEDERATE UNDERGROUND IN NEW YORK AND CANADA...

AS HE PREPARED TO MOVE HIS ACTIVITIES TO A LARGER STAGE.

HE IS NOW THE KEY INSTIGATOR OF A PLOT OF MONUMENTAL PROPORTION...

THE ABDUCTION OF THE PRESIDENT OF THE UNITED STATES!

A PLAN OF LONG STANDING HAS A SMALL BAND TAKING THE ILL-GUARDED PRESIDENT FROM HIS CARRIAGE...

(MOST LIKELY ALONG THE REMOTE ROUTE TO HIS SUMMER RETREAT AT THE SOLDIERS' HOME NORTH OF THE CITY.)

AND CONVEYING HIM ALONG THE BACK ROADS OF SOUTHERN MARYLAND, ACROSS THE POTOMAC AND THENCE TO RICHMOND.

THE CONFEDERATE GOVERNMENT COULD THEN NEGOTIATE THE RELEASE OF THOUSANDS OF SOUTHERN PRISONERS OF WAR.

WHOEVER ACCOMPLISHED THIS WOULD BE ACCLAIMED AS A HERO.

TO THIS END, BOOTH HAS DEDICATED HIMSELF ABSOLUTELY.

AS EARLY AS AUGUST OF 1864, HE BEGAN TO GATHER A CREW OF CONSPIRATORS.

IN BALTIMORE, HE RECRUITED TWO OF HIS CHILDHOOD COMPANIONS:

MICHAEL O'LAUGHLIN, AGE 27.

SAMUEL B. ARNOLD, AGE 28.

THROUGH THE SOUTHERN UNDERGROUND NETWORK, HE CAME IN CONTACT WITH:

DR. SAMUEL A. MUDD, AGE 31, MARYLAND FARMER AND PHYSICIAN.

AND, THROUGH HIM, THE CONFEDERATE COURIER JOHN H. SURRATT, AGE 20.

SURRATT BROUGHT IN THE REMAINING MEMBERS, DEVOTED REBELS ALL:

DAVID E. HEROLD, AGE 23, FORMER DRUG STORE CLERK...

AN AVID HUNTER, WITH INTIMATE KNOWLEDGE OF RURAL MARYLAND.

GEORGE A. ATZERODT, AGE 33, OF PORT TOBACCO, MARYLAND...

A CARRIAGE-MAKER OF PRUSSIAN ORIGIN, EXPERIENCED IN FERRYING BLOCKADE-RUNNERS ACROSS THE POTOMAC.

LEWIS POWELL (ALIAS PAINE), AGE 20, FORMER RAIDER IN THE CONFEDERATE ARMY.

A LOYAL GIANT OF SIMPLE MIND AND FIERCE SPIRIT.

BY FEBRUARY OF 1865, THE GROUP WAS COMPLETE.

SINCE THE FIRST OF THE YEAR, THE CONSPIRACY HAS USED, AS ITS INFORMAL HEADQUARTERS, A BOARDING HOUSE AT 541 H STREET, WHERE JOHN SURRATT IS RESIDENT.

THE BUILDING IS OWNED BY HIS MOTHER, MRS. MARY E. SURRATT, A WIDOW, AGE 42.

THIS ESTABLISHMENT AND THE TAVERN SHE OWNS AT SURRATTSVILLE IN MARYLAND HAVE LONG SERVED AS "SAFE HOUSES" FOR CONFEDERATE SPIES AND SMUGGLERS.

ANOTHER RESIDENT IS ONE LOUIS J. WEICHMANN, A WAR DEPT. CLERK AND FORMER SCHOOL-MATE OF JOHN SURRATT'S

THOUGH NOT A PARTY TO THE CONSPIRACY, HE HAS OCCASION TO NOTE ITS COMINGS AND GOINGS.

PERHAPS TO SATISFY HIS ACTOR'S EGO, BOOTH WANTS TO CAPTURE THE PRESIDENT—WELL KNOWN AS AN AVID PLAYGOER— AS HE WATCHES A THEATRICAL PERFORMANCE...

INCAPACITATE HIM IN BURLAP... LOWER HIM FROM THE BOX TO THE STAGE...

AND CONVEY HIM THROUGH THE REAR DOOR TO A WAITING CARRIAGE.

OR AT LEAST THAT IS HIS DREAM ON THIS MARCH 4, AS HE WATCHES THE DESPISED LINCOLN TAKE THE OATH OF OFFICE.

FRIDAY, MARCH 17, 1865
ON THIS NIGHT, BOOTH HAS BOOKED A ROOM AT GAUTIER'S RESTAURANT ON PENNSYLVANIA AVENUE.
HERE, FOR THE FIRST TIME, ALL SEVEN OF THE CONSPIRATORS ARE TOGETHER.

ALSO, FOR THE FIRST TIME, BOOTH REALIZES THAT NOT ALL OF THEM ARE OF LIKE MIND.

BOTH ARNOLD AND O'LAUGHLIN ARE WAVERING.

TOO MUCH TIME HAS BEEN WASTED, THEY FEEL. SOON IT WILL BE TOO LATE TO ACT.

TO JOHN SURRATT, THE WHOLE PLAN IS TOO DANGEROUS. THE GOVERNMENT IS SURE TO GET WIND OF IT.

IN ANY CASE, THE IDEA OF TAKING LINCOLN FROM A THEATRE SHOULD BE ABANDONED: BETTER TO DO IT OUTDOORS AND AWAY FROM CROWDS.

BOOTH CHALLENGES HIS OVERLY-CAUTIOUS ASSOCIATES. ANGRY WORDS ENSUE.

GENTLEMEN, IF WORSE COMES TO WORST, I KNOW WHAT I SHALL DO!

IF YOU INTIMATE ANYTHING MORE THAN THE CAPTURE OF MR. LINCOLN, I, FOR ONE, WILL BID YOU GOODBYE!

GENTLEMEN, I APOLOGIZE. I FEAR I AM THE WORSE FOR THE CHAMPAGNE.

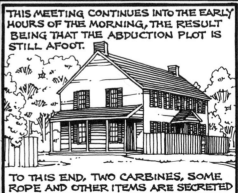

THIS MEETING CONTINUES INTO THE EARLY HOURS OF THE MORNING, THE RESULT BEING THAT THE ABDUCTION PLOT IS STILL AFOOT.

TO THIS END, TWO CARBINES, SOME ROPE AND OTHER ITEMS ARE SECRETED IN THE TAVERN AT SURRATTSVILLE.

SATURDAY, MARCH 18, 1865 BY THIS DATE, LOUIS WEICHMANN HAS INFORMED HIS SUPERIORS AT THE WAR DEPT. OF THE "SECESH" ACTIVITIES IN THE SURRATT BOARDING HOUSE.

HIS REPORT, THOUGH, IS FILED AWAY AND NEVER ACTED UPON.

IN THE EVENING, JOHN WILKES BOOTH MAKES WHAT WILL BE HIS FINAL THEATRICAL APPEARANCE — IN "THE APOSTATE," AT FORD'S THEATRE.

IN THE AUDIENCE ARE JOHN SURRATT, DAVID HEROLD AND LEWIS POWELL.

MONDAY, MARCH 20, 1865 BOOTH, WHO HAS NO FIXED RESIDENCE, IS ACCUSTOMED TO RETRIEVING HIS MAIL AT FORD'S AND VARIOUS OTHER THEATRES.

THIS MORNING, HE LEARNS THAT THE PRESIDENT WILL ATTEND A PERFORMANCE OF "STILL WATERS RUN DEEP" AT THE CAMPBELL HOSPITAL FOR CONVALESCENT SOLDIERS.

LOCATED JUST NORTH OF THE CITY, ITS APPROACH IS SEEMINGLY IDEAL FOR OVERTAKING THE PRESIDENTIAL CARRIAGE.

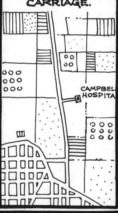

CAMPBEL HOSPITA

IN THE EARLY AFTERNOON, THE CONSPIRATORS GATHER AT SEVENTH ST. AND FLORIDA AVE.

AFTER SEVERAL HOURS, THEY BEGIN TO SUSPECT THAT SOMETHING IS AMISS.

BOOTH RIDES TO THE HOSPITAL AND CASUALLY INQUIRES AS TO THE STATE OF THINGS.

HE IS TOLD OF A CHANGE IN PLAN: MR. LINCOLN HAS CHOSEN NOT TO ATTEND THE PERFORMANCE TODAY.

(IN A TOUCH OF IRONY, THE PRESIDENT IS MEETING AT THIS MOMENT WITH A UNIT OF VOLUNTEERS, AT THE NATIONAL HOTEL.— WHERE THE ACTOR IS CURRENTLY RESIDENT!)

WHEN BOOTH RETURNS AND TELLS THE OTHERS, THEY SCATTER IN PANIC. SURELY THEIR PLOT HAS BEEN DISCOVERED!

FEDERAL TROOPS COULD OVERTAKE THEM AT ANY MOMENT.

IN THE LATE AFTERNOON, BOOTH, POWELL AND SURRATT RETURN SEPARATELY TO THE BOARDING HOUSE.

THE ACTOR, IN A STATE OF ANGER AND AGITATION, PACES THE FLOOR, CURSING HIS FORTUNE.

IN THE DAYS THAT FOLLOW, THE KIDNAP PLOT IS PRONOUNCED DEAD.

ARNOLD AND O'LAUGHLIN RETURN TO BALTIMORE.

JOHN SURRATT DEPARTS FOR RICHMOND.

ONLY POWELL, ATZERODT, AND HEROLD REMAIN LOYAL TO BOOTH AND READY FOR WHATEVER NEW PLAN MIGHT EMERGE TO RE-IGNITE THE DYING SOUTHERN CAUSE.

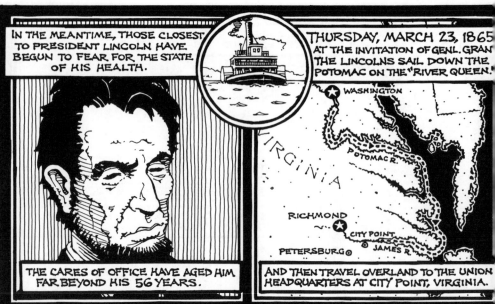

IN THE MEANTIME, THOSE CLOSEST TO PRESIDENT LINCOLN HAVE BEGUN TO FEAR FOR THE STATE OF HIS HEALTH.

THURSDAY, MARCH 23, 1865 AT THE INVITATION OF GENL. GRAN THE LINCOLNS SAIL DOWN THE POTOMAC ON THE "RIVER QUEEN."

THE CARES OF OFFICE HAVE AGED HIM FAR BEYOND HIS 56 YEARS.

AND THEN TRAVEL OVERLAND TO THE UNION HEADQUARTERS AT CITY POINT, VIRGINIA.

THE EVENTS OF THE FOLLOWING SATURDAY WILL HAVE UNFORESEEN REPERCUSSIONS IN THE WEEKS TO COME.

WHILE THE PRESIDENT AND THE GENERAL RIDE AHEAD, MRS. LINCOLN AND MRS. GRANT ARE RELEGATED TO A FIELD AMBULANCE.

THE LENGTHY JOURNEY OVER MUDDY, RUTTED ROADS IS A HUMILIATING ORDEAL FOR BOTH LADIES...

ESPECIALLY FOR MARY LINCOLN, WHO SUFFERS THE ONSET OF ONE OF HER DEBILITATING HEADACHES.

340

THE FIRST LADY ARRIVES AT THE PARADE GROUND LATE AND IN THE FOULEST OF HUMORS.

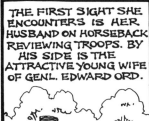

THE FIRST SIGHT SHE ENCOUNTERS IS HER HUSBAND ON HORSEBACK REVIEWING TROOPS. BY HIS SIDE IS THE ATTRACTIVE YOUNG WIFE OF GENL. EDWARD ORD.

THAT WOMAN IS PRETENDING TO BE ME! THE SOLDIERS WILL THINK THAT VILE WOMAN IS ME!

MRS. GRANT ATTEMPTS TO CALM HER, BUT IS REBUFFED.

YOU THINK YOU WILL GET TO THE WHITE HOUSE YOURSELF, DON'T YOU?!

AT THE REVIEWING STAND, MRS. LINCOLN DENOUNCES MRS. ORD AS A WHORE AND DEMANDS THAT HER HUSBAND REMOVE THE GENERAL FROM COMMAND.

THE PRESIDENT BEARS THIS WITH HIS USUAL STOIC RESIGNATION.

NONE WHO ARE PRESENT WILL FORGET THIS DAY, LEAST OF THEM JULIA GRANT.

341

BY NOW IT IS PLAIN TO MOST AMERICANS THAT THE SOUTHERN CAUSE IS DOOMED.

NOT, HOWEVER, TO JOHN WILKES BOOTH, WHO SPENDS SEVERAL DAYS IN NEW YORK AND BOSTON MEETING WITH CONFEDERATE OPERATIVES.

MONDAY, APRIL 3, 1865
THE SOUTHERN CAPITAL OF RICHMOND FALLS TO THE UNION ARMY.

THE NEXT DAY, PRESIDENT LINCOLN TOURS THE DEFEATED CITY — IN AN OPEN CARRIAGE, UNGUARDED.

SUNDAY, APRIL 9, 1865
GENL. LEE SURRENDERS TO GENL. GRANT AT APPOMATTOX COURT HOUSE, VIRGINIA. PRESENT AT THE CEREMONY IS ROBERT TODD LINCOLN, AGE 21, THE PRESIDENT'S ELDEST SON.

FROM THIS MOMENT, THE WAR IS EFFECTIVELY OVER.

THE CITY OF WASHINGTON STAGES A GRAND CELEBRATION THAT WILL LAST SEVERAL DAYS.

LINCOLN RETURNS TO GREAT ADULATION. TO THOSE CLOSE TO HIM, HE SEEMS BUOYANT, TRANSFORMED.

MONDAY, APRIL 10, 1865
ON THIS DAY, HE VISITS THE STUDIO OF ALEXANDER GARDNER FOR A SERIES OF PORTRAITS THAT REFLECT HIS MOOD.

THEY WILL TURN OUT TO BE HIS LAST IMAGES.

TO JOHN WILKES BOOTH AND MANY SOUTHERNERS, HOWEVER, THE WAR IS FAR FROM OVER.

ARE NOT THE FORCES OF GENL. JOSEPH JOHNSTON STILL ARRAYED AGAINST THOSE OF GENL. WILLIAM T. SHERMAN IN NORTH CAROLINA?

TUESDAY, APRIL 11, 1865 ON THIS EVENING, BOOTH IMBIBES AT DEERY'S TAVERN.

LATER, HE JOINS DAVID HEROLD AND LEWIS POWELL AS PART OF THE VAST THRONG THAT GATHERS UPON THE WHITE HOUSE LAWN TO HEAR THE PRESIDENT SPEAK.

FROM A WINDOW BENEATH THE NORTH PORTICO, LINCOLN TALKS OF PEACE...
AND OF RECONCILIATION...
AND OF ENFRANCHISEMENT FOR THE NEWLY-FREE SLAVE POPULATION.

THE IDEA OF CITIZENSHIP FOR THE NEGRO ENRAGES BOOTH.

THAT WILL BE THE LAST SPEECH HE WILL EVER MAKE!

BY NOW HE HAS DECIDED UPON HIS ULTIMATE COURSE.

LATER IN THE EVENING, THE PRESIDENT AND MRS. LINCOLN SIT INFORMALLY WITH A SMALL NUMBER OF GUESTS AT THE WHITE HOUSE.

AMONG THEM IS WARD HILL LAMON, LINCOLN'S OLD FRIEND AND SELF-APPOINTED BODYGUARD.

ALL IN THE ROOM ARE GREATLY DISTURBED, AS THE PRESIDENT RECOUNTS A DREAM FROM THE NIGHT BEFORE.

IN THE DREAM, HE IS AROUSED FROM SLEEP BY MOURNFUL SOBBING AND WAILING SOMEWHERE IN THE WHITE HOUSE.

FOLLOWING THE SOUNDS DOWNSTAIRS, HE ARRIVES AT THE EAST ROOM, WHERE A BLACK COFFIN IS ARRANGED FOR PUBLIC VIEWING.

WHO IS DEAD IN THE WHITE HOUSE?

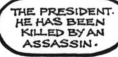

THE PRESIDENT. HE HAS BEEN KILLED BY AN ASSASSIN.

PART III.
GOOD FRIDAY

FORD'S THEATRE

FRIDAY, APRIL 14, 1865
ON THIS MORNING, AT ABOUT 7:00 AM, THE LINCOLNS BREAKFAST AT THE WHITE HOUSE WITH THEIR SONS, ROBERT AND TAD, AGE 9.

ALL ARE CHEERFUL AND TALK OF THE DAY'S ACTIVITIES. THE PRESIDENT ENTREATS ROBERT TO GIVE A FIRST-HAND ACCOUNT OF THE SOUTHERN SURRENDER.

ROBERT SHOWS HIS FATHER GENERAL LEE'S CARTE DE VISITE.

IT IS THE FACE OF A NOBLE, BRAVE MAN. I AM GLAD THIS WAR IS OVER.

MRS. LINCOLN ANNOUNCES THEIR PLAN TO ATTEND A PLAY TONIGHT AT FORD'S THEATRE, ACCOMPANIED BY GENERAL AND MRS. GRANT.

THEY INVITE ROBERT TO JOIN THEM, BUT HE DECLINES, FEELING ILL AND TIRED FROM HIS RECENT DAYS IN THE FIELD.

347

AT THIS VERY HOUR, DAVID HEROLD RAPS UPON THE DOOR OF BOOTH'S ROOM AT THE NATIONAL HOTEL...

228

BUT FINDS NOBODY IN.

PERHAPS THE ACTOR HAS SPENT THE NIGHT WITH ONE OF SEVERAL WOMEN WITH WHOM HE IS KNOWN TO BE INVOLVED...

(ALTHOUGH HE IS UNOFFICIALLY ENGAGED TO MISS LUCY HALE, DAUGHTER OF THE FORMER SENATOR JOHN HALE OF NEW HAMPSHIRE).

LATER ON, HE IS SEEN BREAKFASTING IN THE HOTEL'S DINING ROOM IN COMPANY OF TWO LOVELY LADIES.

AT ABOUT 8:30 AM, BOOTH BRINGS HIS ASSOCIATE GEORGE ATZERODT TO THE KIRKWOOD HOUSE ON PENNSYLVANIA AV.

AND ESTABLISHES HIM IN THE ROOM DIRECTLY ABOVE THAT OF VICE PRESIDENT ANDREW JOHNSON.

IN COMPANY OF HEROLD AND LEWIS POWELL, HE THEN PATRONIZES HIS FAVORITE BARBER, FOR A TRIM OF HIS HAIR AND REFURBISHMENT OF HIS FACIAL BEAUTY.

HE IS NOW READY TO BE MASTER OF HIS DAY!

11:30 AM — AS HE COLLECTS HIS MAIL AT FORD'S THEATRE, BOOTH LEARNS THAT THE LINCOLNS AND THE GRANTS WILL ATTEND TONIGHT.

MISS LAURA KEENE IN A BENEFIT PERFORMANCE OF "OUR AMERICAN COUSIN."

FOR MINUTES THEREAFTER HE CAN BE SEEN SITTING ON THE FRONT STEPS OF THE THEATRE.

RACING THROUGH HIS MIND CAN BE ONLY ONE THING...

NOW IS THE TIME TO STRIKE!

BOOTH RE-ENTERS THE THEATRE TO WATCH THE DRESS REHEARSAL IN PROGRESS.

HE KNOWS THIS POPULAR COMEDY PRACTICALLY BY HEART.

IN THE MEANTIME, EMPLOYEES OF FORD'S ARRANGE THE PRESIDENTIAL BOX.

THE PARTITION BETWEEN BOXES 7 AND 8 IS REMOVED IN ORDER TO PROVIDE A SINGLE LARGE SPACE.

FLAGS ARE DRAPED OVER THE RAILINGS.

COUCHES AND CHAIRS ARE BROUGHT IN.

FOR THE PRESIDENT, A COMFORTABLE ROCKER.

OUTSIDE THE BOX IS PLACED A CHAIR FOR LINCOLN'S BODYGUARD.

AT THIS HOUR, PRESIDENT LINCOLN PRESIDES OVER A CABINET MEETING IN HIS OFFICE AT THE WHITE HOUSE.

GENERAL GRANT IS IN ATTENDANCE.

FREDERICK SEWARD ATTENDS IN THE PLACE OF HIS FATHER, THE SECRETARY OF STATE...

WM. H. SEWARD

WHO WAS SERIOUSLY INJURED IN A CARRIAGE ACCIDENT ON APRIL 5.

TALK AROUND THE TABLE IS OF POSTWAR POLICY TOWARD THE SOUTHERN STATES.

ALL AWAIT WORD OF THE IMMINENT SURRENDER OF GENL. JOHNSTON.

THE PRESIDENT RELATES A DREAM OF HIS FROM LAST NIGHT, ONE THAT RECURS TO HIM ON THE EVE OF MOMENTOUS EVENTS.

IN IT, HE STANDS AT THE PROW OF A HUGE SHIP, AS IT MOVES RAPIDLY TOWARD SOME FAR, INDETERMINATE SHORE.

I HAD THIS DREAM PRECEDING SUMTER, BULL RUN, ANTIETAM, GETTYSBURG...

AFTER THE MEETING, GENL. GRANT INFORMS MR. LINCOLN THAT, REGRETFULLY, HE AND MRS. GRANT MUST DECLINE TO ATTEND THE THEATRE.

THE STATED REASON IS THEIR DESIRE TO LEAVE FOR NEW YORK TODAY TO RE-UNITE WITH THEIR CHILDREN.

UNSTATED, SURELY, IS MRS. GRANT'S EXTREME DISTASTE FOR THE COMPANY OF MRS. LINCOLN.

BOOTH'S ACTIVITIES ON THIS BUSY AFTERNOON CONTINUE UNABATED.

AT PUMPHREY'S STABLE ON PENNSYLVANIA AVENUE, HE RESERVES A SWIFT MOUNT FOR THE EVENING.

HE VISITS MARY SURRATT AT HER BOARDING HOUSE, AS SHE PREPARES TO DEPART ON A BUSINESS ERRAND TO SURRATTSVILLE.

WOULD SHE PLEASE DELIVER A PARCEL FOR HIM TO THE TAVERN THERE?

IN THE PARCEL, UNKNOWN TO THE LADY, IS BOOTH'S FIELD GLASS, PRESUMABLY NECESSARY FOR HIS ACTIVITIES LATER TONIGHT.

MRS. SURRATT SOON LEAVES ON THE 13-MILE JOURNEY, ACCOMPANIED BY LOUIS WEICHMANN.

AT THE TAVERN, SHE HANDS THE PARCEL TO THE BAR-KEEPER, JOHN LLOYD, AND RELAYS A MESSAGE FROM BOOTH —

HAVE THOSE SHOOTING IRONS READY TONIGHT. THERE WILL BE SOME PARTIES CALL FOR THEM.

(THESE WORDS, IN THE MONTHS TO COME, WILL WEIGH HEAVILY UPON THE FATE OF MRS. SURRATT.)

IN THE MEANTIME, BOOTH STOPS BY THE KIRKWOOD HOUSE TO LEAVE A CRYPTIC MESSAGE.

ON A SMALL CARD, HE WRITES:

Don't wish to disturb you. Are you at home? J. Wilkes Booth

HE ASKS THAT IT BE LEFT IN THE BOX OF WILLIAM BROWNING, PERSONAL SECRETARY TO VICE-PRESIDENT JOHNSON.

WHAT IS THE PURPOSE OF THIS MESSAGE? IS IT FOR JOHNSON OR BROWNING?

AT THE WHITE HOUSE, THE CABINET MEETING, HAVING DRAGGED ON INTO MID-AFTERNOON, AT LAST CONCLUDES.

ACCOMPANIED BY HIS BODYGUARD, WM. CROOK, OF THE METROPOLITAN POLICE, LINCOLN WALKS NEXT DOOR TO THE WAR DEPARTMENT.

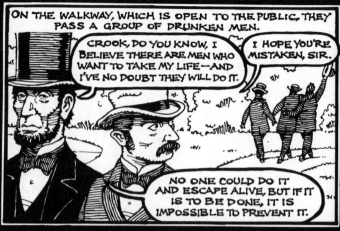

ON THE WALKWAY, WHICH IS OPEN TO THE PUBLIC, THEY PASS A GROUP OF DRUNKEN MEN.

CROOK, DO YOU KNOW, I BELIEVE THERE ARE MEN WHO WANT TO TAKE MY LIFE—AND I'VE NO DOUBT THEY WILL DO IT.

I HOPE YOU'RE MISTAKEN, SIR.

NO ONE COULD DO IT AND ESCAPE ALIVE, BUT IF IT IS TO BE DONE, IT IS IMPOSSIBLE TO PREVENT IT.

AT THE OFFICE OF EDWIN M. STANTON, THE SECRETARY OF WAR, LINCOLN MAKES AN UNUSUAL REQUEST:

I AM LOOKING FOR SOMEONE TO GO TO THE THEATRE WITH ME TONIGHT. GRANT SAYS HE CANNOT ATTEND.

CAN I HAVE YOUR MAN ECKERT?

(HE REFERS TO MAJ. THOMAS ECKERT, THE BURLY CHIEF OF THE WAR DEPARTMENT'S TELEGRAPH OFFICE.)

I CANNOT SPARE HIM. I HAVE IMPORTANT WORK FOR HIM THIS EVENING.

WHY WOULD STANTON REFUSE THE PRESIDENT PROTECTION?

MORE IMPORTANTLY, WHY IS THE NOTORIOUSLY FATALISTIC PRESIDENT SO CONCERNED ABOUT HIS PERSONAL SAFETY ON THIS PARTICULAR EVENING?

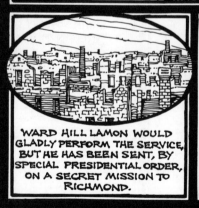

WARD HILL LAMON WOULD GLADLY PERFORM THE SERVICE, BUT HE HAS BEEN SENT, BY SPECIAL PRESIDENTIAL ORDER, ON A SECRET MISSION TO RICHMOND.

ON THE WALK BACK TO THE WHITE HOUSE, LINCOLN OFFERS CROOK A FURTHER CONFIDENCE....

HE HAS LITTLE INTEREST IN ATTENDING THE THEATRE TONIGHT, BUT FEELS HE MUST NOT DISAPPOINT THE PEOPLE.

AT ABOUT 4:00 PM, BOOTH PICKS UP HIS HORSE AT PUMPHREY'S.

HE IS SEEN DRINKING AT DEERY'S TAVERN...

AFTER WHICH HE GOES NEXT DOOR TO GROVER'S THEATRE, WHERE HE PENS A LENGTHY MISSIVE OF UNKNOWN CONTENT.

SOMEWHAT LATER, ALONG PENNSYLVANIA AVENUE, BOOTH HAPPENS UPON HIS FRIEND AND FELLOW ACTOR JOHN MATTHEWS.

HE HANDS THE BULKY LETTER, IN A SEALED ENVELOPE, TO THE SURPRISED MATTHEWS, AND ASKS THAT HE DELIVER IT TOMORROW MORNING TO THE OFFICES OF THE NATIONAL INTELLIGENCER.

(THIS LETTER WILL NEVER BE DELIVERED: ACCORDING TO MATTHEWS, HE WILL LATER OPEN AND READ THE MESSAGE—AND THEN, FEARING HIS OWN INCRIMINATION, DESTROY IT.)

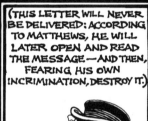

BOOTH SEES THE CARRIAGE OF GENERAL GRANT PASS BY ON THE AVENUE.

HE AT ONCE TAKES OFF IN PURSUIT.

HE RIDES AHEAD OF THE CARRIAGE WHEELS AROUND AND RETURNS, BOTH TIMES PEERING MALEVOLENTLY IN UPON ITS OCCUPANTS.

THOSE INSIDE THE VEHICLE ARE UNNERVED BY THIS INTRUSION.

AN ESPECIALLY STRONG IMPRESSION IS LEFT UPON MRS. GRANT.

BOOTH'S NEXT STOP, AT 5:30 OR 6:00 PM, IS FORD'S THEATRE, A BUILDING TO WHICH HE HAS UNLIMITED ACCESS.

AT THIS TIME OF THE AFTERNOON, REHEARSALS HAVING CONCLUDED, IT IS USUALLY EMPTY.

HE INVITES SOME OF THE STAGE HANDS FOR DRINKS AT TALTAVUL'S TAVERN NEXT DOOR.

HE THEN VENTURES UP TO THE DRESS CIRCLE AND AROUND TO THE PRESIDENTIAL BOX AND ITS OUTER VESTIBULE.

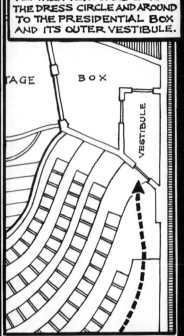

HE PROCURES A TWO-FOOT PINE BOARD (THE UPRIGHT PORTION OF A MUSIC-STAND) TO USE AS A BRACE FOR HOLDING SHUT THE OUTER DOOR...

CUTTING A SMALL NICHE INTO THE WALL TO SECURE IT.

HE THEN USES HIS PENKNIFE TO BORE A TINY HOLE IN THE INNER DOOR TO THE BOX...

THROUGH WHICH HE CAN VIEW THE OCCUPANTS AS THEY WATCH THE PLAY.

HIS PREPARATIONS COMPLETE, BOOTH RETURNS TO THE NATIONAL HOTEL FOR DINNER.

IN THE MEANTIME, AT THE WHITE HOUSE, THE PRESIDENT AND HIS WIFE PREPARE TO TAKE A CARRIAGE RIDE AROUND THE CITY.

AT THIS TIME, CROOK'S REPLACEMENT FOR THE EVENING SHIFT, JOHN F. PARKER, HAS NOT YET ARRIVED.

CROOK VOLUNTEERS TO REMAIN ON DUTY.

BUT LINCOLN ADVISES HIM TO GO HOME AND GET SOME REST.

GOODBYE, CROOK

CROOK THINKS IT ODD THAT HE DOES NOT SAY "GOOD NIGHT," AS IS HIS CUSTOM.

ON THE CARRIAGE RIDE, LINCOLN IS ANIMATED AND EBULLIENT. THE COUPLE TALK OF THEIR FUTURE LIVES, AFTER HIS TERM OF OFFICE.

TO MARY'S MIND, HER HUSBAND IS LOOKING FORWARD ENTHUSIASTICALLY TO AN EVENING AT THE THEATRE.

THEY STOP AT THE NAVY YARD AND ARE GIVEN A TOUR OF THE IRONCLAD WARSHIP "MONTAUK."

THEY ARE BACK HOME BY 7:00 PM FOR DINNER WITH ROBERT AND TAD.

THEIR YOUNGER SON PLANS TO ATTEND GROVER'S THEATRE TONIGHT FOR A PERFORMANCE OF "ALADDIN, OR: HIS WONDERFUL LAMP."

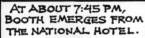

AT ABOUT 7:45 PM, BOOTH EMERGES FROM THE NATIONAL HOTEL.

RESPLENDENT IN BLACK, FOR THE EVENING'S DRAMA.

CONCEALED IN HIS COAT: A SINGLE-SHOT DERRINGER...

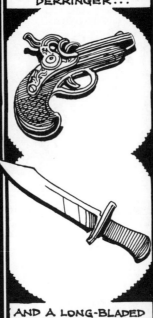

AND A LONG-BLADED HUNTING KNIFE.

AT ABOUT 8:00 PM, THE CONSPIRATORS GATHER FOR A FINAL TIME...

AT THE HERNDON HOUSE, 9TH & F STREETS.

HERE, THEY REVIEW THEIR ASSIGNMENTS:

POWELL, WITH HEROLD AS GUIDE, WILL ASSASSINATE SECRETARY OF STATE SEWARD AT HIS HOME ON LAFAYETTE SQUARE.

WHILE ATZERODT WILL MURDER VICE-PRESIDENT JOHNSON IN HIS ROOMS AT THE KIRKWOOD HOUSE.

(BOOTH SUSPECTS, HOWEVER, THAT THIS MAN HASN'T THE STOMACH FOR THE JOB.)

NEVERTHELESS, THE MEN GO THEIR SEPARATE WAYS IN A SPIRIT OF DETERMINATION.

BOOTH SPURS HIS HORSE TOWARD FORD'S THEATRE.

AT 8:15 PM, THE LINCOLNS DEPART THE WHITE HOUSE.

ACCOMPANYING THEM ARE: EDWARD BURKE, THE COACHMAN, AND CHARLES FORBES, THE PRESIDENT'S PERSONAL ATTENDANT.

THE BODYGUARD JOHN PARKER, HAVING AT LAST REPORTED FOR DUTY, HAS RIDDEN AHEAD TO THE THEATRE TO ARRANGE FOR THE PARTY'S ARRIVAL.

ON THE WAY, THE LINCOLNS' CARRIAGE STOPS AT A RESIDENCE ON H ST. NEAR 15TH, TO COLLECT THEIR LAST-MINUTE GUESTS.

(AFTER THE GRANTS DECLINED THIS MORNING, NO LESS THAN 14 OTHER COUPLES HAVE REFUSED THE PRESIDENTIAL INVITATION.)

EAGERLY ACCEPTING ARE MISS CLARA HARRIS, DAUGHTER OF SENATOR IRA HARRIS OF NEW YORK...

AND HER BETROTHED, MAJOR HENRY R. RATHBONE, ATTACHE OF THE WAR OFFICE.

WHEN THE PRESIDENTIAL PARTY ARRIVES AT FORD'S THEATRE, THE TIME IS 8:30 PM. THE PLAY HAS BEEN IN PROGRESS FOR 30 MINUTES.

ALL ACTION STOPS AS THEY MAKE THEIR WAY TO THE BOX.

THE STAR OF THE PRODUCTION, MISS LAURA KEENE, LEADS THE AUDIENCE IN APPLAUSE.

A FULL HOUSE IS PRESENT: ABOUT 1700 PEOPLE.

THE ORCHESTRA STRIKES UP "HAIL TO THE CHIEF."

THE FOUR ARRANGE THEMSELVES IN THEIR SEATS, AND THE COMEDY CONTINUES.

AT 9:30 PM, BOOTH DISMOUNTS IN THE ALLEY BEHIND THE THEATRE.

HE GIVES HIS HORSE TO EDMAN SPANGLER, A HANDY-MAN AT FORD'S AND AN OLD FRIEND OF THE BOOTH FAMILY.

THE ACTOR SAYS HE WILL RETURN SHORTLY.

AFTER BOOTH ENTERS THE THEATRE, SPANGLER, NEEDING TO RESUME HIS DUTIES, RECRUITS A YOUNG MAN NAMED JOSEPH BURROUGHS (KNOWN AS "JOHN PEANUT") TO MIND THE ANIMAL.

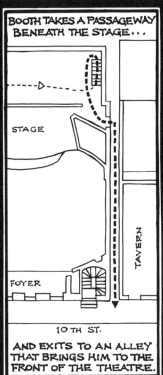

BOOTH TAKES A PASSAGEWAY BENEATH THE STAGE...

STAGE

TAVERN

FOYER

10 TH ST.

AND EXITS TO AN ALLEY THAT BRINGS HIM TO THE FRONT OF THE THEATRE.

HE IS SEEN BY THE TICKET-SELLER NERVOUSLY ENTERING AND RE-ENTERING THE FOYER.

HE ORDERS BRANDY AT TALTAVUL'S NEXT DOOR.

SHORTLY AFTER 10:00 PM, BOOTH CLIMBS THE STAIRS TO THE DRESS CIRCLE AND ROUNDS THE REAR AISLE TOWARD THE PRESIDENTIAL BOX.

SITTING OUTSIDE IT, IN THE GUARD'S CHAIR, IS THE ATTENDANT, CHARLES FORBES, UNARMED.

AS TO THE WHEREABOUTS OF JOHN PARKER, THE POLICE BODYGUARD, NOBODY IS QUITE CERTAIN.

AT VARIOUS TIMES DURING THE EVENING, HE IS SEEN WATCHING THE PLAY FROM THE FRONT OF THE BALCONY...

LOITERING ON THE SIDEWALK IN FRONT OF THE THEATRE...

AND DRINKING AT TALTAVUL'S.

AS THEY ENJOY THE COMEDY, THE LINCOLNS ARE UNCHARACTERISTICALLY AFFECTIONATE.

WHAT WILL MISS HARRIS THINK OF MY HANGING ON TO YOU SO?

SHE WON'T THINK ANYTHING ABOUT IT.

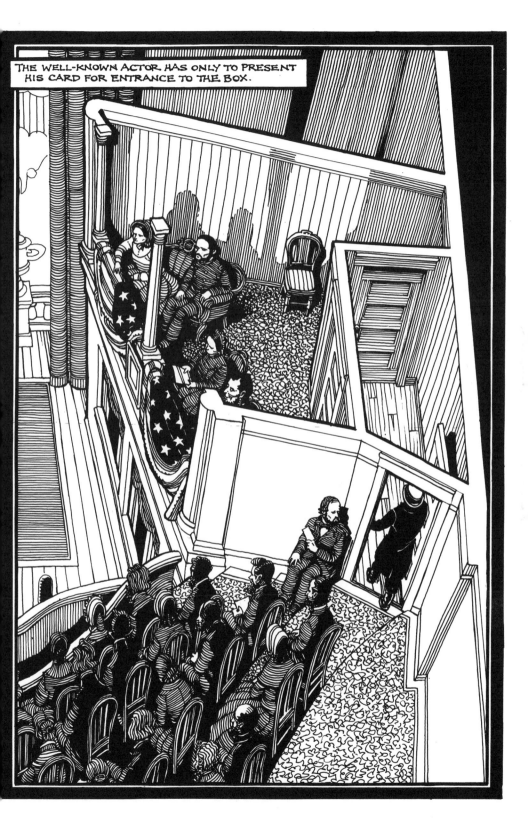

THE WELL-KNOWN ACTOR HAS ONLY TO PRESENT HIS CARD FOR ENTRANCE TO THE BOX.

INSIDE THE VESTIBULE, HE USES THE PINE BOARD TO PREVENT FURTHER INTRUSION.

HE PEERS THROUGH THE HOLE HE HAS BORED IN THE INNER DOOR...

AND SIGHTS HIS TARGET.

AT ABOUT 10:15 PM, HE SLOWLY PUSHES THE DOOR OPEN — AND AWAITS THE CRUCIAL MOMENT.

IT IS ACT III, SCENE 2, AND THE SINGLE ACTOR ONSTAGE (HARRY HAWK AS "ASA TRENCHARD") DELIVERS A LINE THAT NEVER FAILS TO BRING UPROARIOUS LAUGHTER.

DON'T KNOW THE MANNERS OF GOOD SOCIETY, EH? WELL, I GUESS I KNOW ENOUGH TO TURN YOU INSIDE OUT, OLD GAL — YOU SOCKDOLOGIZING OLD MAN TRAP!

LINCOLN TURNS HIS HEAD SLIGHTLY TO THE LEFT, AS IF LOOKING AT SOMEONE IN THE AUDIENCE...

WHILE BOOTH BRINGS THE DERRINGER TO WITHIN MERE INCHES.

IT FIRES NOW — SENDING A HALF-INCH BALL OF LEAD DEEP INTO THE SKULL OF ITS VICTIM.

THE PROJECTILE TAKES A PATH FROM THE LEFT TO THE RIGHT, THROUGH THE MASS OF THE BRAIN...

AND LODGING BEHIND THE RIGHT EYE.

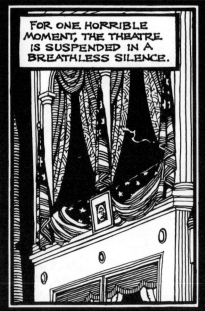

FOR ONE HORRIBLE MOMENT, THE THEATRE IS SUSPENDED IN A BREATHLESS SILENCE.

THE PRESIDENT, HAVING LOST ALL MOTOR FUNCTION, SLUMPS FORWARD IN HIS ROCKER.

HIS STILL-BEWILDERED WIFE ATTEMPTS TO KEEP HIM UPRIGHT.

BOOTH DROPS THE PISTOL AND MAKES FOR THE RAILING OF THE BOX. MAJOR RATHBONE LEAPS INTO ACTION, LUNGING AT THE ASSAILANT...

ONLY TO RECEIVE A VICIOUS GASH TO HIS ARM FROM THE ASSASSIN'S BLADE.

BOOTH VAULTS THE RAILING AND LEAPS THE 12 FEET TO THE STAGE.

IN THE PROCESS, HIS SPUR CATCHES ON ONE OF THE FLAGS DRAPED OVER THE BALUSTRADE.

THROWN OFF BALANCE, HE HITS THE BOARDS AWKWARDLY, BREAKING HIS LEFT LEG JUST ABOVE THE ANKLE.

HE TURNS TO THE AUDIENCE AND SHOUTS AN APPROPRIATE SLOGAN: THE MOTTO OF THE STATE OF VIRGINIA...

SIC SEMPER TYRANNIS!*

*THUS EVER TO TYRANTS.

A SCREAM ISSUES FROM THE PRESIDENTIAL BOX...

AND THE THEATRE AWAKENS TO WHAT IS HAPPENING.

BOOTH LIMPS ACROSS THE STAGE, TOWARD THE REAR DOOR THROUGH WHICH HE ENTERED...

THREATENING ANY WHO STAND IN HIS WAY.

IN THE ALLEY, HE GRABS THE REINS FROM YOUNG BURROUGHS...

GIVING THE LAD A VIOLENT KICK FOR GOOD MEASURE.

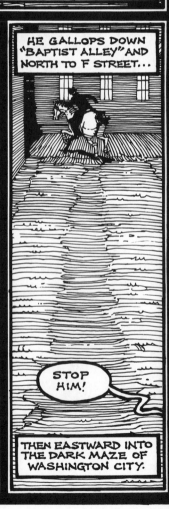

HE GALLOPS DOWN "BAPTIST ALLEY" AND NORTH TO F STREET...

STOP HIM!

THEN EASTWARD INTO THE DARK MAZE OF WASHINGTON CITY.

AT THE SAME MOMENT THAT BOOTH ENTERS THE PRESIDENT'S BOX, ANOTHER DRAMA UNFOLDS ON LAFAYETTE SQUARE.

LEWIS POWELL AND DAVID HEROLD ARRIVE AT THE HOME OF WILLIAM H. SEWARD.

HEROLD WAITS IN THE STREET WHILE POWELL KNOCKS ON THE DOOR, POSING AS A MESSENGER FROM SEWARD'S PHYSICIAN.

ONCE INSIDE, POWELL LEAPS UP THE STAIRS...

ONLY TO BE CONFRONTED BY FREDERICK SEWARD.

THE INTRUDER AIMS HIS REVOLVER...

BUT IT FAILS TO FIRE.

HE THEN USES IT TO BELABOR THE POOR MAN ABOUT THE HEAD.

HE MAKES HIS WAY TO SEWARD'S BEDROOM, WHERE THE SECRETARY HAS LAIN IMMOBILE SINCE HIS ACCIDENT...

ATTENDED BY HIS DAUGHTER, FANNY, AND A SOLDIER-NURSE, GEORGE ROBINSON.

POWELL PULLS OUT A BOWIE KNIFE AND SETS UPON THE HELPLESS STATESMAN. THE STEEL BRACE ABOUT SEWARD'S NECK SAVES HIS LIFE — BUT CANNOT PREVENT SEVERAL GASHES TO HIS FACE IN THE ONSLAUGHT.

ROBINSON AND THE SECRETARY'S OLDER SON AUGUSTU ATTEMPT TO INTERVENE — ONLY TO RECEIVE DEEP STAB WOUNDS FOR THEIR TROUBLE.

DAVID HEROLD, WAITING OUTSIDE, HEARS SCREAMS AND COMMOTION FROM WITHIN THE HOUSE.

ASSUMING THAT THE ATTEMPT HAS GONE AWRY, HE GALLOPS AWAY IN A PANIC.

I AM MAD! I AM MAD!

POWELL, SOAKED IN BLOOD, BOUNDS DOWN THE STAIRS, RAISING HIS KNIFE TO ANY WHO STAND IN HIS WAY.

ONCE OUTSIDE, HE FINDS THAT HEROLD HAS DESERTED HIM...

AND, UNFAMILIAR WITH THE STREETS OF THE CAPITAL, RIDES MADLY OFF INTO THE NIGHT.

GEORGE ATZERODT, FOR HIS PART, HAS BY NOW ABANDONED THE IDEA OF KILLING ANDREW JOHNSON — AND INSTEAD WANDERS THE STREETS FROM TAVERN TO TAVERN.

BACK AT FORD'S THEATRE, CHAOS AND CONFUSION DOMINATE.

MISS HARRIS CALLS FOR WATER... AND A DOCTOR.

RATHBONE RECOVERS HIS SENSES ENOUGH TO REMOVE THE BOARD SECURING THE OUTER DOOR.

THE FIRST DOCTOR INTO THE BOX IS CHARLES LEALE, AGE 23. THE SECOND IS CHARLES TAFT, ALSO 23. TOGETHER, THEY GENTLY MOVE THE PRESIDENT ONTO THE FLOOR.

LEALE FINDS AND PROBES THE WOUND. HE SEES LITTLE REASON FOR HOPE.

HIS WOUND IS MORTAL.

HE CANNOT SURVIVE.

NEVERTHELESS, HE STILL BREATHES SHALLOWLY, AND A FAINT HEARTBEAT CAN BE MEASURED.

MISS LAURA KEENE SOMEHOW MAKES HER WAY INTO THE BOX. SHE CRADLES LINCOLN'S HEAD IN HER LAP.

MARY LINCOLN, SOBBING UNCONTROLABLY, PAYS HER NO ATTENTION.

369

BEFORE LONG, IT IS DECIDED THAT THE VICTIM MUST BE MOVED TO A MORE COMFORTABLE LOCATION.

SIX MEN VOLUNTEER TO CARRY HIM DOWN THE STAIRS AND OUT OF THE THEATRE.

THE WHITE HOUSE BEING TOO DISTANT, ONE OF THE RESIDENCES ACROSS 10TH ST. SEEMS THE LIKELIEST DESTINATION.

THE STREET IS A SEA OF CURIOUS, UNBELIEVING FACES, AND THE PARTY MAKES ITS WAY BUT SLOWLY.

OUT OF THE WAY!

FROM THE BOARDING HOUSE OWNED BY WILLIAM PETERSEN, A YOUNG TENANT, HENRY STAFFORD, OFFERS A ROOM.

BRING HIM IN HERE!

THE MEN STRUGGLE WITH THEIR BURDEN UP THE FRONT STEPS, DOWN A NARROW HALLWAY, AND INTO A TINY BACK ROOM — BARELY 9 BY 17 FEET!

HERE HE IS LAID DIAGONALLY UPON THE BED... AND THE LONG NIGHT BEGINS.

BY 10:45 PM, JOHN WILKES BOOTH HAS MADE HIS WAY THROUGH THE STREETS OF WASHINGTON TO THE NAVY YARD BRIDGE ACROSS THE ANACOSTIA RIVER.

ALTHOUGH THE BRIDGE STILL ENFORCES A 9:00 PM CURFEW, HE HAS LITTLE TROUBLE PERSUADING THE SENTRY TO LET HIM PASS.

I LIVE IN MARYLAND AND HAVE BEEN DELAYED IN THE CITY!

ONLY MINUTES LATER, DAVID HEROLD IS LIKEWISE GIVEN LEAVE TO CROSS THE BRIDGE.

THE TWO MEET AT A PRE-ARRANGED SPOT NOT FAR INTO MARYLAND...

AND RIDE SOUTH TOWARD SURRATTSVILLE — THE FULL MOON LIGHTING THEIR ESCAPE.

PART IV.

THE ESCAPE

THE GARRETT FARM

SATURDAY, APRIL 15, 1865
INSIDE THE PETERSEN HOUSE, THE DEATH-WATCH CONTINUES THROUGH THE MORNING'S EARLY HOURS.

IN THE BACK ROOM, AS MANY AS 16 PHYSICIANS LABOR TO MAKE THE PRESIDENT'S LAST HOURS AS COMFORTABLE AS POSSIBLE. HIS CLOTHING IS REMOVED, A MUSTARD PLASTER APPLIED.

ANOTHER BEDROOM BECOMES THE DE FACTO SEAT OF THE U.S. GOVERNMENT, PRESIDED OVER BY THE SECRETARY OF WAR, EDWIN McMASTERS STANTON.

THE FRONT PARLOR IS THE PROVINCE OF THE INCONSOLABLE MARY LINCOLN...

WHILE A STEADY STREAM OF GOVERNMENT OFFICIALS AND OTHER VISITORS DRIFTS IN IN AND OUT OF THE FRONT DOOR. UPWARDS OF 100 PEOPLE THROUGHOUT THE NIGHT!

375

STANTON HIMSELF INTERVIEWS DOZENS OF WITNESSES BROUGHT OVER FROM THE THEATRE.

NOBODY IS IN DOUBT THAT THE MURDERER IS THE WELL-KNOWN ACTOR JOHN WILKES BOOTH.

TAKING INTO ACCOUNT THE ATTACK ON SEWARD, STANTON THINKS IT LIKELY THAT A WIDE CONSPIRACY IS IN MOTION—PERHAPS THE PRECURSOR TO A LARGE-SCALE CONFEDERATE INSURGENCY...

AND HE ACTS ACCORDINGLY.

ROADBLOCKS ARE ERECTED ABOUT THE CITY... BRIDGES ARE CLOSED...

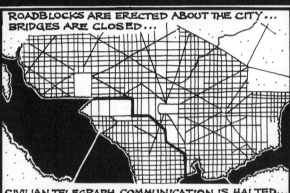

CIVILIAN TELEGRAPH COMMUNICATION IS HALTED... TRAINS AND SHIPS HEADING SOUTH ARE DETAINED...

DOZENS OF PEOPLE ARE ARRESTED THIS NIGHT ON LITTLE OR NO EVIDENCE...

INCLUDING MISS LAURA KEENE AND THE COMPANY OF "OUR AMERICAN COUSIN."

BOOTH'S ASSOCIATES ARE SOUGHT OUT. AT SOME POINT, HIS NAME BECOMES LINKED TO THAT OF JOHN SURRATT, KNOWN TO BE A SOUTHERN COURIER.

AT ABOUT 2:00 AM, CITY DETECTIVES ARRIVE AT THE SURRATT BOARDING HOUSE IN SEARCH OF BOOTH AND JOHN SURRATT, WHO IS BELIEVED TO BE SEWARD'S ATTACKER.

LOUIS WEICHMANN EXPERIENCES A MOMENT OF REVELATION.

MY GOD... I SEE IT ALL NOW!

MRS. SURRATT EXPLAINS THAT HER SON IS IN CANADA...

AND PRODUCES A LETTER FROM HIM AS PROOF.

BOOTH AND HEROLD, IN THE MEANTIME, TARRY ONLY BRIEFLY AT SURRATTSVILLE...

WHERE THEY RETAIN THE TWO RIFLES HIDDEN THERE PREVIOUSLY.

ALSO: A BOTTLE OF WHISKEY.

THE CONTINUING AGONY OF BOOTH'S BROKEN LEG FORCES THE FUGITIVES TO ALTER THEIR SOUTHWARD COURSE.

WASHINGTON

MARYLAND

INIA

SURRATTSVILLE

INTENDED ROUTE

AT ABOUT 4:00 AM, THEY ARRIVE AT THE FARM OF DR. SAMUEL A. MUDD.

ALTHOUGH BOOTH AND MUDD HAVE MET SEVERAL TIMES — AND MUDD IS NO LESS STAUNCH A REBEL — THE ACTOR WEARS A FALSE BEARD AND CALLS HIMSELF "TYSON" DURING THE ENCOUNTER.

(PERHAPS HE DOES NOT WISH TO IMPLICATE THE DOCTOR — WHO COULD NOT YET KNOW OF THE ASSASSINATION.)

MUDD SETS THE FRACTURE AS BEST HE CAN.

HE ORDERS A CRUTCH FASHIONED FOR THE PATIENT...

WHOM HE ALLOWS TO REST IN AN ATTIC ROOM.

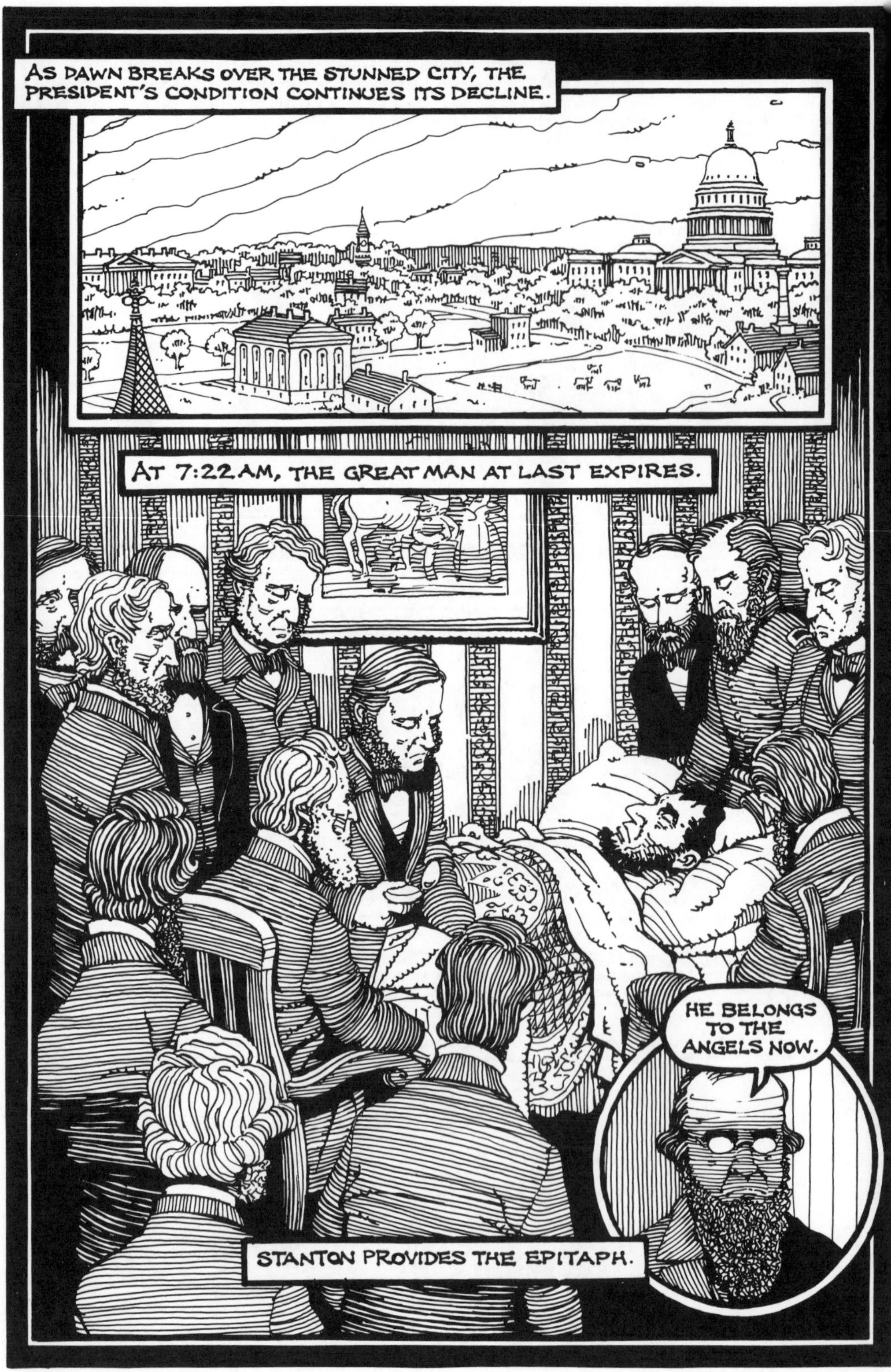
AS DAWN BREAKS OVER THE STUNNED CITY, THE PRESIDENT'S CONDITION CONTINUES ITS DECLINE.
AT 7:22 AM, THE GREAT MAN AT LAST EXPIRES.
HE BELONGS TO THE ANGELS NOW.
STANTON PROVIDES THE EPITAPH.

SHORTLY AFTER LINCOLN'S DEATH IS CONFIRMED, CHIEF JUSTICE SALMON P. CHASE ARRIVES AT THE HOTEL ROOM OF VICE PRESIDENT JOHNSON...

AND SWEARS HIM IN AS PRESIDENT OF THE UNITED STATES.

A CHILLY RAIN FALLS AS THE PRESIDENT'S BODY IS BORNE BACK TO THE WHITE HOUSE.

IN A GUEST ROOM ON THE SECOND FLOOR, A PARTIAL AUTOPSY IS CONDUCTED BY THE SURGEON GENERAL, DR. JOSEPH BARNES, AND FIVE OTHERS.

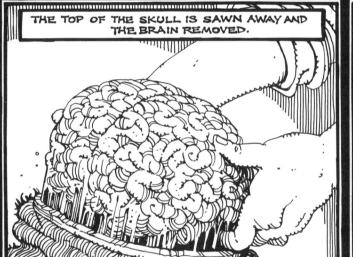

THE TOP OF THE SKULL IS SAWN AWAY AND THE BRAIN REMOVED.

DURING THIS PROCEDURE THE FLATTENED BULLET IS DISLODGED, CLATTERING INTO A BASIN BELOW.

NOT LONG THEREAFTER, THE EMBALMERS GO TO WORK.

IN THE AFTERNOON, STANTON SUPERVISES THE DRESSING OF THE CORPSE, IN PREPARATION FOR A MASSIVE STATE FUNERAL.

TOWARD EVENING, BOOTH AND HEROLD AT LAST TAKE THEIR LEAVE OF DR. MUDD'S FARM.

THE DOCTOR, WHO LEARNED OF THE ASSASSINATION WHILE VISITING BRYANTOWN THIS AFTERNOON, DECLINES TO TURN THEM IN.

INSTEAD, HE DIRECTS THEM SAFELY SOUTHWARD, INTO THE CARE OF HIS COMPATRIOT, COL. SAMUEL COX.

MUDD FARM

BRYANTOWN

PORT TOBACCO

PINE THICKET

COX FARM

COX HIDES THE FUGITIVES IN A PINE THICKET ON HIS PROPERTY.

AND HERE THEY WILL REMAIN IN MISERABLE WEATHER, FOR THE NEXT FIVE NIGHTS.

THEY ARE WATCHED OVER BY THE FORMER CONFEDERATE AGENT THOMAS JONES...

WHO BRINGS THEM FOOD, BLANKETS AND THE LATEST NEWSPAPERS.

BOOTH IS SURPRISED AND DISAPPOINTED TO FIND THAT HE IS NOT HAILED AS A HERO IN THE SOUTH.

The Richmo

IN FACT, HE IS UNIVERSALLY CONDEMNED AS A VILLAIN!

MONDAY, APRIL 17, 1865
ON THIS DAY, THE REMAINS OF ABRAHAM LINCOLN BEGIN THEIR PUBLIC DISPLAY. AFTER A PRIVATE VIEWING ON THE SECOND FLOOR, THE COFFIN IS MOUNTED ON A CATAFALQUE IN THE EAST ROOM.

TUESDAY, APRIL 18
THE PUBLIC STREAMS IN TO PAY ITS RESPECTS.

WEDNESDAY, APRIL 19, 1865
AT 12 NOON, A FUNERAL SERVICE IS CONDUCTED, AFTER WHICH THE COFFIN IS BORNE, IN A LONG, SLOW PROCESSION DOWN PENNSYLVANIA AVE. TO THE CAPITOL.

THURSDAY, APRIL 20
THE PUBLIC, IN A DOUBLE LINE OF NEVER-ENDING GRIEF, PASSES THROUGH THE GREAT ROTUNDA TO LOOK BRIEFLY UPON THE FACE OF ITS FALLEN LEADER.

FRIDAY, APRIL 21, 1865
AT 8:00 AM, IN A DREARY RAIN, THE FUNERAL TRAIN DEPARTS WASHINGTON FOR ITS LONG JOURNEY WESTWARD.

ALSO ON THE TRAIN: THE DISINTERRED REMAINS OF THE LINCOLNS' YOUNG SON WILLIE, WHO DIED FROM TYPHOID IN 1862.

BY THIS TIME, MOST OF BOOTH'S FELLOW CONSPIRATORS HAVE BEEN TRACKED DOWN BY FEDERAL AUTHORITIES.

ON MONDAY, APRIL 17, SAMUEL ARNOLD AND MICHAEL O'LAUGHLIN ARE ARRESTED IN BALTIMORE.

ON THE SAME DAY, LEWIS POWELL, HAVING WANDERED THE STREETS OF WASHINGTON FOR THREE DAYS, AT LAST MAKES HIS WAY TO SURRATT'S BOARDING HOUSE...

ONLY TO BE TAKEN INTO CUSTODY ALONG WITH MRS. SURRATT.

THURSDAY, APRIL 20: GEORGE ATZERODT IS FOUND HIDING AMONG RELATIONS AT BARNSVILLE, MARYLAND.

ON FRIDAY, APRIL 21, DR. SAMUEL MUDD IS ARRESTED AT HIS FARM.

A REWARD OF $100,000 IS OFFERED FOR THE REMAINING FUGITIVES...

SURRAT.   BOOTH.   HAROLD.

War Department, Washington, April 20, 1865.

$100,000 REWARD!

THE MURDERER

(STILL WRONGLY IDENTIFYING JOHN SURRATT AS ONE OF THEM.)

AS A DETACHMENT OF CAVALRY FOLLOWS BOOTH'S TRAIL SOUTHWARD.

THE FUNERAL TRAIN, IN THE MEANTIME, PROGRESSES NORTHWARD, WITH STOPS IN BALTIMORE, HARRISBURG—AND PHILADELPHIA...

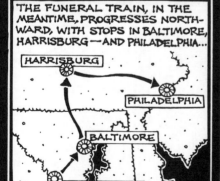

HARRISBURG

PHILADELPHIA

BALTIMORE

WASHINGTON

WHERE THE BODY LIES ON DISPLAY AT INDEPENDENCE HALL.

SATURDAY, APRIL 23 THE EAGER PUBLIC BECOMES SO TIGHTLY CROWDED THAT A RIOT ERUPTS.

ORDER IS RESTORED ONLY WITH DIFFICULTY.

FRIDAY, APRIL 21, 1865 ON THIS NIGHT, BOOTH AND HEROLD ATTEMPT TO CROSS THE POTOMAC, IN A FLAT-BOTTOMED FISHING BOAT SUPPLIED BY THOMAS JONES.

A FEDERAL GUNBOAT BLOCKS THEIR WAY DOWN-RIVER, FORCING THEM TO TURN ABOUT.

THEY END UP BACK ON THE MARYLAND SHORE, AT NANJEMOY CREEK.

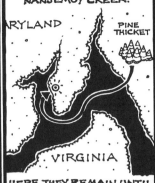

HERE THEY REMAIN UNTIL THE FOLLOWING EVENING.

SAT.-SUN., APRIL 22-23 THEIR ATTEMPT TONIGHT IS SUCCESSFUL. THEY LAND AT MATHIAS POINT IN VIRGINIA.

IN THE AFTERNOON, A CONFEDERATE OPERATIVE GUIDES THEM TO THEIR SHELTER FOR THE NIGHT:

THE CABIN OF A FORMER SLAVE, WILLIAM LUCAS, HIS WIFE AND SIX CHILDREN.

THE RACIST BOOTH FORCES THE ENTIRE FAMILY TO SLEEP OUTSIDE.

MONDAY, APRIL 24, 1865 IN THE MORNING, BOOTH PAYS THE OLDEST LUCAS BOY TO TRANSPORT HEROLD AND HIMSELF, HIDDEN UNDER STRAW, IN A WAGON TO PORT CONWAY.

HERE, FATE BRINGS THE FUGITIVES INTO CONTACT WITH A TRIO OF CONFEDERATE VETERANS:

MORTIMER RUGGLES, ABSALOM BAINBRIDGE, AND WILLIAM JETT.

THE THREE SEE THEM SAFELY ACROSS THE RAPPAHANNOCK RIVER TO PORT ROYAL.

SOUTH OF PORT ROYAL, THE FUGITIVES ARE TAKEN IN AT THE FARM OF RICHARD GARRETT, WHERE THEY POSE AS RETURNING SOLDIERS. BOOTH CALLS HIMSELF JAMES BOYD.

HIS BLACK AND SWOLLEN LEG GIVES CREDENCE TO THE STORY.

TONIGHT, THE ASSASSIN OCCUPIES AN UPPER BEDROOM.

IT WILL BE HIS LAST COMFORTABLE NIGHT.

TUESDAY, APRIL 25, 1865 IN THE MORNING, BOOTH RELAXES ON THE GARRETT PORCH.

HE TALKS BRIEFLY WITH ANNIE, THE FAMILY'S TEENAGED DAUGHTER.

THEY AGREE THAT THE MURDER OF PRESIDENT LINCOLN WAS "MOST UNFORTUNATE."

AT THE SAME MOMENT, THE CRACK UNIT OF FEDERAL SOLDIERS RIDES SOUTH FROM PORT ROYAL.

ORGANIZED BY STANTON'S MAN LAFAYETTE BAKER AND MADE UP OF 25 TROOPS OF THE 16TH NEW YORK CAVALRY.

ACTING ON A TIP, THEY BYPASS THEIR QUARRY AND PROCEED TO BOWLING GREEN.

RAPPAHANNOCK

LUCAS CABIN

PORT CONWAY

PORT ROYAL

GARRETT FARM

BOWLING GREEN

HERE, THEY FIND WILLIAM JETT, WHO POINTS THEM IN THE RIGHT DIRECTION.

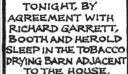

TONIGHT, BY AGREEMENT WITH RICHARD GARRETT, BOOTH AND HEROLD SLEEP IN THE TOBACCO DRYING BARN ADJACENT TO THE HOUSE.

WEDNESDAY, APRIL 26 AT 2:00 AM, THE PURSUERS AT LAST ARRIVE.

THEY QUICKLY ASCERTAIN THE WHEREABOUTS OF THEIR QUARRY AND SURROUND THE BARN.

YOU'VE TEN MINUTES TO COME OUT!

I'LL FIGHT YOU SINGLE-HANDED, BUT I WILL NEVER SURRENDER!

FIVE MINUTES MORE AND MY MEN WILL TORCH THE BARN!

THIS IS ENOUGH FOR DAVID HEROLD.

HE EMERGES INTO THE ARMS OF HIS CAPTORS.

THE STRUCTURE IS SET ABLAZE...

YET BOOTH, STILL WELL-ARMED, SHOWS NO INCLINATION TO SURRENDER.

A SHOT FROM SOMEWHERE BRINGS HIM DOWN.

THE DYING ASSASSIN IS DRAGGED FROM THE BARN TO THE GARRETTS' PORCH.

A SARGEANT NAMED BOSTON CORBETT CLAIMS CREDIT FOR THE SHOT — ACTING, HE SAYS, UNDER A COMMAND FROM GOD.

SOME ARE LEFT TO WONDER, HOWEVER, IF BOOTH COMMITTED THE DEED HIMSELF.

THE ACTOR CLINGS TO CONSCIOUSNESS FOR A FEW MINUTES LONGER.

TELL MY MOTHER THAT I DIE FOR MY COUNTRY...

I DID WHAT I THOUGHT WAS BEST...

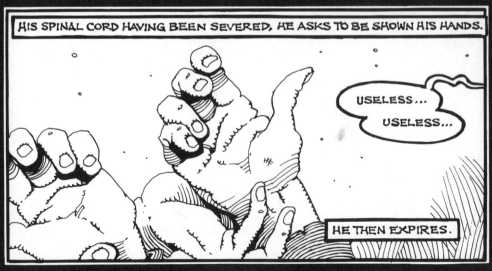

HIS SPINAL CORD HAVING BEEN SEVERED, HE ASKS TO BE SHOWN HIS HANDS.

USELESS...

USELESS...

HE THEN EXPIRES.

PART V.
LAID TO REST

FUNERAL CARRIAGE

MONDAY, APRIL 24, 1865
AS ABRAHAM LINCOLN'S MURDERER IS HUNTED DOWN, THE FUNERAL TRAIN CONTINUES ITS PROGRESS: FROM PHILADELPHIA, THROUGH TRENTON, TO JERSEY CITY.

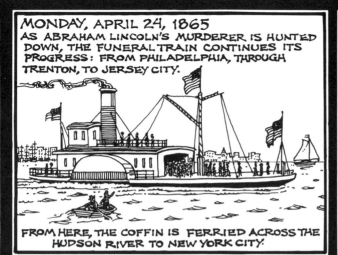

FROM HERE, THE COFFIN IS FERRIED ACROSS THE HUDSON RIVER TO NEW YORK CITY.

A SLOW, SAD PROCESSION BRINGS IT DOWN BROADWAY TO THE CITY HALL...

WHERE IT LIES ON DISPLAY IN THE GREAT ROTUNDA.

BEFORE THE PUBLIC IS ALLOWED INSIDE, AN ENTERPRISING PHOTOGRAPHER TAKES AN IMAGE OF THE CORPSE.

BUT, UNDER ORDERS FROM EDWIN M. STANTON, THE PLATES ARE SEIZED AND DESTROYED.

TUESDAY, APRIL 25
AT 2:00 PM, ANOTHER PROCESSION MAKES ITS WAY TO THE RAIL DEPOT AT 9TH AVENUE AND 34TH ST.

THE TRAIN DEPARTS NORTHWARD FOR ALBANY (WITH STOPS AT WEST POINT AND POUGHKEEPSIE)

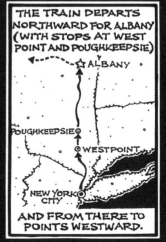

AND FROM THERE TO POINTS WESTWARD.

WEDNESDAY, APRIL 26
THE BODY OF JOHN WILKES BOOTH IS CARRIED BY STEAMER UP THE POTOMAC TO ALEXANDRIA, VIRGINIA, AND THENCE BY TUGBOAT TO THE WASHINGTON NAVY YARD.

THURSDAY, APRIL 27
EARLY THIS MORNING, IT IS BROUGHT ABOARD THE IRONCLAD "MONTAUK," WHERE THE OTHERS OF THE CONSPIRACY ARE INCARCERATED.

(BY GRIM COINCIDENCE, THIS IS THE VERY SHIP THAT PRESIDENT LINCOLN TOURED ON HIS LAST DAY OF LIFE.)

THE AUTOPSY IS PERFORMED BY SURGEON GENL. BARNES.

THE VERDICT: DEATH FROM A PISTOL BALL.

THE DOCTORS REMOVE THE DAMAGED SEGMENT OF THE DEAD MAN'S SPINE, TO ILLUSTRATE THE PATH OF THE MISSILE.

WITH THE AUTOPSY CONCLUDED, SEVERAL OF BOOTH'S ACQUAINTANCES (ABOUT 10 IN ALL) ARE INVITED ON BOARD TO IDENTIFY THE REMAINS.

DESPITE THE MUDDY AND BURNT CONDITION OF THE BODY, A POSITIVE IDENTIFICATION IS MADE BY NEARLY ALL.

MOST POINT TO THE CRUDE INITIALS ON HIS RIGHT HAND, CARVED THERE IN CHILDHOOD, AND NOTICED BY EVERYONE WHO KNEW HIM.

DURING THIS TIME, A SMALL GROUP OF SOUTHERN SYMPATHIZERS MANAGE TO GET ABOARD FOR A GLIMPSE OF THEIR HERO.

ONE LADY SNIPS A LOCK OF HAIR BEFORE THEY ALL ARE EJECTED.

AMONG THE ITEMS RECOVERED FROM BOOTH'S POCKETS...

PHOTOGRAPHS OF FIVE LOVELY WOMEN — FOUR OF THEM ACTRESSES, THE FIFTH HIS "FIANCEE," MISS LUCY HALE.

AN APPOINTMENT CALENDAR WHICH HE USED FOR A DIARY DURING HIS 12 DAYS AS A FUGITIVE. (THIS JOURNAL IS BROUGHT TO STANTON, IN WHOSE POSSESSION IT WILL VANISH, ONLY TO RESURFACE IN TWO YEARS — WITH 18 PAGES MISSING!)

AFTER DARK, THE ASSASSIN'S BODY IS TAKEN TO THE OLD PENITENTIARY BUILDING ON THE GROUNDS OF THE WASHINGTON ARSENAL.

HERE, IT IS BURIED, QUICKLY AND WITHOUT CEREMONY, IN THE DIRT FLOOR OF AN AMMUNITION STORAGE ROOM.

NO MARKER IDENTIFIES THE SPOT.

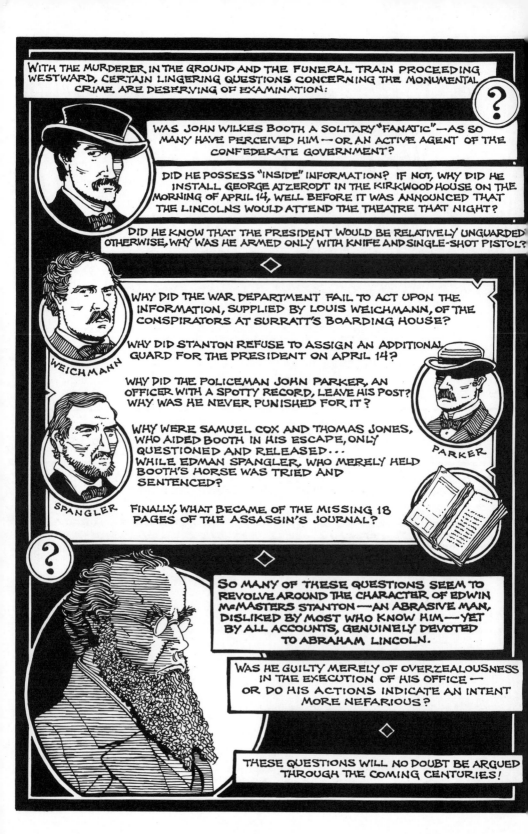

WITH THE MURDERER IN THE GROUND AND THE FUNERAL TRAIN PROCEEDING WESTWARD, CERTAIN LINGERING QUESTIONS CONCERNING THE MONUMENTAL CRIME ARE DESERVING OF EXAMINATION:

WAS JOHN WILKES BOOTH A SOLITARY "FANATIC"—AS SO MANY HAVE PERCEIVED HIM — OR AN ACTIVE AGENT OF THE CONFEDERATE GOVERNMENT?

DID HE POSSESS "INSIDE" INFORMATION? IF NOT, WHY DID HE INSTALL GEORGE ATZERODT IN THE KIRKWOOD HOUSE ON THE MORNING OF APRIL 14, WELL BEFORE IT WAS ANNOUNCED THAT THE LINCOLNS WOULD ATTEND THE THEATRE THAT NIGHT?

DID HE KNOW THAT THE PRESIDENT WOULD BE RELATIVELY UNGUARDED? OTHERWISE, WHY WAS HE ARMED ONLY WITH KNIFE AND SINGLE-SHOT PISTOL?

WHY DID THE WAR DEPARTMENT FAIL TO ACT UPON THE INFORMATION, SUPPLIED BY LOUIS WEICHMANN, OF THE CONSPIRATORS AT SURRATT'S BOARDING HOUSE?

WEICHMANN

WHY DID STANTON REFUSE TO ASSIGN AN ADDITIONAL GUARD FOR THE PRESIDENT ON APRIL 14?

WHY DID THE POLICEMAN JOHN PARKER, AN OFFICER WITH A SPOTTY RECORD, LEAVE HIS POST? WHY WAS HE NEVER PUNISHED FOR IT?

PARKER

WHY WERE SAMUEL COX AND THOMAS JONES, WHO AIDED BOOTH IN HIS ESCAPE, ONLY QUESTIONED AND RELEASED... WHILE EDMAN SPANGLER, WHO MERELY HELD BOOTH'S HORSE WAS TRIED AND SENTENCED?

SPANGLER

FINALLY, WHAT BECAME OF THE MISSING 18 PAGES OF THE ASSASSIN'S JOURNAL?

SO MANY OF THESE QUESTIONS SEEM TO REVOLVE AROUND THE CHARACTER OF EDWIN McMASTERS STANTON — AN ABRASIVE MAN, DISLIKED BY MOST WHO KNOW HIM — YET BY ALL ACCOUNTS, GENUINELY DEVOTED TO ABRAHAM LINCOLN.

WAS HE GUILTY MERELY OF OVERZEALOUSNESS IN THE EXECUTION OF HIS OFFICE — OR DO HIS ACTIONS INDICATE AN INTENT MORE NEFARIOUS?

THESE QUESTIONS WILL NO DOUBT BE ARGUED THROUGH THE COMING CENTURIES!

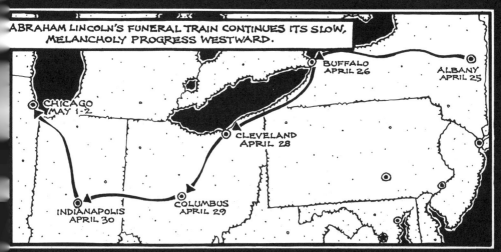

ABRAHAM LINCOLN'S FUNERAL TRAIN CONTINUES ITS SLOW, MELANCHOLY PROGRESS WESTWARD.

ALBANY
APRIL 25

BUFFALO
APRIL 26

CHICAGO
MAY 1-2

CLEVELAND
APRIL 28

COLUMBUS
APRIL 29

INDIANAPOLIS
APRIL 30

AT EACH STOP, GREAT THRONGS BRAVE DRENCHING RAINS TO PAY TRIBUTE.

MONDAY, MAY 1, 1865
AT 11:00 AM, THE TRAIN ARRIVES AT CHICAGO, FOR A SOLEMN PROCESSION THROUGH THE CITY...

ACE, NOBLE SOUL, PAT

AND DISPLAY OF THE REMAINS AT THE COOK COUNTY COURT HOUSE.

THE PUBLIC FILES BY THROUGH THE NIGHT AND INTO THE FOLLOWING AFTERNOON.

TUESDAY, MAY 2
AT 9:30 PM, THE TRAIN LEAVES CHICAGO ON THE FINAL SEGMENT OF ITS SORROWFUL JOURNEY.

CHICAGO

SPRINGFIELD

393

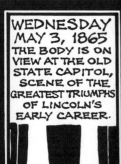

WEDNESDAY MAY 3, 1865 THE BODY IS ON VIEW AT THE OLD STATE CAPITOL, SCENE OF THE GREATEST TRIUMPHS OF LINCOLN'S EARLY CAREER.

HERE, HIS FACE IS SCRUTINIZED BY OLD FRIENDS AND ENEMIES.

THURSDAY MAY 4, 1865 AT 10:00 AM, A PROCESSION OF THOUSANDS LEAVES FOR OAK RIDGE CEMETERY.

MRS. LINCOLN, WHO HAS ATTENDED NONE OF THE CEREMONIES, REMAINS IN SECLUSION.

AFTER A BRIEF SERVICE, ABRAHAM LINCOLN IS PLACED WITHIN A SIMPLE HILLSIDE VAULT.

IN THE WEEKS THAT FOLLOW, THE REMAINING MEMBERS OF BOOTH'S CONSPIRACY ARE PUT ON TRIAL BEFORE A MILITARY COURT.

SAMUEL ARNOLD, MICHAEL O'LAUGHLIN AND SAMUEL MUDD ARE SENTENCED TO LIFE AT HARD LABOR.

THEY ARE SENT TO THE PRISON AT FT. JEFFERSON IN THE DRY TORTUGAS, FLORIDA.

THE UNFORTUNATE EDMAN SPANGLER IS GIVEN A 6-YEAR TERM.

(O'LAUGHLIN WILL DIE IN PRISON; ARNOLD, MUDD, AND SPANGLER WILL BE PARDONED BY PRESIDENT JOHNSON IN 1869.)

DAVID HEROLD, LEWIS POWELL, GEORGE ATZERODT, AND MARY SURRATT ARE SENTENCED TO THE GALLOWS.
FRIDAY, JULY 7, 1865
THEY ARE PUT TO DEATH.

IN 1869, THE BODY OF JOHN WILKES BOOTH IS REMOVED FROM THE PRISON FLOOR AND GIVEN OVER TO HIS FAMILY.

BOOTH

IT IS CONSIGNED TO AN UNMARKED GRAVE WITHIN THE FAMILY PLOT AT GREEN MOUNT CEMETERY IN BALTIMORE.

LINCOLN

A GRAND MONUMENT NOW STANDS OVER THE REMAINS OF ABRAHAM LINCOLN.

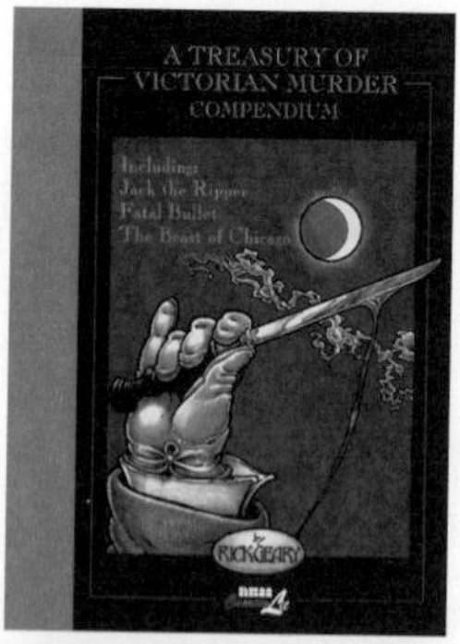
A TREASURY OF
VICTORIAN MURDER
COMPENDIUM
Including:
Jack the Ripper
Fatal Bullet
The Beast of Chicago
RICK GEARY

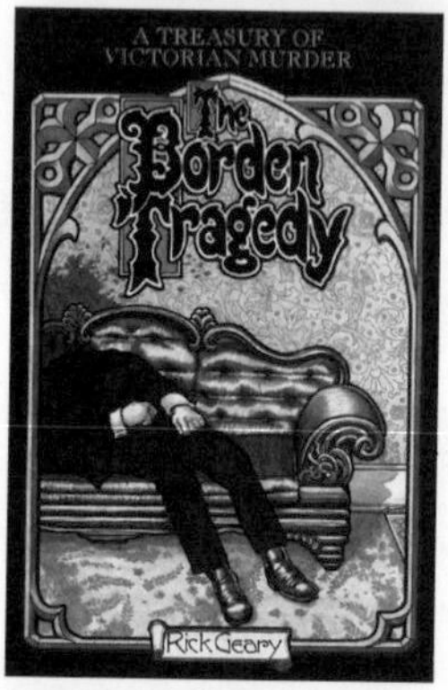
A TREASURY OF
VICTORIAN MURDER
The Borden Tragedy
Rick Geary

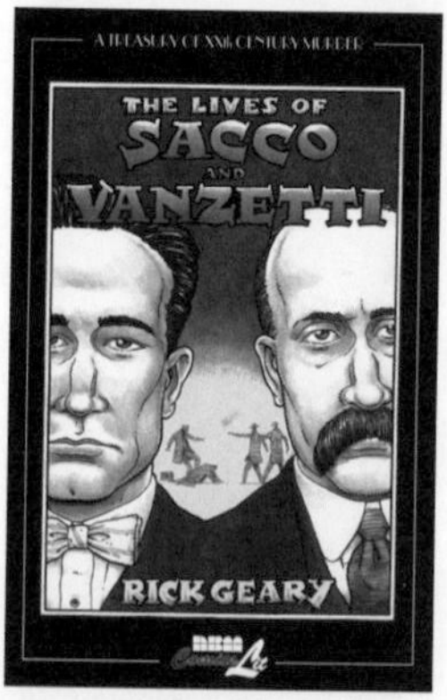
THE LIVES OF
SACCO
AND
VANZETTI
RICK GEARY

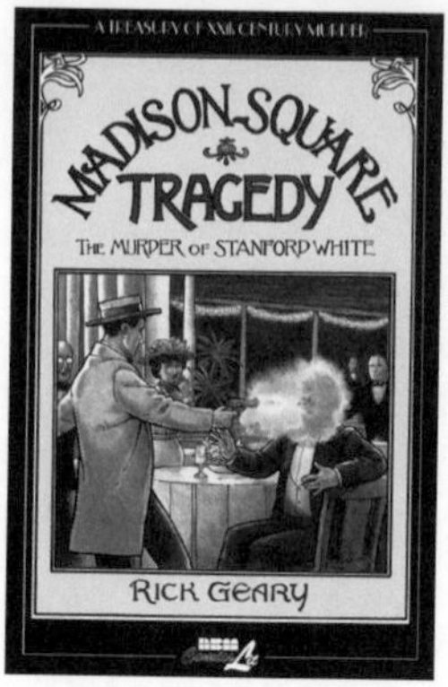
MADISON SQUARE
TRAGEDY
THE MURDER OF STANFORD WHITE
RICK GEARY

Rick Geary was born in 1946 in Kansas City, Missouri and grew up in Wichita, Kansas. He graduated from the University of Kansas in Lawrence, where his first cartoons were published in the University Daily Kansan.

He worked as staff artist for two weekly papers in Wichita before moving to San Diego in 1975.

He began work in comics in 1977 and was for thirteen years a contributor to the Funny Pages of National Lampoon. His comic stories have also been published in Heavy Metal, Dark Horse Comics and the DC Comics/Paradox Press Big Books.

During a four-year stay in New York, his illustrations appeared regularly in The New York Times Book Review. His illustration work has also been seen in MAD, Spy, Rolling Stone, The Los Angeles Times, and American Libraries.

He has written and illustrated three children's books based on The Mask for Dark Horse and two Spider-Man children's books for Marvel. His children's comic Society of Horrors ran in Disney Adventures magazine from 1999 to 2006.

His graphic novels include three adaptations for CLASSICS ILLUSTRATED. He has also done various biographies for Farrar, Straus and Giroux.

In 2007, after more than thirty years in San Diego, he and his wife Deborah moved to the town of Carrizozo, New Mexico.